Classical Swedish

ARCHITECTURE AND INTERIORS

1650–1840

The Classical America Series
in Art and Architecture

The Golden City by Henry Hope Reed
The American Vignola by William R. Ware
The Architecture of Humanism by Geoffrey Scott
The Decoration of Houses by Edith Wharton and Ogden Codman, Jr.
Italian Villas and Their Gardens by Edith Wharton
The Classic Point of View by Kenyon Cox
What is Painting? by Kenyon Cox
Man As Hero: The Human Figure in Western Art by Pierce Rice
Greek and Roman Architecture in Classic Drawings by Hector d'Espouy
Monumental Classic Architecture in Great Britain and Ireland by Albert E. Richardson
Monograph of the Work of McKim, Mead & White, 1879–1915, Student Edition
The Library of Congress: Its Architecture and Decoration by Herbert Small
Letarouilly on Renaissance Rome by John Barrington Bayley
The New York Public Library: Its Architecture and Decoration by Henry Hope Reed
The Elements of Classical Architecture by Georges Gromort
Palaces of the Sun King: Versailles, Trianon, Marly, The Chateaux of Louis XIV by Berndt Dams and Andrew Zega
Bricks and Brownstone: The New York Row House 1783–1929 by Charles Lockwood
The Architecture of the Classical Interior by Steven W. Semes
Classical Architecture for the Twenty-first Century by Jean-François Gabriel

The Institute of Classical Architecture and Classical America
is the organization dedicated to
the classical tradition in architecture and the allied arts in the United States.
Inquiries about the mission and programs of the organization should be addressed to:
The Institute of Classical Architecture and Classical America
www.classicist.org

Classical Swedish

ARCHITECTURE AND INTERIORS

1650–1840

JOHAN CEDERLUND

TRANSLATED BY LANI SUMMERVILLE-STERNERUP

In association with

THE INSTITUTE OF
CLASSICAL ARCHITECTURE AND CLASSICAL AMERICA

W. W. NORTON & COMPANY

New York • London

To Constanza and Maria

Printed in Singapore
First Edition

For information about permission to reproduce selections from this book, write to Permissions, W. W. Norton & Company, Inc., 500 Fifth Avenue, New York, NY 10110

Manufacturing by KHL Printing
Book design by Abigail Sturges
Production Manger: Leeann Graham

Library of Congress Cataloging-in-Publication Data

Cederlund, Johan.
Classical Swedish architecture and interiors : 1650–1840 / Johan Cederlund ; translated by Lani Summerville-Sternerup.
p. cm.
Includes bibliographical references and index.
ISBN-13: 978-0-393-73172-9
ISBN-10: 0-393-73172-3
1. Architecture—Sweden. 2. Interior decoration—Sweden. 3. Decorative arts—Sweden. I. Title.

NA1284.C43 2006
720.9485'0903—dc22

2005058545

ISBN 13: 978-0-393-73172-9
ISBN 10: 0-393-73172-3

W. W. Norton & Company, Inc., 500 Fifth Avenue,
New York, N.Y. 10110
www.wwnorton.com
W. W. Norton & Company Ltd., Castle House, 75/76 Wells St.,
London W1T 3QT
1 2 3 4 5 6 7 8 9 0

Contents

Preface and Acknowledgments / 7

CHAPTER ONE
Historical Overview / *9*

CHAPTER TWO
The Baroque / *27*

CHAPTER THREE
The Late Baroque / *74*

CHAPTER FOUR
The Rococo / *125*

CHAPTER FIVE
Neoclassicism / *168*

CHAPTER SIX
The Empire Style / *226*

Notes / *256*

Glossary of Selected Terms / *260*

Index / *262*

Credits / *270*

Monuments of Sweden 1650-1840

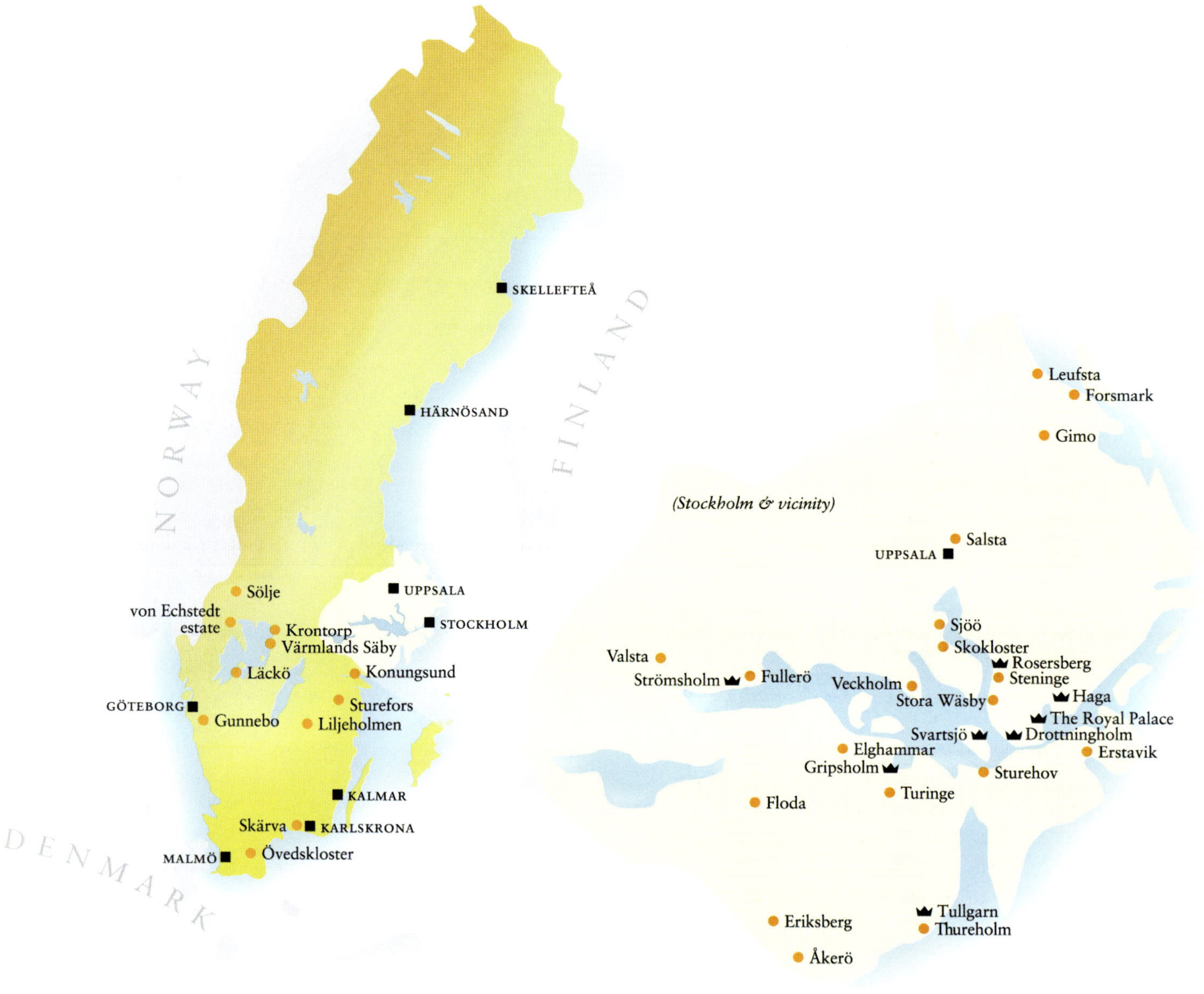

- ■ Cities and towns
- ♛ Royal palaces & other royal residences
- ● Aristocratic residences, manor houses, & churches

Preface and Acknowledgments

Despite a recent increase in interest in the history of Swedish architecture, interior design, and the decorative arts, the literature in English has remained quite limited. Scholars and other authors who are knowledgeable in this area generally write for readers of Swedish—a relatively small public—leaving their knowledge inaccessible beyond the borders of Sweden. Of particular note is a lack of broad overviews, in which buildings and their interiors, and the architects and designers who created them, are presented in their historical context. This book is thus an attempt to fill a twofold gap.

The title *Classical Swedish Architecture and Interiors 1650–1840* calls for a word of explanation. Geographically, the book treats only the Sweden demarcated by today's boundaries, which have been in place since the early nineteenth century. In fact, however, the Swedish state possessed all of Finland for more than six centuries starting in the middle ages, and during a period of imperial expansion in the seventeenth century, she annexed several sizable Baltic states plus a few small ones in today's Germany. The historical buildings in Finland and Sweden's lesser holdings are not discussed here, though some of them could arguably be included as part of Sweden's architecture heritage.

The term "classical," too, requires an explanatory note. As used most of the time, classical applies mostly to a set of fundamental design ideals formulated and applied in Greek and Roman antiquity, which were recalled and revitalized during the Renaissance, and which have found prominence throughout western art and architecture ever since. Most of the buildings and interiors considered in this book do fit this definition: for instance, the Royal Palace in Stockholm, which exemplifies baroque classicism, and the neoclassical Governor's residence in the city of Härnösand. Other buildings discussed here, however, can hardly be called classical in the sense of a reflection of antiquity; an obvious example is the Chinese Pavilion at Drottningholm. In this case, "classical" is used to mean more or less traditional and of lasting cultural value. The high quality and significance of such buildings make them examples of classical Swedish architecture.

After an introductory historical overview as the context of Sweden's architectural development, *Classical Swedish Architecture and Interiors* proceeds chronologically. Starting around 1650, the book takes in nearly two centuries during which Sweden underwent four distinct historical and political periods. At the start of that span, Swedish building design and decoration caught up with and became dominated by the prevalent style of Continental Europe: the Baroque. Then they underwent a series of transformations, all reflecting reverence for the styles and techniques of foreign countries, especially Italy and France: the late Baroque, the Rococo, and the Neoclassical. Finally, in the early nineteenth century with the Empire style, design and decoration began to give way to a nationalistic Swedish spirit.

Classical Swedish Architecture and Interiors grew out of a longtime friendship and the shared interests of the author and Lani Summerville-Sternerup. The original idea for the book came from Ms. Summerville-Sternerup, who has also translated and adapted the original Swedish manuscript; I owe her my deepest thanks. I would also like to acknowledge the essential contributions of photographers Åke E:son Lindman and Lars Hallén, and those of Jan Teeland and Joy Hayes for their help in preparing the manuscript. Thanks also go to Åke Nilsson and Niels Hofman-Bang, who assisted with graphics and digital editing. And finally, for assembling all the parts, transforming them into this book, and bringing it to an English-reading audience, I owe thanks to Nancy N. Green of W. W. Norton and to Johanna Zacharias, who edited the final text.

I am especially indebted to The Institute of Classical Architecture & Classical America and H. M. King Gustav VI Adolf's Foundation for Swedish Cultural Activities for their financial support of the photography. In addition, I owe special thanks to the owners of the palaces and manor houses, who graciously opened their doors to photographers to enable inclusion of their homes in this book.

Historical Overview

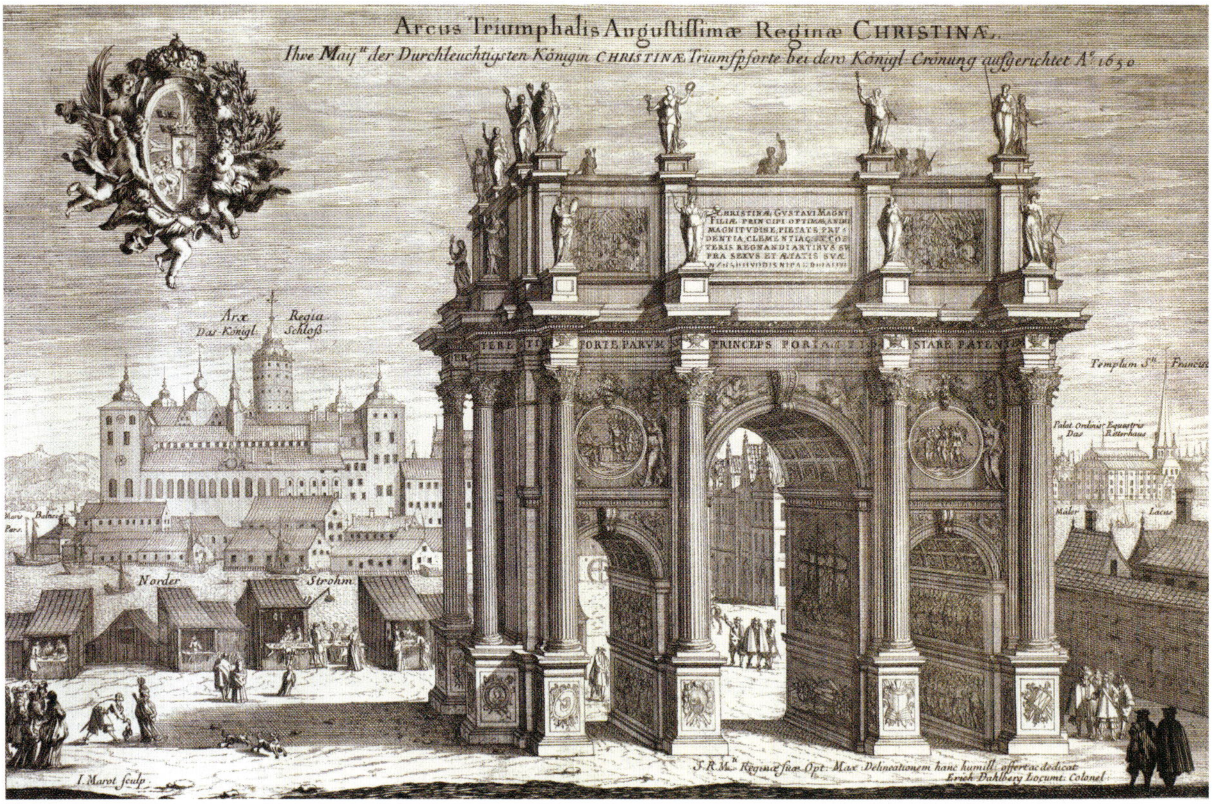

In 1650, the only daughter of King Gustav II Adolf of the Vasa dynasty was crowned Queen Christina of Sweden. As part of the scene set for the ceremony a triumphal arch modeled after the ancient Arch of Constantine in Rome was erected in the center of Stockholm. Made of wood and canvas rather than of marble, Queen Christina's arch nonetheless connoted supremacy. How better to assert the new superpower's might than through classicism?

The arch stood in sharp contrast to the capital's medieval houses and church spires, and to the antiquated royal castle, Three Crowns (*Tre kronor*). Thus it prominently showed the direction that Sweden's architecture would take for the rest of the seventeenth century.

THE AGE OF GREATNESS (1611–1718)

By the time of Christina's coronation, Sweden had risen from her earlier humble position among nations to become one of Europe's great military powers. King Gustav II Adolf and his field generals had laid the groundwork with their successful campaigns during the Thirty Years War (1618–48). In this seemingly endless and devastating war, Sweden, alongside various German princely houses, had fought against the papist Holy Roman Empire—that is to say, against the Hapsburgs of Austria and their cousin on the throne of Spain, as well as several minor German states that also practiced Catholicism. Led by Cardinal Richelieu, France too sought to undermine the power of the Hapsburgs and did so in part by augmenting the forces of Protestant Sweden. For France, the result was a strengthened position in Europe. Sweden, meanwhile, increased her territory by conquering several provinces on the Baltic Sea (besides Finland, which already was part of Sweden). Thus the Swedish empire reached its zenith around the middle of the seventeenth century, a rank it then held for more than fifty years. In Swedish history, this epoch is referred to as the Age of Greatness.

The bold expansionist stance that Sweden had taken demanded considerable changes in society. New government offices were to be created, the judicial administration

PAGES 8–9 *Drottningholm Palace outside Stockholm, designed by Nicodemus Tessin the Elder and begun in 1662, exemplifies Sweden's architectural ambitions in the Age of Greatness.*

FACING PAGE *For her coronation in 1650, Queen Christina had a triumphal arch built of wood and canvas modeled after the ancient Arch of Constantine in Rome. In the background to the left is the north facade of the old royal castle, Three Crowns. (Engraving from Erik Dahlbergh's* Suecia antiqua et hodierna).

RIGHT *Arch of Constantine, early fourth century.*

modernized, and the military organization made more effective. Achieving all these objectives required a great many loyal servants. Because Sweden's high offices were accessible only to the nobility, noblemen were generously allotted land and riches as reward for their dedication to the state. When there were too few men of noble birth to fill the state offices, able commoners were chosen and elevated to nobility. Ennoblement and the distribution of fiefdoms owing allegiance to the Crown reached an all-time high during Queen Christina's reign.

Architecture provided a visual expression of the power of the nobility. Private palaces that were constructed throughout the country exhibited a level of magnificence never before seen in Sweden. The building boom culminated during the 1660s and '70s, led primarily by Chancellor of the Realm (*rikskansler*) Magnus Gabriel De la Gardie, one of the period's luminaries. In 1674, De la Gardie was said to be building in some fifty different places in Sweden and its provinces, in addition to the many churches that he built or repaired.

Aspiring to compete with the luxury and refinement of Continental Europe's upper classes, the Swedish nobility and the state itself drew inspiration and professional help from abroad. Although Swedish architecture already relied on imported expertise—canal and fortifications engineers from the Netherlands, for example, and German sculptors and master builders—design in Sweden was to a great extent guided by utilitarian rather than esthetic considerations. This pragmatism was not strict or universal, however, and especially in Stockholm some houses were erected with attention to ornamental details. North German and Dutch influences contributed to a Swedish synthesis of late-Gothic and Mannerist Renaissance styles that resulted in houses built with brick-red exteriors adorned with rich decorative window quoins and sandstone rustication, and topped with steep roofs and high gables.

The first architect in the modern sense of the word—that is, a professional with intellectual education and special training that placed him on an equal social footing with his patrons—the Frenchman Simon de la Vallée raised the stan-

ABOVE *The House of Nobility in Stockholm was originally designed by Simon de la Vallée, but the project progressed under the direction of other architects. This drawing, from about 1666, is almost certainly the work of Simon's son Jean de la Vallée, who was involved in the building's completion and influenced its final appearance.*

BELOW *The anatomy theater at the University of Uppsala was designed by scientist-architect Olof Rudbeck and built in 1662–63 as a hall for medical students to observe dissections. This woodcut comes from Rudbeck's book,* Atlantica.

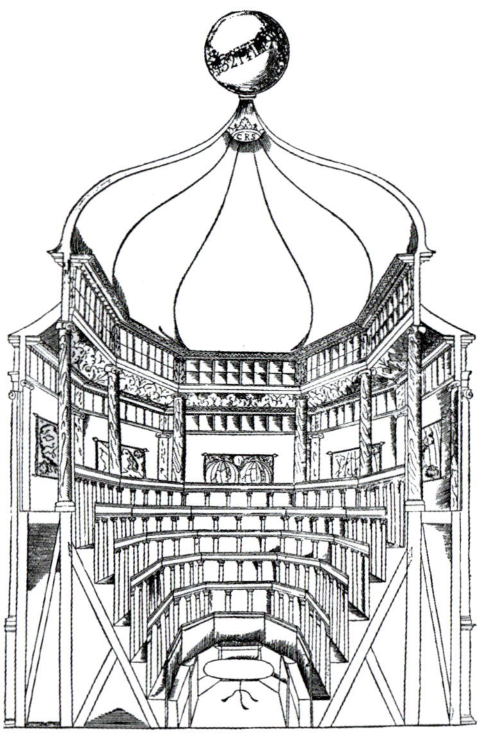

dard of Swedish architecture from the time of his arrival in 1637. Simon de la Vallée's most important commission was a new meeting place for the noblemen, the House of Nobility (*Riddarhuset*) in Stockholm. The architect based his original proposals on French palace architecture, but as the project progressed under later architects, its style came close to contemporary Dutch classicism. With its distinct classical elements and an original roof design, however, the House of Nobility exerted a significant influence on Swedish architecture.

During the intensive building period that followed, Jean de la Vallée, son of Simon, and Nicodemus Tessin the Elder became prominent as Sweden's two leading architects. Both had been trained in France and Italy, and both knew theory and the classical motifs as well as the trends taking shape in the cultural centers of Continental Europe. As a result of their work for the monarchy and the nobility, both rose to great heights in Swedish society. Through them, international architecture was seriously introduced into Sweden.

In 1662, for Dowager Queen Hedvig Eleonora, Nicodemus Tessin the Elder designed Drottningholm Palace, the most grandiose Swedish composition ever created (see pages 8–9). Erected just outside Stockholm beside Lake Mälaren, the splendid baroque palace was a manifestation of Sweden's newly attained position of power. At the same time, it also symbolized the new dynasty that claimed the throne with the coronation in 1654 of Queen Christina's cousin, King Karl X Gustav, by whose name the new Palatine royal line became known as the Karolinian. Drottningholm represented something truly new in Sweden: a precise, symmetrically organized building following the classical vocabulary and set amid an elaborate, formal, baroque garden parterre and park. The pattern realized at Drottningholm served as a prototype for the country palaces and manor houses later erected for Swedish aristocrats.

Elsewhere, beneath the anomalous and striking exterior of a copper-clad cupola atop the University of Uppsala's Gustavianum, a superb anatomy theater (1662–63) offers an example of the Swedish fascination with classical antiquity. Its architect, the versatile scientist Olof Rudbeck the Elder, shaped the auditorium's interior as an octagonal amphitheater with steps radiating upward from the stage supporting the dissection table. A series of pilasters adorning the rows of seats and representing the classical orders of architecture attest to Rudbeck's affinity with the architecture of antiquity.

The strong attraction of both ancient and contemporary Rome for the young Swedish superpower is evident not only in the allusions in the art and architecture of the period but also in the growing numbers of travelers to the Eternal City. While it became almost obligatory for an artist or architect with ambitions to visit Rome, noblemen as well, thirsting for cultivation and refinement, made their way there. (After abdicating the throne in 1654, Queen Christina too set out for Rome, propelled by both her admiration for Continental European culture and her Catholicism.) And there was another culture the Swedes wished to adopt: the French, especially as it flowered during the glorious reign of the Sun King, Louis XIV. In the late seventeenth century, Versailles became the leading model in interior furnishings, gardens, theater, and ceremonial life.

The Swedes did their best to copy all things French, though they were also eager to show that they stood apart. In emulation of the French use of the Sun as a symbol for King Louis XIV, the Swedes designated the Polar Star a symbol of their monarchy; it was usually accompanied by a proud motto, *Septentrioni Ortum quod Merito nescit Occasum*, meaning that, as the Polar Star never sets, so the Swedish empire guaranteed world harmony and order.

THE SWEDISH MONARCHY: 1650–1840

During the span covered in this book, Sweden came under the rule of monarchs from five royal houses, or dynasties. The rule of the Vasa dynasty in fact began long before the present discussion, with King Gustav I (1521/23–60). The Bernadotte dynasty has endured many generations past the death of Karl XIV Johan, to the present day. While a monarch-to-be was underage and yet to be crowned, authority sometimes rested with an advisor or advisory council, that is, a regent; the period of a regent's control was the years of regency of a crown prince or princess. As the list below indicates, royal marriages, often guided by political concerns, invariably crossed national boundaries.

VASA DYNASTY

GUSTAV II ADOLF (reign 1611–32) married Maria Eleonora of Brandenburg 1620

CHRISTINA (regency 1632–44, reign 1644–abdication 1654)

PALATINE DYNASTY

KARL X GUSTAV (reign 1654–60) married Hedvig Eleonora of Holstein-Gottorp 1654

KARL XI (regency 1660–72, reign 1672–97) married Ulrika Eleonora of Denmark 1680

KARL XII (regency 1697, reign 1697–1718)

ULRIKA ELEONORA (reign 1719–20) married Fredrik of Hesse 1715

HESSE DYNASTY

Fredrik I of Hesse (reign 1720–51)

HOLSTEIN-GOTTORP DYNASTY

ADOLF FREDRIK (reign 1751–71) married Lovisa Ulrika of Prussia 1744

GUSTAV III (reign 1771–92) married Sophia Magdalena of Denmark 1766

GUSTAV IV ADOLF 1792 (regency 1792–96, reign 1796–1809) married Fredrika of Baden 1797, divorced 1812

KARL XIII (reign 1809–18) married Hedvig Elisabet Charlotta of Oldenburg 1774

BERNADOTTE DYNASTY

KARL XIV JOHAN (reigned 1818–44) married Désirée Clary 1798

The Royal Palace in Stockholm by Nicodemus Tessin the Younger replaced the old Three Crowns. This engraving from the 1750s by architect Jean Eric Rehn depicts the palace from the northeast.

The same national self-assertion was a force driving the building activity during the Age of Greatness. This was displayed especially clearly in Erik Dahlbergh's *Suecia antiqua et hodierna* (Sweden in Antiquity and Today), an impressive collection of engravings that presented Sweden's newly erected palaces and manor houses to the rest of Europe and attested to the Nordic nation's greatness and honor. Today the book, compiled in 1715, still provides a rich source of knowledge about seventeenth-century Swedish architecture. To be sure of capturing the precision and elegance of architects' original concepts, Dahlbergh sometimes followed the initial drawings instead of depicting what was actually built. In some cases, therefore, Dahlbergh's renderings give a somewhat loftier impression than do the buildings themselves.

In 1672, Karl XI, then just seventeen years old, claimed the throne after the country had been controlled for twelve years by a regency led by Magnus Gabriel De la Gardie, Karl's uncle by marriage. The young king became engaged to a Danish princess, but this did not dissuade Denmark from declaring war on Sweden, which successfully defended her domination of the Baltic during the Scanian War (1675–79). Not three decades after the end of the Thirty Years War, the new hostilities plunged Sweden into acute financial crisis. One result was a call for an inquiry into the administration of the previous regency. Another was a demand for a *reduktion* (Reduction), meaning a return to the Crown's control of all the lands recently granted to the expanded nobility. Although the estates of the old nobility were relatively unaffected, many newly rich clans that had attained noble status only in exchange for pledges of loyalty to the Crown now faced financial ruin. Magnus Gabriel De la Gardie was probably the person most affected: In a single sweep, he lost nearly all his properties. Though the land-owning nobility managed to save many of their belonging, their power was diminished, and a new privileged class—men with skills and competence but no high titles—took their place.

The Reduction had been supported by the clergy, the burghers, and the peasants, that is, the three lower of the four Estates that constituted the Parliament. Since the days of Gustav II Adolf, the king, though holding a strong position, had formally reigned with the advice of a Council and the Parliament—the latter being especially influential on decisions concerning war, taxes, and conscription. Now, however, parliamentary support gave absolute power to the king and led during the 1680s to the foundation of a royal autocracy.

With the royal autocracy in power, the architectural initiative shifted to the state. Much of Sweden's labor force now became engaged in national defense. Under the leadership of Erik Dahlbergh, Swedish fortifications underwent their own great age, and activities in fortress building along the country's borders intensified. Large sums of money went toward the main fortified cities such as Göteborg and Karlskrona, with the latter founded as a new base for the Royal Navy in 1680. Karlskrona was built on an ideal baroque city plan, with a grand boulevard and streets radiating from an open public square. Meanwhile, a nationwide military allotment system (*indelningsverket*) instituted by Karl XI enabled the creation of an army of professional soldiers and the construction of housing for them. Proper houses were built for officers; for lower-ranking soldiers, crofts were provided, all on the economic base created by the Reduction. Moreover, in peacetime, Swedish agriculture had the benefit of soldiers' working as farmers.

Karl XI also harbored a strong interest in religion and declared himself head of the Swedish Protestant church. During his reign, which lasted until 1697, baroque church building reached its pinnacle. While the king's involvement with the church was rooted in his own deep piety, it also had another goal: every citizen's regular participation in church services. From the pulpit, one could easily disseminate not only religious messages but also political propaganda. Church interiors that were open and that had good sight lines as well as good acoustics offered the advantage that the minister could be seen and heard by all. The aristocracy's main contribution to ecclesiastical architecture was mostly limited to mausoleums erected at old country churches.

Nicodemus Tessin the Younger, son of Tessin the Elder, took charge of the great majority of the royal autocracy's artistic undertakings. His great competence and political loyalty were qualities that the Crown needed and could appreciate. In exchange for high titles and honors, the architect glorified the monarchy through all aspects of architecture and elevated ceremonial court life to a level comparable to that of the leading nations of Continental Europe. Though Tessin ranks among the most important baroque architects in Europe, he was also a pragmatic ideologue and politician. His most prestigious work, the Royal Palace in Stockholm, became the most prominent symbol of the Swedish empire.

In 1697, the same year that the old Three Crowns was destroyed by fire and work began on the new royal palace, Karl XI died. The throne was claimed by his son, who, as Karl XII, became the third and last king of the Palatine dynasty. Three years later, an alliance of Denmark, Poland, and Russia attacked Sweden, and the young king left Stockholm at the head of his army. This was the beginning of the Great Nordic War (1700–21).

During the first few years at war, Sweden received regular victory messages from the front on the far shore of the Baltic Sea, but soon her luck changed. At the battle of Poltava in 1709, the entire Swedish army was captured by Czar Peter the Great and herded to Russia. Karl XII escaped to Turkey, where he remained isolated for five years. In Stockholm, construction on the Royal Palace halted, and the country stood on the verge of economic ruin.

After Karl XII's return to Sweden, the country's last resources were mobilized in an attempt to invade Norway. At the siege of the Fredriksten Fortification on November 30, 1718, the king was shot through the head and killed. Whether the shot was fired by an enemy or came from one of his own men remains a question. His death brought to an abrupt end to both the Crown's absolute rule and the Age of Greatness.

Pressured by the Russian navy's raids along the Baltic coast (1719–21), Sweden was forced into a very costly peace treaty. The Baltic provinces were lost, along with most of the German territories; only Finland remained Swedish. Sweden reverted to her humble position as a minor state.

THE AGE OF LIBERTY (1719-1772)

Freed from the grip of royal autocracy, Sweden started life afresh, with a new constitution, social structure, and spirit. "Here everyone is behaving like flies that have survived the winter and come to life again" is how one citizen described the political mood in Stockholm in 1718, shortly after the king's death.

In the new Sweden that was taking shape, power was divided between the Council (i.e., the government) and the Parliament. Karl XII's younger sister Ulrika Eleonora was elected queen but only after renouncing all claims to absolute power, and she quickly relinquished the throne to her husband, Fredrik I of Hesse. Fredrik, in turn, settled for a limited role in politics as chairman of the Council. In time, a parliamentary system similar to that of Great Britain was developed; it was characterized by frictions between the two parties, the Hats (*hattarna*) and the Caps (*mössorna*).

The Hats, led by military officers, public officials, and large company holders, allied themselves with France and against Russia and governed the country for thirty years. Active economic policies were at the top of the Hats' agenda. The cautious and realistic Caps, representing the lower ranks of the bourgeoisie, the land-owning nobility, the clergy, and the peasants, took over in 1765. Through foreign policy, the Caps were more closely allied with England, Denmark, and Russia. The political oppositions turned what Swedish history refers to as the Age of Liberty into a disorderly epoch, but one that laid the foundation for a more peaceful Sweden.

The style of interior decoration at Hammarby, the summer house purchased in 1758 by Carl Linnaeus, lies midway between late baroque and rococo. Botanical prints cover the bedroom walls, on one of which hangs a painting, a gift from King Adolf Fredrik, of a pet guenon monkey given to the great botanist by Queen Lovisa Ulrika.

Though the wars and hardships of the Karolinian period had drastically depleted both the country's economy and its population, recovery occurred quickly. Several years of abundant harvests and the swift development of many newly established manufacturers stimulated the Swedish economy, largely because of the Hat party's politics. Most of the measures undertaken benefited Swedish society. In 1735, the Royal Drawing Academy was founded, laying the foundation for the later Royal Academy of Fine Arts. Four years later came the establishment of the Royal Academy of Science, founded with an explicit objective of furthering the nation's interests. Within fourteen years, Sweden also had its Royal Academy of Arts and Letters.

Meanwhile, in 1739, the Parliament had created the Department of Manufacturing to promote domestic production, especially of decorative materials such as silk and faience. From the standpoint of the national economy, these enterprises were of relatively little significance, but for artistic and cultural life, the influence of the new department was great.

In terms either of corporate profits or the penetrating effect that a single company had on the times, no firm compared to the Swedish East India Company, which had been established in 1731 with headquarters in Göteborg. Under the firm's auspices, Chinese goods poured into Sweden throughout the century, generating immense profits for the company's owners and promoting a lively interest in East Asia that spread deep into the Swedish countryside.

Sweden's clock had turned from twelve to one: Karl XII fell, and Fredrik I rose. A new period began with renewed spirit and promising potential. To be sure, peace in Sweden always faced challenges; now the main threat came from Russia. Strengthening the defense of the country's eastern parts therefore became an important task for the Age of Liberty's leading politicians. On a rocky island off the Finnish coast at Helsinki, a great fortress, Sveaborg, was constructed. The builders of Sveaborg aspired to make it impregnable, and the fortress became Sweden's biggest building project of the period.

Some of Sweden's greatest contributions to the world at large were products of the Age of Liberty, most notably in the fields of science, letters, and culture. The Age of Liberty coincided with the Age of Enlightenment, which had its origins in England and flowered in France. The broad swing in Continental Europe away from superstition, prejudice, and unquestioning acceptance of authority and toward reason, logic, and learning occurred in Sweden as well, although it affected only a minority of the people. France's influence on

Svindersvik, the summer house of wealthy merchant Claes Grill, appears to the left in this 1748 gouache by Michael Andries. Designed by Carl Hårleman, Svindersvik is one of Sweden's finest rococo sites.

Sweden grew stronger than ever before, at least at the court and among aristocrats and intellectuals, who took a lively interest in the writings of Voltaire and Rousseau. Members of the Swedish middle classes, meanwhile, were particularly attracted to England's more utilitarian and bourgeois outlook. Swedish academicians of the time attained a stature comparable to that of the great thinkers and investigators abroad, most especially in the natural sciences. The Age of Liberty produced such eminent Swedish scientists as Anders Celsius (astronomer and physicist), Emanuel Swedenborg (philosopher, theologian, and natural scientist), and Carl Linnaeus (botanist)—all fathers of modern science.

Tranquility, economic progress, and widespread optimism led to a renewed interest in building. The development of discernable new stylistic ideals took time, though. The late baroque style still dominated the architecture of manor houses as well as provincial churches, though a new tone different from the earlier one gradually emerged. As a result of the newly invigorated ambition to build, the Parliament voted in 1727 to resume work on the Royal Palace after a standstill of nearly two decades. This action, however, encountered an unforeseen complication. Completion of the palace required a massive work force, and the lack of qualified craftsmen was obvious. Count Carl Gustav Tessin, the son of Nicodemus Tessin the Younger and his father's successor as superintendent of buildings, and court architect Carl Hårleman, who took the greater role in the completion of the palace, decided to recruit the needed manpower in France; it was there that Hårleman had become familiar with the new Rococo style. Soon, French artisans and craftsmen in the workshops around the palace were ably rendering the Swedish palace's rococo carvings and paintings from Carl Hårleman's drawings.

Through his architecture and furnishings based on French prototypes, Carl Hårleman created an ideal, simple, and restrained style that set the tone for most eighteenth-century Swedish architecture. This is especially beautifully expressed in his manor houses, which certainly contributed to shaping what today is considered the Swedish style.

As the marriage of Fredrik I and Ulrika Eleonora produced no children, the Parliament was compelled to seek a suitable heir to the throne elsewhere. After pressure from Russia, it was decided in 1743 that Adolf Fredrik, a scion of the north German ducal dynasty of Holstein-Gottorp, would be the new Swedish heir. Not only was Adolf Fredrik a grandson of Karl XII's elder sister, but also and more important, he was a relative of the Russian empress, Elisabeth. As Russia had just defeated Sweden in battle (1741–43), the victor got its way: access to the Swedish throne. In the following year, the crown prince married Lovisa Ulrika, sister of Frederick the Great of Prussia. The couple produced four lively children, all of whom reached adulthood: Gustav (the third of that name), Karl (the thirteenth), Fredrik Adolf, and Sophia Albertina. In 1751, Adolf Fredrik was crowned king of Sweden.

Raised in autocratic Prussia, Lovisa Ulrika had more trouble finding her way in the Swedish political system than did her quiet, good-natured husband, and she made several attempts to strengthen the power of the monarchy. She was discovered as the instigator of a coup d'état, albeit unsuccessful, in 1756. The royalist aristocrats involved with the conspirators were executed, and the royal couple threatened with dethronement and exile. After some embarrassing reprimands, however, the alleged insurgents were pardoned.

The Prussian princess made her greatest contributions to Sweden in art and culture. She brought about the refurbishment and enlargement of Drottningholm Palace as a modern summer residence for the royal family, and she participated in developing the exotic Chinese Pavilion nearby. She pursued such cultural interests as book collecting, theater, and the study of natural history, which resulted in a series of milieus that are considered the most exquisite of eighteenth-century Swedish creations. It was she who founded the Royal Academy of Arts and Letters, where annual gatherings were held on her birthday. Virtually without political power and access to government funds, the royal family had to make do with the palaces that already existed. Nevertheless, the royals were in a class of their own when it came to constructing buildings and commissioning art.

During the eighteenth century another group of patrons arose from the internationally oriented bourgeoisie. Together with office holders from the lower nobility, these wealthy merchants and industrial leaders assumed the initiative in most areas. Carl Gustav Tessin—a diplomat and art collector, and by now a leading Hat politician and Sweden's Court Marshal—belonged to this group and counted as one of the most illustrious personalities of the eighteenth century. Carl Gustav Tessin's country house, Åkerö, housed an exceptional collection of French art and in all respects exhibited the ultimate in good taste and refinement. His collections today constitute an important basis for the National Museum of Fine Arts in Stockholm.

For Sweden to rise from the poor condition in which it began the Age of Liberty to the commercial, scientific, and cultural level of many other European countries took just fifty years. Throughout these decades, Sweden's population continued to grow steadily, reaching more than two million in 1770. The population of Swedish-held Finland, meanwhile, reached 600,000. Ten percent of the population in both countries lived in the cities, Stockholm being the largest, with 75,000, followed by Göteborg and Karlskrona, with about 10,000 each. The remaining towns were small and rural. The nobility made up about five percent of the population. Nine out of ten Swedes lived in the country and under meager conditions.

Social change characterized the final years of the Age of Liberty. But the initial, ebullient optimism had cooled down. Disputes between the political parties increased, while divisive antagonisms between the aristocracy and the lower classes deepened. Open criticism of aristocratic privileges was on the rise, as were corruption and misuse of power. It was time to go in a new direction—but which way?

THE GUSTAVIAN AGE (1772–1809)

Crown Prince Gustav was attending the theater in Paris one evening in 1771 when he received the news of the death of his father, King Adolf Fredrik. Upon his return to Sweden, the prince was crowned King Gustav III, Sweden's second ruler from the Holstein-Gottorp dynasty. In the following year, on August 19, King Gustav took advantage of the current political instability and carried out a bloodless coup d'état. In one swift moment Sweden's political system changed dramatically. A new constitution was established, which essentially reintroduced the principles of sovereignty, and the parliamentary government was replaced by Gustav III's own royal autocracy.

During the next twenty years, nearly everything that occurred, was said, or was thought in Sweden was influenced by Gustav III. Gifted, egocentric, and frenetically busy, he controlled both domestic and foreign politics while enthusiastically leading the country's cultural life as well. Some people viewed him as the country's savior, others as an evil tyrant.

The first decade of his regime was politically calm, and the French-oriented Gustav III stood out as one of Europe's most enlightened monarchs. But the 1780s saw growing tensions between the king and his opposition. Paradoxically, it was within the nobility that power struggles ruffled the most feathers. In an attempt to regain popularity and break the opposition's power, Gustav III attacked Russia, the official rationale being to regain some of the Finland's Baltic provinces that had been lost earlier. The Russian War (1788–90) ended in a status quo ante bellum, but it led to a group of noblemen's openly opposing the king. Gustav III summoned the Parliament, and in 1789 he pushed through a new form of government, reinstating an absolute monarchy. Although the French Revolution, which occurred in the same year, won little support in Sweden, the king nevertheless decided to stem any attempt at insurgency by introducing censorship, curtailing the nobility's privileges, and giving the lower estates more rights.

Though opinions of Gustav III's political contributions vary, his reign was indisputably a period of unprecedented artistic flowering in Sweden. Gustav III consciously used art and culture for patriotic purposes. Inspired by the cultural institutions in France, he founded the Royal Academy of Music, reinvigorated the newly established Royal Academy of Arts and Letters, and founded the Swedish Academy, the eighteen members of which were bidden not only to groom the language but also to honor the regent. The Royal Academy of Fine Arts experienced a golden age during his reign, and both opera and theater won the king's favor and were awarded a national stage. No other Swedish monarch had had so great an interest in theater, and no other had promoted it as he did. Gustav III is still known today as "the Theater King."

As absolute monarch, Gustav III was able to initiate various building projects and to fulfill his elaborate architectural dreams without interference from the Parliament. Despite this, he left behind no royal palace of monumental scale. Haga, the king's pavilion outside Stockholm, which occupied his interest during his last decade, still stands out as a gem in Swedish architecture; however, the enormous palace intended for the site never advanced beyond a foundation.

Gustav III left so great a mark on both art and architecture that even today Swedes refer to the Gustavian style. This style, which replaced the rococo, is often thought of as the Swedish national counterpart to the French fine and decorative arts of King Louis XVI. The lines and shapes that char-

King Gustav III was thirty-one years old when he was portrayed by Lorens Pasch the Younger (1777).

acterize the Gustavian style had in fact been developed several years before Gustav III's coronation, but it was the monarch—greatly influenced by French art and culture—whose patronage contributed to the style's popularity and dissemination. Elegant and restrained, the Gustavian style is still widely regarded as the ultimate expression of Swedish good taste.

Gustav III's journey to Italy in 1783–84 is usually seen as the preface to the Late Gustavian style. As the king's tastes changed, architecture and interior decoration in Sweden developed toward a more stern and international form of neoclassicism. The Late Gustavian style, on which the king himself exerted an especially strong personal influence, continued well after Gustav III was gone.

As it had in the mid-seventeenth century, eighteenth-century Rome attracted more Swedes than the king. For architects, the journey to Rome was nearly obligatory. Many continued south to Naples and to the excavations of the ancient cities of Herculaneum and Pompeii, or still further,

This Gustavian ballroom housed in a 1780 annex to Svindersvik appears today almost exactly as it did more than two centuries ago.

to Paestum and Sicily, where they came into direct contact with Greek originals. The results reached Sweden quickly. Swedish churches and other public buildings were soon adorned with heavy Doric columns and pilasters. Palaces and manor houses, meanwhile, were being furnished in the style seen in Roman wall paintings. Circular temples, figures of ancient deities, and obelisks emulating those that Roman conquerors had hauled home from Egypt appeared in Swedish parks and gardens. The sight amazed foreign visitors. During a visit to the Gunnebo estate outside Göteborg, the English feminist writer and traveler Mary Wollstonecraft could not contain her astonishment over the Swedes' need to install, in this untouched Nordic landscape, not only columns but also, "Venuses and Apollos condemned to lie in snow three parts of the year."

In keeping with his enthusiasm for Italy, Gustav III acquired a collection of ancient sculptures. The most admired pieces were a figure of the sleeping Endymion and a sculptural group representing Apollo and the Muses. Awaiting the completion of the new residence at Haga, the sculptures were installed in a gallery in the Royal Palace. Years later, the king's collection was moved to a pair of galleries in the lower northeast wing, where it constituted Sweden's first public museum, dedicated to Gustav III.

Within the noble circle as well as among more radically minded citizens, the king's autocratic behavior eventually provoked a drastic reaction that led to a decisive step: the murder of the king. The last act of Gustav III's life played out in a theater—or rather, in the opera house in Stockholm that the king himself had commissioned. At a masquerade ball on March 16, 1792, the

Stockholm Monuments

1. Royal Palace
Stockholms slott
2. Tessin palace
Tessinska palatset
3. Oxenstierna palace
Oxenstiernska palatset
4. Royal Mint
Kungliga mynthuset
5. Bonde palace
Bondeska palatset, present Supreme Court
6. House of Nobility
Riddarhuset
7. Rosenhane palace
Rosenhaneska palatset, present Court of Appeals
8. Riddarholm church
Riddarholmskyrkan
9. The Exchange
Börsen
10. Swedish National Bank
Gamla riksbanken
11. Customs House
Tullpackhuset
12. Skeppsholm church
Skeppsholmskyrkan
13. Royal Opera House
Kungliga operan
14. Sophia Albertina's Palace
Arvsfurstens palats, present Swedish Foreign Ministry
15. Garrison Hospital
Garnisonssjukhuset, present Stockholm County Concil
16. Karlberg
Present Military Academy Karlberg
17. Drottningholm
18. Adolf Fredrik's Church
Adolf Fredriks kyrka
19. Haga
20. Rosendal
21. Katarina Church
Katarina kyrka

The Royal Museum opened in 1794 as Sweden's first public museum. The visitor today can view King Gustav III's collection of antique sculptures as it was originally displayed in two galleries designed by Carl Fredrik Sundvall in the Royal Palace.

king was mortally wounded by a pistol shot in the back, and he died two weeks later. The murderer, Captain Johan Anckarström, was publicly executed in front of the House of Nobility; no other suspects were apprehended. The deceased king's brother, Prince Karl, found it in his best interest to close the case quickly.

The assassination of Gustav III failed, however, in the sense that the absolute monarchy continued with his son, Gustav IV Adolf. Under the new king, Sweden again became unstable, with politics deeply affected by the Napoleonic wars. Gustav IV Adolf's disgust both for the revolt and for Napoleon contributed to his decision, in 1805, to enter into a war with Russia and England against France. The French easily captured the Swedish province of Pomerania on the far side of the Baltic Sea, and, when Napoleon and the Czar agreed to peace in 1807, Sweden was ordered to break off her alliance with England. When Sweden refused to comply, Russian troops invaded Finland. The war of 1808–9 ended in complete defeat for Sweden. Finland was once and for all lost to her, and Stockholm waited for the enemy's approach.

In light of this situation, a group of civil and military officers deemed Gustav IV Adolf incapable of ruling, and in March 1809, before the war was over, the king was arrested and deposed. A parliamentary session quickly formed a new constitution, which, to a great extent, is still in effect today. While the deposed monarch was driven into exile, the late Gustav III's brother was nominated to succeed Gustav IV Adolf as King Karl XIII. The Gustavian absolute monarchy was abolished. Sweden was now a constitutional monarchy.

THE KARL JOHAN PERIOD (1810–44)

In 1810, the French Field Marshal Jean Baptiste Bernadotte was elected to be heir to the Swedish throne. He was met with great enthusiasm when he arrived in his new country, where he was adopted by the childless King Karl XIII. Within months of Bernadotte's arrival, Désirée, the wife of Sweden's French crown prince, followed. The lady radiated a glamorous aura owing in part to her prior engagement to Napoleon. But Désirée had a difficult time with the Swedish climate, and almost immediately, she went home to France. Not until 1823, for the marriage of her son Oscar, did she return to Sweden.

Though Bernadotte was not crowned until 1818, under the name Karl XIV Johan, he had in reality been acting as regent for eight years. He immediately took control of politics, skillfully leading a badly damaged Sweden through the difficult aftermath of the Napoleonic Wars. From a cautious distance, Sweden participated in the great coalition of countries that, in 1813, finally triumphed over Napoleon's troops in Leipzig.

Many Swedes had hoped to reclaim Finland, but Karl Johan had other plans. Instead of marching on Finland, he turned his troops against Denmark, which, in 1814, was forced to relinquish control of Norway to Sweden. Faced with the superiority of Sweden's weapons, the reluctant Norwegians had no choice but to enter into a ninety-year union with their neighbor. Thereafter, peace dominated the Scandinavian peninsula.

The Karl Johan period, which continued until 1844, was a time that historians characterize with the military expression, "marching in place." The opposition complained about the lack of actual change and about what they called the king's "bedchamber regency" (Karl Johan made a habit of addressing advisors and government representatives

Rosendal, the Stockholm summer palace of King Karl XIV Johan, was designed by Fredrik Blom and built in the 1820s.

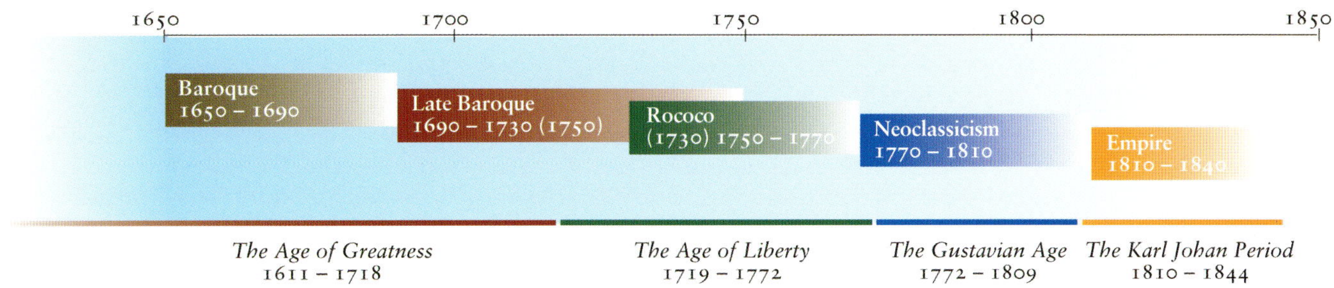

Timeline of Swedish history.

in his bedchamber as he prepared to rise in the afternoon.) Despite this, there were a number of substantial advances in the social and economical spheres, as well as in the cultural, but they often took place in silence and therefore went largely unnoticed.

The arts from the Karl Johan period have always stood in the shadow of the artistic achievements of the Gustavian age. Neoclassicism continued to color academic art well into the nineteenth century, and the same applied in architecture. The country manor houses that were built reflected a taste for moderation, with their foremost traits being simplicity and good proportions, although they were not entirely without monumental elements. Columns continued to be the prevalent symbol of power and status. In the growing cities, classicism, well balanced and somberly expressed, reached its full height during the first half of the century.

The harsh times called for utilitarian buildings such as hospitals, barracks, and schools. Most of these were erected in a severe, toned-down style. Function was the watchword. The period's largest undertaking involved something as pragmatic as the Göta Canal (1810–32), which linked the country's east and west coasts via waterways. The canal was an enormous project, led by military officers and carried out by soldiers. Construction of the Karlsborg military fortress in southwest Sweden was closely connected to the building of the Göta Canal and was intended to be the main fortress for Sweden's troops. Such projects demonstrated that the military was in charge.

Bernadotte's time as crown prince and regent coincided with the French Empire style, which in Sweden was named for him: the Karl Johan style. The two terms are almost interchangeable, though the Swedish version is usually lighter and somewhat simpler than its French counterpart. It is, in effect, a continuation of European neoclassicism, with inspirations still drawn from antiquity, mostly from the Roman Empire.

The style was applied primarily in interiors. Rooms were painted to imitate marble or cloaked in textiles to give the impression of a military tent. Furniture of dark mahogany, gilt ormolu bronzes, vibrant colors, and shiny fabrics—everything that characterizes the style—is evident at Karl Johan's summer palace in Stockholm. Called Rosendal, it is considered the most harmonious and best-preserved Empire environment in Sweden.

Toward the end of the Karl Johan period, there was no longer any dominant ideal style in Sweden. Academic classicism in architecture went into eclipse. New technical and practical advantages allowed architects to experiment freely with shape and form, and to explore other sources of stylistic ideas. The derivative "neo" styles, such as neo-Gothic and neo-Renaissance, permeated Swedish architecture throughout much of the nineteenth century.

Awareness of the national heritage that developed during the Karl Johan period found expression beyond architecture. Native Nordic gods and heroes took up the fight with imported classical Greek and Roman gods. As his predecessor acquired sculptures of Apollo and the nine muses, Karl Johan ordered colossal sculptures of the ancient Nordic Asa gods. He also had a frieze painted in one of the salons at Rosendal depicting the Scythian chieftain Oden, founder of the Asa line, coming to Sweden and saving the country. The allegorical connection between the king and the mythological figure was obvious. Karl Johan was most assertive that his life as king was unlike that of any other living being. As he said on his deathbed, *Personne n'a fourni une carrière semblable à la mienne*—No one has completed a path comparable to mine.

CHAPTER TWO

The Baroque

PAGES 26–27 *Skokloster castle, begun in 1654 on a plan by German architect Caspar Vogel but completed by other architects, was in its day Sweden's largest private residence. It still stands as a monument to its patron, Field Marshal Carl Gustav Wrangel, and to the grand building traditions of Sweden's Baroque period.*

RIGHT *Most of the costly baroque interiors of Skokloster survive intact, such as the King's Hall, with its brightly colored plaster ceiling ornament depicting Saint George and the Dragon and its equestrian portraits of kings.*

During the mid-seventeenth century, the Continental Baroque style permeated Swedish architecture. Plans for elaborate palaces and other buildings of major public significance were drawn from models in Italy, France, Holland, and Germany—not infrequently with elements from several different prototypes intermingled. The bold, dramatic forms usually associated with the Baroque style were relatively restrained in Sweden, however, at least in architecture, in which the visual vocabulary and design principles of antiquity exerted strong influence. Thus, though the term Baroque serves throughout Europe to define both the historical period and the prevalent style of the latter 1600s, Swedish architecture from this time can more aptly be termed baroque classicism.

In interiors and furnishings from the period, classicism was heavily overlaid with baroque pomp and grandeur. Splendid stucco work with swelling, curving forms adorned ceilings and chimney pieces, while walls were decorated with gilt leather, lush tapestries, and paintings depicting myths, allegories, moral principles, and lofty personages both real

and fantastic. In general, Swedish architecture and interior design, which had been dominated by the sometimes stern German style, gave way to the extravagant elegance of the French.

THE BEGINNING OF BAROQUE CLASSICISM

In 1632, Charles Ogier, a delegate in the French legation dispatched by Cardinal Richelieu, did not conceal his consternation over the Sweden he encountered. It was a country, he wrote, in which the aristocracy lived in cold, drafty stone houses with simple wooden furniture and unadorned walls, surrounded by barren, inhospitable nature. Indeed, Jacob De la Gardie, the father of Magnus Gabriel and one of the five regents ruling Sweden during Queen Christina's minority, lived in a house that was no better than those outside Paris occupied by craftsmen and merchants. From such conditions, Swedish monumental architecture rose in only a matter of decades to a level that compared favorably with that of the leading European nations.

This transformation was first seen in the palaces and manor houses of masonry constructed in the provinces at the center of the Swedish empire as well as in Stockholm itself. Forty years after Ogier's visit, the capital city boasted buildings that, according to another foreigner, the Florentine diplomat, Lorenzo Magalotti, had no equals outside Italy. "Not with respect to the quantity or size," wrote Magalotti, "but with regard for the consistency that equals the Italian building traditions and consequently that of Roman antiquity."

The fortunes made in Sweden during the seventeenth century provided the economic base for such superior building. Land was considered the safest investment, and tax deferments as well as other benefits assured that property belonging to the aristocracy could be built to a noble standard.

Besides the economic, there were also ideological motivations. What a nobleman built was a manifestation of himself and his family, and often a representation of his class as well. Furthermore, to build on a grand scale was also seen as a way of honoring the fatherland. Erik Dahlbergh's great volume of engravings, *Suecia antiqua et hodierna*, is indicative of how patriotism could be a motive for building. This noteworthy tome gives not only an impression of Sweden's topography and dwellings during the second half of the seventeenth century, but also a reflection of how the nation wished the rest of the world to see her.

Skokloster Castle, built for Carl Gustav Wrangel, exemplifies the nobility's use of architecture to display status. Wrangel had been a most successful field marshal during the Thirty Years War before rising to great heights in the state bureaucracy. Sweden's largest private building, Skokloster took two decades to build (1654–74) and is today one of the best-preserved seventeenth-century castles in Europe, providing an invaluable record of the period. It still contains nearly all of its original baroque furnishings, art, and textiles, as well as library, armor, and scientific instruments.

Several architects were involved with the design of Skokloster, but the quite elderly German, Caspar Vogel, was responsible for the general plan. Erected on the site of a former medieval cloister, this imposing building consisted of four wings with octagonal towers at each corner and enclosing a central courtyard. Its lavish interiors give a vivid impression of the style of living enjoyed by the newly rich Swedes of the period. Here, Wrangel lived like a German prince in luxurious splendor and surrounded by objects of art and curiosities. Lorenzo Magalotti, however, found the castle too much and too showy, preferring a more refined aesthetic taste—such as the Italian. With its conservative—even old-fashioned—architecture, however, Skokloster did not serve as a model for buildings. Architecture was already evolving in a different direction.

An important step toward a renewal of Swedish architecture was taken in the mid-seventeenth century by Simon de la Vallée (ca. 1600–1642). Born in Paris, de la Vallée began his career under the direction of his father, Marin, one of the architects working for Dowager Queen Marie de Médicis; Marin had participated in such prestigious projects as the Hôtel de Ville and the Luxembourg Palace in Paris. In 1633, Simon left France to work for the Dutch prince of Orange, and four years later, he moved to Sweden.

The first trained, professional architect to practice in Sweden, Simon de la Vallée attracted numerous commissions from private clients. As word of his gifts spread in his newly adopted country, he found himself sought after for public commissions as well. By 1639, indeed, he was named to the position of Royal Architect.

During his tenure in Sweden, Simon de la Vallée initiated many projects, but relatively few were completed. With these, he replaced the architecture influenced by German and Dutch late-Renaissance styles with a French-Dutch classicism, which was then taken up by his successors. The House of Nobility in Stockholm became Simon de la Vallée's most prominent work.

This 1641 perspective drawing of the House of Nobility is the work of Simon de la Vallée. The building was gradually reduced in size during a long construction process, to consist in the end of just the central block.

For many years, when noblemen convened in Stockholm for political deliberations, they had to crowd into old-fashioned quarters. This situation was to change, however, with the offer of a parcel of land by the renowned Axel Oxenstierna, who had been appointed Chancellor of the Realm by Gustav II Adolf and who, in this powerful office, effectively ruled Sweden throughout Christina's years as a minor. Oxenstierna's generosity made possible a suitably splendid meeting place for the nobility on the waterfront to the west of the Royal Palace. The commission for the House of Nobility went to Simon de la Vallée and yielded the earliest example of Swedish architecture in which one can follow the complete design and construction process through drawings.

In 1641, the architect presented two different proposals for the building. The larger one shows a three-story main structure with corner pavilions and four projecting wings, along with a lower entrance wing. The facade, of alternating red brick and sandstone, rusticated pilasters, and a decorative balustrade along the roof, has clear similarities to city palaces in Paris. His inspiration may have come in part from French architect Jacques Androuet du Cerceau's 1576–79 work, *Les plus excellents bastiments de France* (*The Most Excellent Buildings of France*).

The career of Simon de la Vallée came to an abrupt and violent end in 1642, when he was struck down one November evening and left for dead on the public square, Stortorget, in Stockholm. His attacker, a young colonel, was a nephew of Axel Oxenstierna; a settlement was quickly reached between the powerful Oxenstierna family and the architect's heirs.

During the long building period between 1642 and 1674, the House of Nobility was slowly modified to consist only of the central block. A Dutch architect, Justus Vingboons, was called to Sweden to complete the project ten years after de la Vallée's death. Vingboons gave the facade of the building its final, harmonious, classical appearance, with colossal Corinthian pilasters of light gray sandstone contrasting against the brick red walls (originally stuccoed and painted brick red with white joinery imitating masonry). The end result closely resembled buildings in Vingboons's native Holland, such as the Mauritshuis in The Hague or the Trippenhuis in Amsterdam. The House of Nobility was thus transformed into a genuine example of Dutch classicism.

The building was finally completed by Jean de la Vallée (1620–1696), Simon's son, who took over the project in

PRIATIVM
ORDINIS
EQVESTRIS

LEFT *The House of Nobility in Stockholm (1641–74), often cited as Sweden's most beautiful building, was begun on a design by the French-born architect, Simon de la Vallée. With contributions by other architects, it became Sweden's foremost example of Dutch classicism. Before it stands a bronze statue of King Gustav I, the first monarch of the Vasa dynasty. The sculptor, Pierre Hubert L'Archevêque, completed the work in 1774.*

Designed around 1633 by the Dutch architect Pieter Post, the Mauritshuis in The Hague was a model for the House of Nobility. Engraving from Les oeuvrages d'architecture de Pierre Post, *1714.*

Jean de la Vallée, son of Simon, attempted to copy the House of Nobility in wood at Fullerö manor in Västmanland. The panels imitate elements in a classical masonry facade.

1656. Jean de la Vallée cleverly took advantage of the rich facade and added a magnificent roof, which he divided into two sections with a vertical intermediary part and an elegantly curved lower section. A simplified version of this uniquely Swedish roof form—the *säteri* roof—came to dominate the aristocratic manor houses and palaces built over the course of seven decades.

Latin inscriptions along the frieze named the virtues and obligations of the nobility and complemented the roof's allegorical figures. The classical virtues of Honor, Strength, and Wisdom were displayed in the pediment, while the entrance was flanked by the Roman deities, Minerva and Mars, holding aloft a shield. For all who entered this space, the classical gods' message was that, through art and war, the nobility who served as civil officials and military officers thus advanced the cause of their country.

The roof of the House of Nobility, as well as the motifs in the facade decorations, recurred on a smaller scale in many other places. Jean de la Vallée himself was responsible for translating the architectural vocabulary used in the House of Nobility into wood for the manor house Fullerö, in Västmanland (which in fact was completed even before its supposed prototype in Stockholm). With its colossal pilasters, a pediment, a Doric entablature, and painted in colors meant to imitate brick and sandstone, Fullerö imparted a Dutch classicism to the architecture of the Swedish countryside.

THE LEADING ARCHITECTS

Jean de la Vallée was well prepared to take over the House of Nobility project. As the first of many recipients of royal travel stipends, he had gone to France and Italy in the late 1640s and would surely have remained abroad longer had he not been called home to Stockholm for the important task of preparing the city for Queen Christina's coronation. In connection with this event (see also Chapter One), he created, in fact, two triumphal arches in the capital, both made of impermanent materials, of which the better known echoed the Arch of Constantine in Rome.

Soon thereafter, Jean de la Vallée received the title of Royal Architect and with it, responsibility for the city's building projects. His main task was to be to continue building the empire's capital and the Royal Palace; for various reasons, none of these projects could be carried out. Instead, he took on a steady stream of wide-ranging and prestigious commissions from private clients belonging to the aristocracy.

Despite many delays with drawings, Jean de la Vallée was met with much appreciation. After his appointment in 1671 as Stockholm's Mayor of Building, administrative duties displaced the actual practice of architecture. He was awarded a noble title for both his own and his father's architectural achievements and for his administrative contributions to Sweden.

A peer and competitor of Jean de la Vallée, Nicodemus Tessin the Elder (1615–1681), came from Stralsund, in Germany (then part of Sweden), where he had been educated in building fortifications. As an assistant to Simon de la Vallée, he had become well grounded in civil building, although his future development was greatly influenced by a study tour through Europe in 1651–53 sponsored by Queen Christina. Like Jean de la Vallée, Tessin received many commissions from the high nobility, but unlike his rival, he managed his career carefully and was better focused on his goals. While Jean had trouble delivering drawings on time, Tessin carried his tasks to completion. In 1661, after fifteen years as Royal Architect, he took over from Jean responsibility for the Royal Palace and was given the title of Stockholm's first City Architect. Later, King Karl XI elevated Tessin the Elder to the nobility.

Thanks to his skill and tenacity, and to whole troops of assistants, Tessin managed to produce over three decades some thirty great country houses, as well as a number of churches and palaces in Stockholm. He was the supreme master of his time, and with his classically composed architecture he was able to realize his clients' architectural ambitions. While Tessin looked to France, Holland, and Italy for prototypes, his models came primarily from the sixteenth-century Italian architect, Andrea Palladio, whose books on architecture wielded great influence throughout Europe. Tessin traveled in northern Italy to study Palladio's famous villas, in which the Italian master had brilliantly melded visions of the houses and temples of antiquity. Eventually, all of Tessin's time was consumed by the one project for which he is most renowned: Drottningholm, today the residence of Sweden's royal family.

ARCHITECTURE FOR THE MONARCHY

When Dowager Queen Hedvig Eleonora took over Drottningholm in 1661, the palace was owned by Chancellor of the Realm Magnus Gabriel De la Gardie. On the same lakeside site stood a palace erected nearly a century before by the Vasa King Johan III for his wife, Katarina Jagellonica. It was for her that the palace on Lake Mälaren came to be called "the Queen's Islet."

Shortly after Hedvig Eleonora bought the property, the old palace was destroyed by fire. The queen turned to Nicodemus Tessin the Elder and ordered him released from his other royal duties to prepare drawings for a new palace. Tessin made use of the foundation and the surviving walls and laid out a pair of larger rooms—the so-called guards' rooms—plus a stair hall and a vestibule. Around this core, two state apartments with the most prestigious rooms were linked by a gallery facing the sea. All this was contained in a rectangular building with a recessed central section looking toward the garden. The second floor followed a similar arrangement.

Soon after the new foundations were laid in 1662, the queen decided to enlarge the palace. Four two-story corner pavilions were now added, as well as single-story, flat-roofed wings that enclosed two inner courtyards. At the outer corners stood two smaller pavilions to which were affixed, as accenting finials for the building, two domed towers; the southern tower housed the palace kitchen, the northern one was to house the palace chapel (though it was not completed until 1728). Tessin's ability to divide the building's volume into small, well-proportioned, interconnected segments gave the palace a harmonious rhythm while sustaining its overall

Commissioned by Dowager Queen Hedvig Eleonora and designed by Nicodemus Tessin the Elder, Drottningholm Palace, here seen from the east, is Sweden's most impressive baroque creation. Today it is the royal family's residence and, since 1991, has been a designated UNESCO World Heritage site.

architectural integrity. The exterior was completed around 1671.

When completed, the palace consisted of a central, three-story main block facing the water, with only two stories on a low base facing the garden. Above the rusticated ground floor, the facade was articulated by pilasters and moldings. The main portico toward the lake—the formal entrance—was flanked by paired Doric columns and adorned with Sweden's coat-of-arms. On the opposite side of the building, a double stairway provided an imposing passage to the garden. The walls around the three arched openings that formed the entrance were capped by a cornice, with, among other things, console brackets, lion heads, and the Swedish and the Holstein-Gottorp dynasty's coats-of-arms. The architect gave the corner pavilions on this side more elaborate facades, columns, and pediments, while the lower wings were completely rusticated. From the beginning, the stucco walls were pale red with the articulation in gray.

Tessin was able to combine prototypes from different places at Drottningholm to create a personal and independently interpreted baroque classicism. That Tessin possessed detailed knowledge of his classical sources of inspiration is evident in his floor plan for Drottningholm, which derives from Palladio's villas but with a French baroque palace serving as intermediary, or perhaps another prototype, the Dutch

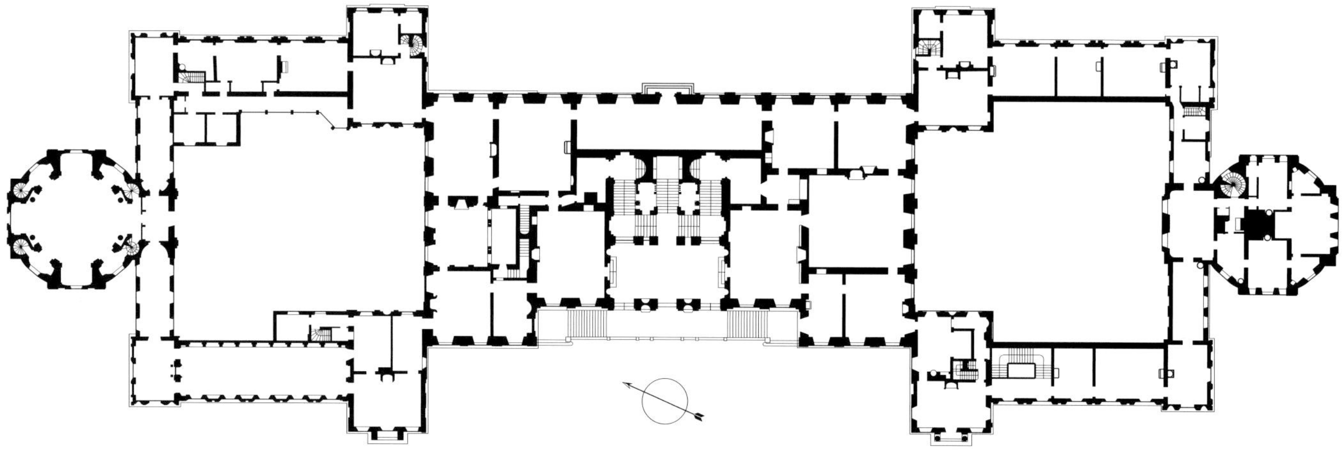

Plan of the main floor at Drottningholm. The central core consists of the main stairs, a vestibule with larger rooms for guards on either side, and a long gallery that stretches along the palace's water side and connects to suites of rooms. Wings projecting from the corner pavilions surround two large interior courtyards and connect the main part of the building to two domed towers; the tower at the south end once housed the kitchen; the one facing north still houses the palace chapel.

FACING PAGE *Dowager Queen Hedvig Eleonora's state bedchamber at Drottningholm, completed in 1683, is one of the finest baroque interiors in Sweden.*

palace, Huis ten Bosch, in The Hague. Just as the system of corner pavilions was inspired by French models such as Luxembourg Palace, the idea to extend the Swedish palace lengthwise may have been derived from Villa Doria Pamphili in Rome; the latter, which also exhibits similar characteristics, was just being completed when Tessin was there. A likely prototype for the garden facade was the Villa Borghese in Rome, with its arcade and loggia.

The central core of Drottningholm palace contains a stairwell, a vestibule, and on the two main floors, long galleries, the lower one of which takes the form of an interior loggia. On either side of this core, on the two upper stories, is a suite of rooms. The lower north suite was furnished as the dowager queen's state apartment and consisted of a small antechamber next to a guards' room, a small audience hall, a state bedchamber (though in fact not for sleeping, and hence referred to instead as the alcove), a large audience hall called "the Ehrenstrahl salon" for the court painter, many of whose works adorn the walls, and a state antechamber. The most distinguished suite, the king's apartment, was to be on the top floor, but the rooms were not completed during the seventeenth century.

During more than a half century, the aging Hedvig Eleonora was occupied with the construction and furnishing of the palace, with the work in her apartment going on for thirty years. It was here that the most important room of the palace was located: Hedvig Eleonora's state bedchamber. The room was designed in a strict classical manner with a flat ceiling above walls articulated with pilasters and with an overabundance of gilding, stucco carvings, and marquetry. Here David Klöcker Ehrenstrahl depicted in allegorical paintings the history of the queen's marriage and the life of her young son, later King Karl XI.

The interior feature most admired during the seventeenth century was the magnificent stairway, which reaches up through the full height of the palace. In this space, all forms of art were combined to create a splendor never before seen in Sweden, with robust stucco reliefs, marble sculptures, as well as perspective fresco paintings by Johan Sylvius. These depicted guests in the garb of faraway places gazing out over the stairway. Geatish kings from Nordic mythology, along with deities and muses from antiquity, were associated with contemporary theories that Sweden was the origin of all European civilizations. The decoration in all the great halls at Drottningholm carried significant symbolism and propaganda. Johan Philip Lemke, the battle-scene painter, depicted the Palatine kings' war deeds in the two galleries, while in the state rooms Ehrenstrahl glorified the

LEFT *The grand stairway at Drottningholm Palace with its stucco ornament, marble sculptures, and perspective paintings, represents a high point of Nicodemus Tessin the Elder's career.*

FACING PAGE *The decoration of Karl XI's gallery on the upper floor at Drottningholm includes Johan Lemke's painted battle scenes depicting the victorious king. Painter Johan Sylvius, brought to Sweden from London where he had worked at Windsor Castle, decorated the ceiling.*

Holstein-Gottorp dynasty's good deeds for the people and the kingdom. The architecture and furnishings combine to make a grand testimonial to the greatness of the dynasty and of the fatherland.

Upon Tessin's death in 1681, work on Drottningholm's interiors was taken over by his son, Nicodemus Tessin the Younger (1654–1728), who completed them with great respect for his father's earlier achievements. For the garden, Tessin the Younger designed a new general scheme that was a free interpretation of André le Nôtre's landscaping at Vaux-le-Vicomte and Versailles. As if by magic, the architect transformed the rocky, swampy land surrounding the palace into parterres, bosks, fountains, and allées. Particularly striking are the many bronze sculptures by the Dutch mannerist artist Adriaen de Vries, which were, in fact, plunder from Prague and Denmark's Fredriksborg castle. (Today, they have been replaced by copies, and the originals reside in a nearby museum.)

Well before Louis XIV transformed Versailles and before the construction of such famous palaces as Schönbrunn in Vienna and Charlottenburg in Berlin, Drottningholm Palace was heralded throughout Europe for its artistic achievements. Its balanced composition and magnificent stairwell astounded foreign visitors, and Drottningholm came to

FACING PAGE *Nicodemus Tessin the Elder designed Strömsholm Palace for Dowager Queen Hedvig Eleonora during the 1670s as a reduced and simplified version of Drottningholm Palace.*

RIGHT *In this drawing for a manor house (ca. 1670), Nicodemus Tessin the Elder tested several approaches for the facade. His experimental ideas demonstrate the architect's knowledge of the classical vocabulary.*

stand as a symbol of Sweden's newly acquired position of power among nations.

Also for the dowager queen, Tessin the Elder designed Strömsholm Palace in the province of Västmanland, a smaller and simpler version of Drottningholm. When Her Majesty had been presented with the property as her husband's wedding gift, it had only a dilapidated sixteenth-century stone house on the grounds. Although drawings of a more up-to-date palace—which included a French baroque garden—were finished in 1668, it was not until twelve years later that Strömsholm Palace was completed. The strict and regular design for the palace called for a central stairwell and four cubical corner pavilions topped by lanterns. Only a projecting forepart, crowned by a tower on the garden side, breaks the austerity of the facade, which was originally most likely brown with grayish-white pilasters and a pale red base.

Strömsholm palace's symmetrical plan resembled that of Drottningholm. One difference, however, was Strömsholm's central great salon (situated on the same side as the gallery at Drottningholm), which projected from the facade. This design admitted light from three sides and allowed closer contact with the garden, a model that Tessin repeated in many palaces. The great salon on the upper floor was to house a chapel, which was not completed, however, until the eighteenth century. None of the interiors were furnished during Hedvig Eleonora's time; rather, during her visits to Strömsholm she stayed in a simple log house near the construction site.

RESIDENTIAL ARCHITECTURE

Drottningholm Palace, and likewise, Strömsholm, set the tone for future aristocratic country houses in Sweden. The older, enclosed system of courtyards was abandoned in favor of an independent central block, in many instances with free-standing wings arranged symmetrically in pairs. Facades were articulated with pilasters and pilaster-strips, and were often decorated with such classical motifs as swags and garlands. Graceful *säteri* roofs replaced the earlier tall, heavy roofs. Foreign models provided inspiration, but in comparison, Swedish palaces and manor houses gave the impression of being subdued, and by Continental standards, somewhat less refined.

Normally, country manor houses were composed of three stories. A ground floor housed the kitchen and servants' quarters; the middle floor, the main apartments; the top floor, the state apartments and guest suites. The upper two

Eriksberg, in Södermanland province, is one of the grandest and most elaborately furnished private country mansions from Sweden's Age of Greatness. Its design has been attributed to either Nicodemus Tessin the Elder or to Mathias Spihler.

stories often had similar floor plans, with suites of rooms arranged symmetrically around a great salon on the central axis, each suite normally consisting of an antechamber, bedchamber, and cabinet that, even if exquisitely decorated, served mostly private purposes.

The estates boasted magnificent and very costly grounds and gardens. The French garden style introduced into Sweden by Simon de la Vallée was first documented in writing and published in 1657 by Queen Christina's gardener, the Frenchman André Mollet, in *Le Jardin de Plaisir* (The Pleasure Garden). These gardens, containing pathways, allées, parterres, and flowerbeds in elaborate patterns, were greatly admired and became an important status symbol for aristocrats.

If one were to combine the composition of Strömsholm with facade decoration based on Dutch classicism, the result could easily be Eriksberg, one of the largest and most elaborately furnished country mansions in Sweden from the Baroque period. Eriksberg used to be considered a typical Tessin country mansion; today, though, it is often attributed to Mathias Spihler (1640–1691), son-in-law of Jean de la Vallée, who often worked under Tessin. More than likely, both architects were involved in the design of Eriksberg, since, despite its harmonious exterior, the architecture of this great house cannot be considered a unified creation. The basis was an existing four-story masonry structure with tall, stepped gables, which were rebuilt and altered in several stages. For instance, the old gables were torn down and four high, connecting wings were added. Eriksberg was probably completed in 1687, the same year that its owner, the military and public official Christoffer Gyllenstierna, was given the title of count.

FACING PAGE *The magnificent octagonal bathing room at Eriksberg has a pool enclosed in an octagonal balustrade. Openings in the elaborately decorated stucco dome above admit light.*

RIGHT *The chapel at Eriksberg is housed in one of the main building's four connecting wings. It closely resembles Nicodemus Tessin the Elder's Kalmar Cathedral (see page 68).*

FOLLOWING PAGES *Beside Lake Mälaren, Nicodemus Tessin the Elder's palatial Sjöö manor house (1670–79) presents three stories on the entrance side but only two at the rear because of the sloping terrain. The open loggia of the main entrance has been glassed in in modern times.*

The best-known interior at Eriksberg is the bathing room that was fitted out in one of the connecting wings. The room, an octagon, has a recessed pool at the center, under a cupola with ornate plaster decoration by the Italian sculptor Carlo Carove (unknown–1697), who worked at Swedish sites for thirty years. The pool is surrounded by vaulted arches with Corinthian pilasters and niches with putti; in one niche is a bathing Venus. Carlo Carove was also responsible for the rich stucco decor in the state bedchamber, a magnificent room with an alcove and a proscenium.

Another of the connecting wings houses a two-story chapel, which during the 1600s was called a *chapel à la romane* because of its classical composition. The chapel echoes the majestic interior of the cathedral of Kalmar, created by Tessin the Elder a few years earlier. Its walls were adorned with Ionic pilasters, and its ceiling was coffered. The window niches contain paintings copied from work by Rubens.

The most modern country residence of its time was probably Sjöö (1670–79) on the shores of Lake Mälaren. Sjöö was built for Johan Gabriel Stenbock, who was Marshal of the

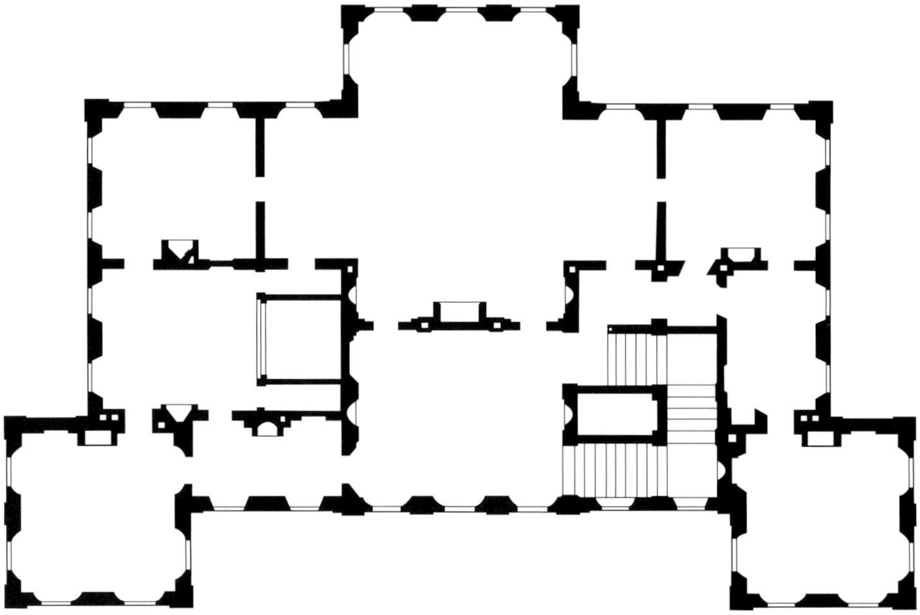

The architect's plan for the upper story at Sjöö shows the imposing cruciform salon, which was inspired by the Italian architect Andrea Palladio's villa designs. The salon was flanked by suites for important guests.

FACING PAGE *The vestibule on the upper floor of Sjöö mansion house, begun in 1670 on a plan by Nicodemus Tessin the Elder, is shaped as a guards' room, with light entering through clerestory windows. The severity of the whitewashed walls starkly contrasts with the elaborate stucco ceiling executed by the Italian master Carlo Carove.*

Realm and a favorite of King Karl XI. The composition of the main building and pavilions was typical for Tessin, although the mansion exhibited some new tendencies, such as the French hip roof (originally with curved edges) and the main entrance in the form of an open loggia similar to that at Drottningholm. A series of freestanding, paired wings marked the way to the main entrance for those arriving by sea.

In the state apartment on the upper floor, prominent guests were met by an imposing, cross-shaped salon comparable only to rooms in a Palladian villa such as Villa Foscari (La Malcontenta) outside Venice. The Sjöö salon had no counterparts or equals in Swedish architecture. Unlike the other important rooms in the house, the salon's ceiling was not finished with stucco ornament but was painted in grisaille and adorned with seven plafond paintings by the Dutch artist, Gerrit van Honthorst, which were booty taken from Denmark during the war.

It is known that Tessin did not have the time personally to supervise the work at Sjöö; oversight was therefore left in the hands of Mathias Spihler. A Frenchman was hired to execute the grounds and gardens. The main attraction was a bronze by Adriaen de Vries called *Psyche Born Aloft by Cupids* (1590–92), which can be seen today at the National Museum of Fine Arts in Stockholm.

The harsh landscape surrounding Sjöö needed a few sophisticated, artistic features. This may have been why the builder allowed a sculpture of a helmeted woman (possibly a personification of Rome), to be placed on the mansion's roof. The sculpture, of volcanic tuff, could have been acquired by Johan Gabriel Stenbock on a tour through Italy during his younger years and later mounted atop his mansion as a fond reminder of Europe's classical South.

Count Nils Bielke, a military hero during the Age of Greatness and another of King Karl XI's favorites, resided not far from Sjöö, at Salsta. As chief of the king's personal horse guard, Bielke had participated in the bloody Battle of Lund (1679), where, sword in hand, he led his regiment to a decisive victory over the Danes. "Today, Sweden's crown has danced on Bielke's sword," were the king's famous words after the battle.

Like many Swedes, Bielke harbored an early and lifelong admiration for everything French, and he served as Sweden's

ambassador to the French court for the period 1679–82. Erected in the 1670s, Salsta can be seen as directly inspired by French architecture, with its corner pavilions, projecting wings, and a protruding central bay facing the garden and the water. The exterior was slightly more cube-like than that of the French prototypes, owing in part to the fact that Salsta was built on the foundation of an earlier building. Salsta was considered for many years to be Tessin's work, but general opinion now attributes this, too, to the little-known Mathias Spihler in the roles of both architect and builder.

The floor plan too adhered to a French pattern, with the state rooms symmetrically arranged on either side of the salon. On the first floor, a large vestibule leads to the King's Hall, which is adorned with royal equestrian portraits. Above is the elaborate Knights' Salon, with gilt red leather wall coverings obtained in France by Bielke, as well as a collection of the highest quality gilt baroque furniture, which may have been a gift from King Louis XIV.

With Karl XI's death, Bielke lost his protector. He was deprived of his positions, put on trial, and convicted of high treason. Having lost his honor and all personal property in 1705, Bielke was sentenced to execution. He was pardoned, however, and allowed to keep two of his properties, one of which was Salsta, where he spent his last years.

One can hardly think about Swedish art and architecture during the Baroque era without considering the outstanding Magnus Gabriel De la Gardie (1622–1686). No other Swedish aristocrat held sway over such widespread proper-

FACING PAGE *The French Château de Berny, reconstructed by François Mansart in the 1620s, provided a sumptuous model for Swedish aristocrats to imitate in planning estates for themselves. Engraving from J. Rigaud,* Recueil choisi des plus belles vues de Paris et les environs *(ca. 1730).*

RIGHT *Plan of Count Nils Bielke's Salsta mansion showing the entrance level. Beyond the great arc of the stairs, a large vestibule projects from the front; the projection at the rear houses the King's Hall.*

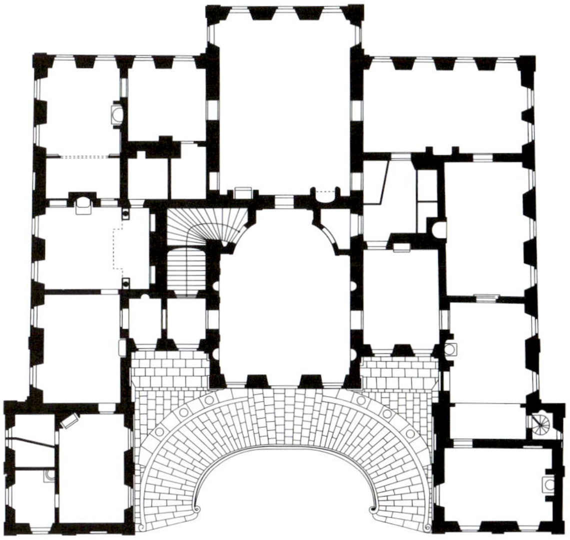

BELOW *Built in the 1670s and reflecting the experience of its owner, Count Nils Bielke, as ambassador to France, Salsta manor is an early example of French-inspired planning for estate houses, with symmetrical wings flanking a grand entrance.*

Salsta manor houses a collection of gilt baroque furniture such as these chairs, upholstered with French textiles. These were most likely gifts from King Louis XIV during Bielke's tenure as Sweden's ambassador to the French court.

ties, nor was there another patron of the arts equal to him. De la Gardie was Chancellor of the Realm and a favorite of Queen Christina. After her abdication, De la Gardie led Karl XI's guardian regency, for which he would later have to answer.

In his description of Sweden from his travels in 1674, Lorenzo Magalotti wrote that De la Gardie was the worst household manager and the most wasteful person in the world. Though the claim that he was building in forty or fifty locations at once was probably an exaggeration, it does attest to De la Gardie's ambitions. His father's city palace, Makalös, just opposite the Royal Palace in Stockholm, and Läckö Castle in the province of Västergötland were included in his vast holdings. While under De la Gardie's care, this beautiful medieval castle almost surrounded by water was expanded and richly furnished. Because Läckö was a feudal property

A·MARIA·MAURITIA·

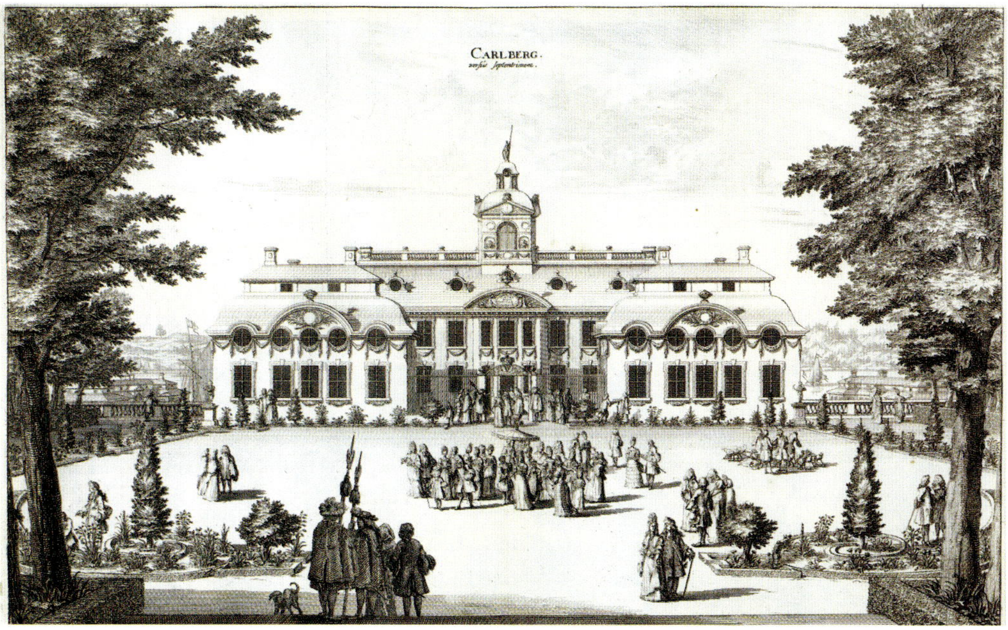

FACING PAGE *Karlberg palace, created during the 1660s by Jean de la Vallée for Count Magnus Gabriel De la Gardie, presents a stately, quite austere facade on the side that fronts on an inlet.*

LEFT *The courtyard facade of Karlberg palace is elaborate and very festive—a sharp contrast to the palace's sedate waterside aspect. Engraving from Erik Dahlbergh's* Suecia antiqua et hodierna.

BELOW *Of the rooms in Karlberg palace, the Cabinet of Rarities is the one that has changed least since the time of De le Gardie. This is where the count kept his most precious art objects.*

belonging ultimately to the crown, the interiors indicate that De la Gardie quite rightly regarded the castle more as a national possession than as his own private residence. De la Gardie's private apartment on the third floor was designed not only to glorify his own family but also to laud the achievements of the Swedish superpower with depictions of battle scenes, war trophies, and officers' portraits.

Karlberg, which the count purchased in 1669, reflected De la Gardie's personal tastes more than did any of his other properties. The estate was located just outside Stockholm on one of the city's waterways. The intention was to create a grand milieu in which De la Gardie, in his capacity as a leader of the guardian regency, could meet with King Karl XI. Karlberg was therefore designed to accommodate a very large staff—at times, some 180 people. From a stone house on the property architect Jean de la Vallée designed an H-shaped building with four wings, which was more in keeping with the current style. The side of the courtyard exhibits a festive character, with round windows adorned with swags and garlands of stucco and a curving *säteri* roof. The elaborate facade decoration was painted a reddish brown to contrast with the whitewashed stucco walls.

The eastern end of the house was furnished to suit the count's personal taste and the western end for his wife and daughters. The master apartment consisted of antechamber,

audience room, bedchamber, and cabinet. To these was added a suite of rooms containing the count's most precious possessions: a library with portraits of the prominent scientists and other intellectual leaders whom he had met; a gallery with plaster reproductions of emperors from Roman antiquity;

Imposing Roman buildings such as the Palazzo Borghese, constructed in the early 1600s, served as prototypes for Jean de la Vallée's Oxenstierna palace. Engraving from Giuseppe Vasi's Vues de Rome *(1754–61).*

FACING PAGE *With the Oxenstierna Palace (1653–57), architect Jean de la Vallée introduced to Stockholm the design principles of Roman Renaissance and baroque palaces.*

and, finally, a cabinet of treasures, with paneled, faux marble walls and a stucco ceiling.

Magnus Gabriel De la Gardie enjoyed his splendid home for less than a decade. In 1684, he was forced to relinquish the property, including the mansion that he so carefully and expensively completed. The king's Reduction (see Chapter One) was knocking at his door, announcing the dissolution of De la Gardie's entire estate.

CITY PALACES

The routines of country life were often interrupted by work and political deliberations in Stockholm, at least for persons belonging to the powerful nobility. Councilmen were required to have residences in the capital, near the Royal Palace and their place of work. Within a relatively short time, therefore, a semicircular zone of councilmen's houses was built around the palace. The growth and transformation that Stockholm underwent during the seventeenth century was remarkable, but it was not accomplished without sacrifice. Many less-well-off Stockholm residents witnessed the razing of their wooden houses to make way for expansion of the palaces.

The transformation of Stockholm provided abundant opportunity for a gifted architect to apply his skills. Upon Jean de la Vallée's return from a long study tour abroad, he was given the title of Royal Court Architect and with it, responsibility for updating the king's palace and for transforming the surrounding areas. Uniform rows of government offices and private palaces were planned on the south and west sides of the Royal Palace, and directly to the north, the architect projected a long, grand avenue—a concept that found its way into city planning for Stockholm for many generations to come.

As a reminder of these ambitious plans stands the palace (or rather, a corner section of it since the plans were never fully realized) that Jean de la Vallée designed for Axel Oxenstierna. It was intended to be the first and largest building west of the Royal Palace. Inspired by Roman baroque buildings such as the Palazzo Borghese, the Oxenstierna palace's monumental facade and recessed mezzanine floors represented something truly new for the Swedes. It was completed, however, with certain non-Roman features such as a triangular gable and a steep roof (which was later changed). The facade was colored a warm, brick red.

The largest concentration of palaces was, and remains today, located on Riddarholmen, a small island between

In this view toward the island of Riddarholmen, the Bonde palace and the House of Nobility can be seen on the left; on a cliff to the far right stands Rosenhane Palace. Boats are at the ready to ferry owners to their country estates. Detail of an engraving from Erik Dahlbergh's Suecia antiqua et hodierna.

FACING PAGE *The Rosenhane palace, probably by Nicodemus Tessin the Elder, is distinguished by its white marble walls high on the island of Riddarholmen.*

Stockholm's Old Town and Lake Mälaren. The island had long ago been used as grazing fields for goats belonging to residents of Stockholm, and later it became the site of a Franciscan cloister. During the seventeenth century, the area was transformed into the capital's most exclusive residential quarter. To the far south stood Carl Gustav Wrangel's impressive, towered palace, with its system of ramps leading to the water and a boat landing. From here, Wrangel could easily reach Skokloster castle

by boat, as could the other Riddarholmen residents with country estates along the shore.

On the highest point of the island stood a palace built in the beginning of the 1650s for the public official and diplomat Schering Rosenhane, one of the most cultivated Swedes of his time. The interiors of Rosenhane's palace reflected the taste of an intellectual and the style of a high official. Probably designed by Nicodemus Tessin the Elder, this three-story building, with its cubic form and rusticated exterior, displays a discreetly restrained classicism. Inside, the rooms are clustered around a central stairway and a simple courtyard that is little more than a light well. As in country manor houses, the utilitarian rooms were located on ground level and the family's private apartments were on the story above. The top floor was reserved for a banquet hall and guest suites. Everything in the house was carefully thought

Both Nicodemus Tessin the Elder and Jean de la Vallée participated in the design of the impressive Bonde Palace (1662–73) in Stockholm. Engraving from Erik Dahlbergh's Suecia antiqua et hodierna.

The Bonde palace's original sheet-copper roof and tower cupolas were destroyed by fire in 1710 and replaced during reconstruction with the low säteri *roof it has today. After another fire, in 1752, an attic story was added, as well as the south-facing wings seen here.*

FACING PAGE *The Swedish National Bank (1657–82) in Stockholm, designed by Nicodemus Tessin the Elder, is an outstanding example of how Italian Renaissance and baroque buildings at this time influenced architecture north of the Alps. Engraving from Erik Dahlbergh's* Suecia antiqua et hodierna.

through following a Palladian pattern and, most likely, the patron's own taste and wishes. In the upper gallery, Rosenhane could explain to educated guests the meaning of the series of paintings with emblematic motifs that were created to illustrate his own ideas. Today, these are all that remain of the original interiors.

The Rosenhane palace was considered noteworthy in its own time. When Magnus Gabriel De la Gardie spoke in 1665 on the question of a new exchange building in Stockholm, he stated that it should be not "costly and magnificent, but beautiful and modestly elegant—like the house of the deceased Councilor of the Realm, Schering Rosenhane."

Close to Riddarholmen on a parcel of land next to the water and neighboring the House of Nobility, Gustav Bonde, the Treasurer of the Realm, built his palace in 1662. It became one of Stockholm's greatest palaces of the period. The building exhibits the expanded French plan that can be seen in Simon de la Vallée's proposal for the House of Nobility: a main building with corner towers, four projecting wings, and an enclosed portico. A garden and a boat landing were probably planned to face the sea.

Gustav Bonde engaged both Tessin the Elder and Jean de la Vallée to work on the project. Tessin gave the palace its principal characteristics: the facade's classical composition, which consisted of a rusticated base and colossal pilasters in the upper level. Jean de la Vallée worked out the remaining details—a project that nearly cost him his life. He got into such a violent dispute with the major who was leading the daily work that the officer attempted to murder the architect and his family by mixing arsenic into their food. The architect recovered after some months; the major was charged with attempted murder, sentenced to death, and executed.

In 1667, at the time of Bonde's death, only the main building of his palace was completed and, despite his widow's attempts to carry out the plans, the building was not finished during the seventeenth century. The impressive structure depicted in Dahlbergh's *Suecia antiqua et hodierna* showed the palace as it was planned, and this was sufficient to win international admiration. When King Charles II of England first saw Dahlbergh's engravings in 1668, he proclaimed that Bonde's palace had hardly an equal in all Europe, except perhaps in Paris.

In his will and testament, Gustav Bonde expressed his desire for the palace to remain forever in his family's possession, since he had built it more for the honor of his family than for his own comfort. Family legacy was an important element in the building traditions of the period. Thus, the house became a monument to the late Treasurer of the Realm and his family. Great sums were spent on the external appearance, but the interiors were often left in a relatively primitive state. The family's living quarters occupied only a portion of the house; some of the remaining space was reserved for the staff, and other rooms were rented out. The palace even contained office space for the accountants and bookkeepers who took care of the owner's finances; from these offices, vast properties could be managed.

The Stockholm palaces from the Baroque period have met with different fates. Today, the Rosenhane Palace is occupied by the Swedish Court of Appeals (*Svea hovrätt*), while the Bonde palace houses the offices of the Supreme Court (*Högsta domstolen*). As early as the 1670s, Axel Oxenstierna's palace came to serve as the headquarters of the Swedish National Bank (*Riksbanken*). Soon, however, the bank acquired its own building, designed in 1676 by Tessin the Elder. As with the Oxenstierna palace, only one portion of the Swedish National Bank building had been completed, on a narrow lot next to a small square, Järntorget, in Old Town; construction was not resumed until 1699.

The Swedish National Bank building is considered one of the most Roman structures built north of the Alps. The balance of the facade's horizontal and vertical elements, the recessed mezzanine floors, the pediments over the windows, and the low roof all contribute to its Roman character. The robust doorway is directly inspired by the famous Villa Farnese in Caprarola outside Rome, designed by the architect Vignola in the mid-sixteenth century. It is not impossible that Nicodemus Tessin the Younger had a certain influence on the bank building's appearance. He was studying in Rome during the 1670s and could have sent reports and drawings home to his father. After all, it was he, more than anyone else, who was responsible for spreading the Roman style in Swedish architecture.

The Katarina Church in Stockholm, built to fulfill a longtime ambition of King Karl X Gustav, was designed by Jean de la Vallée in 1656. This drawing by the architect depicts the church with its original roof construction.

FACING PAGE *The huge, unbroken space of the Katarina Church's interior was a great artistic achievement that offered fine acoustics as well as a clear view of the priest. A fire ravaged the church in 1990, but the excellent reconstruction followed the original architectural plans of Jean de la Vallée.*

CHURCH ARCHITECTURE

Well into the seventeenth century, churches built in Sweden followed a conservative tradition rooted in the Middle Ages. The new power of the country, however, paved the way for a church architecture shaped by new sources of inspiration and a new architectural vocabulary. Here, too, Jean de la Vallée and Tessin the Elder were the forerunners.

The Katarina Church (*Katarinakyrkan*) in Stockholm, Jean de la Vallée's most prestigious project, represented a true innovation. Designed in 1656, this church was part of King Karl X Gustav's grandiose plans to transform the heights south of the Old Town into a new royal quarter. The position of the church and its monumental architecture bear witness to its intended purpose.

In the Katarina Church, Roman Catholic prototypes merged with the architect's experiences in Reformed and Calvinistic Holland. The result was the first central-plan church (i.e., in the form of a Greek cross) built from the ground up in Sweden and, for a Protestant house of worship, a remarkable achievement in its time. This original and

The Katarina Church provides a splendid landmark in Stockholm's skyline.

independent creation consisted of a tall central chamber with short, wide arms, and high cubical corner pavilions. The composition—nearly a pyramid—included a facade dominated by Doric pilasters and arched windows, steeply pitched roof, tall octagonal corner towers, and a slightly sloped dome crowned by a lantern. The color scheme followed that of the House of the Nobility.

The Katarina Church's interior is an architectural and technical work of art, consisting only of one large room without supports. Following the convention of central-plan churches in Italy, Jean de la Vallée's intention was to place the altar and the pulpit at the crossing—that is, at the exact center of the room and directly under the light entering from the dome. This idea raised adamant protests from the congregation, however, which demanded a traditional placement of the altar in the east. By the time the church was completed in the 1690s, the architect's idea for the ritual furnishings had been abandoned.

In 1723, a fire destroyed the original wooden dome. The church was then given a tall masonry baroque dome, designed by Stockholm's city architect, Göran Josuæ Adelcrantz (discussed in Chapters Four and Five). After nearly three centuries, another fire left the entire church in ashes in 1990. Today, however, the church has been excellently reconstructed and it once again stands as a striking landmark in the capital's cityscape.

For Swedish church architecture in general, Katarina Church became an important model during the decades that followed Jean de la Vallée's plan. It can be seen as a precursor to central-plan churches found in cities such as Kungsör, Söderhamn, and Karlskrona. In the countryside, churches

following the same pattern were built of timber and wood, often with successful results.

Drawings that have been preserved make clear that even Nicodemus Tessin the Elder was interested in the idea of central-plan churches. Kalmar Cathedral, his most important ecclesiastical work—and Sweden's greatest Baroque achievement—combined the central plan with the traditional oblong church.

The old town of Kalmar, with its medieval streets and alleys, lay inland in a half circle north of the city's great castle. For military reasons, the town was moved in 1650 to the nearby island of Kvarnholmen and fortified according to the period's defense principles. The new city was planned on a grid, with a central square in which the proposed church would provide a landmark visible from the sea. Tessin finished the drawings for this project in 1660, but work progressed slowly and was not finished until 1699, many years after the architect's death.

In designing the cathedral of Kalmar, Tessin could refer to drawings and sketches that he had brought home from Rome. The Jesuit church Il Gesù has often been considered Tessin's prototype for Kalmar, and it is telling that a church nearly a century older offers the best comparisons. Tessin was not attracted to the dramatic forms of high baroque architecture; rather, as a classicist, he preferred to compose exteriors with clearly differentiated elements.

This engraving, from Erik Dahlbergh's Suecia antiqua et hodierna, *shows Kalmar Cathedral as seen from the city square south of the church.*

FACING PAGE
Kalmar Cathedral (1660–99), designed by Nicodemus Tessin the Elder, stands as Sweden's foremost baroque ecclesiastical building. The church clearly reflects the inspiration of Roman prototypes.

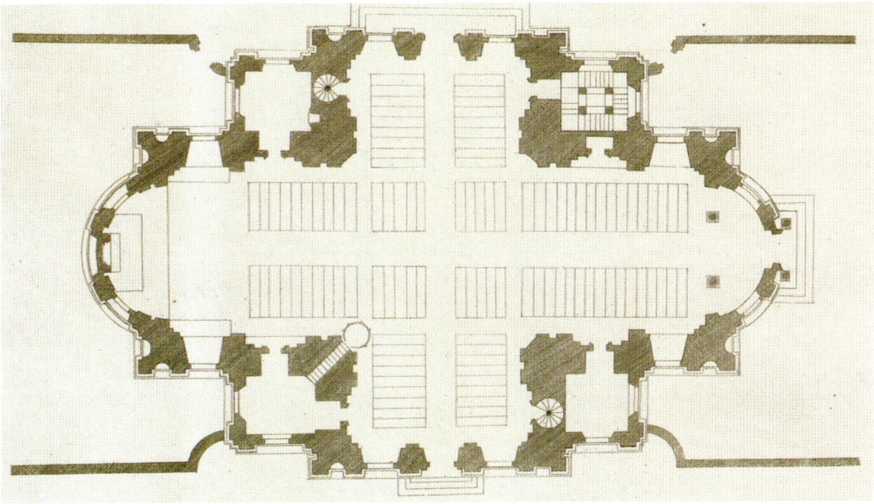

Plan for Kalmar Cathedral from Erik Dahlbergh's Suecia antiqua et hodierna.

Tessin's point of departure was the Greek cross plan, which he extended to the east and west, finishing off the composition with semicircular apses. To the south and the north the wide cross arms form magnificent two-story screen facades completed by pediment scrolls. The arm to the south was most likely planned as the main entrance from the town square. From the cross arms' pavilions rose twin clock towers. The church may have been planned to have a dome, but none was ever built. The entire exterior is unified by Doric pilasters and a powerful entablature.

Though the exterior of the church recalls the symmetry of the central-plan church, the interior has oblong features, such as a monumental barrel-vaulted ceiling. Paired Ionic pilasters dominate the walls. Everything is whitewashed; ornate plasterwork and variegated marbles were alien elements in a Protestant church. From the large windows, a soft light filters into the church. Classical architecture is here suffused with the piety of the Karolinian time.

An urgent matter during the Age of Greatness was the construction of mausoleums to honor military commanders and noblemen. These were strictly a privilege of wealthy patrons and are rarely mentioned in church protocol. They were constructed near existing churches as freestanding structures with their own architecture. All the symbolic adornments of a funeral procession—funeral escutcheons, ancestral coats-of-arms, and flags of mourning—were placed

Fashioned with strongly classical features, the Kagg mausoleum at Floda Church in Södermanland province was built during the 1660s after a design by Erik Dahlbergh.

FACING PAGE *The interior of the Kagg mausoleum is richly decorated with carved plaster ornamentation by the Italian sculptor Carlo Carove.*

along with the deceased's sarcophagus. The coffin was kept in the crypt beneath the floor.

The Gustavian mausoleum at Riddarholm Church in Stockholm played an important role in the development of this Swedish tradition. It was built just after the death of Gustav II Adolf in 1632, in his honor, and the oldest mausoleums derive from this period. Most are nearly cubic buildings, crowned by a spire and with windows on three sides. The architecture is as simple as possible.

In the following years, demands for mausoleums increased. Architects received commissions for grandiose buildings crowned by domes, with exteriors prominently displaying their functions. In the interiors, the worldly mixed with the spiritual. Exploits of war were intermingled with the hope of resurrection and eternal blessedness.

One of the most elaborate mausoleums of the time was built in 1666 at Floda Church in the province of Södermanland for the Field Marshall Lars Kagg and his wife Agneta Ribbing. The architect of the Kagg mausouleum was Erik Dahlbergh (1625–1703), who was by this time beginning his travels in Sweden for his work *Suecia antiqua et hodierna*. It was his journeys farther from home, however—especially to Italy—that were to become a determining factor for Dahlbergh's architectural ideas. As the country's fortification supervisor and with his large-scale book project in the works, Dahlbergh had little time for private commissions, but the few that he undertook exhibit originality and independence. King Karl XI's harsh characterization of Dahlbergh as a man who "consists of himself" suits both the man and the artist.

The Kagg mausoleum is a cruciform building in the Doric order with pediments, pilasters, and luxurious *trofée* groups, and it is crowned by a dome. The overall impression is elaborate and yet somber. The rich, light-filled room is framed by Corinthian pilasters embellished with a series of eight allegorical figures depicting the virtues. Above flows an exuberant, highly symbolic stucco ornament executed by Carlo Carove. His creations are reminiscent of those in sixteenth-century Italian country villas and grottos.

As to the number of mausoleums executed, Tessin the Elder dominated the field. His first datable project is the 1658 chapel at Veckholm church, which Magnus Gabriel De la Gardie intended to erect in honor of his father. Tessin

The mausoleum proposed by Nicodemus Tessin the Elder at Veckholm Church (ca. 1659) for the family of Magnus Gabriel De la Gardie was cathedral-like in its grandeur.

The mausoleum of Gustav Bonde at Spånga church in Stockholm, built 1667–73 following Nicodemus Tessin the Elder's drawings, has its original reddish yellow facade.

FACING PAGE *The interior of the Bonde mausoleum at Spånga church still offers a rare, compact view into a baroque interior.*

planned a domed structure of impressive size, with cross arms articulated with pediments, pilaster-strips, and niches. From the architect's drawing, one could think that the project at hand was a cathedral, but the Reduction curtailed the completion of the grandiose plans. What was to be a crescendo rising in the east of the church was abbreviated at the level of the cornice, and a simple, pyramidal roof served as the terminal feature.

The mausoleum that Tessin designed ten years later at Spånga Church in Stockholm for Count Gustav Bonde displays great similarities to the De la Gardie mausoleum at Veckholm church. Bonde's mausoleum, however, is more modest in size, and the overall impression is of a more compact building. The facades of the cross arms are articulated by pilasters, which continue upward to a domed, octagonal tambour. A lantern originally graced the dome. The well-preserved interiors, with their multicolored funeral escutcheons and rich plasterwork, display a rarely seen condensed baroque ambience.

The construction of mausoleums reached its culmination with buildings such as these. The Reduction, however, drastically changed the conditions for all types of grandiose funereal pomp and splendor, and, indeed, for noble manifestations in general.

CHAPTER THREE

The Late Baroque

PAGES 74–75 *Thureholm mansion, in the province of Södermanland, was designed in 1729 by Carl Hårleman and erected the following decade for Count Thure Gabriel Bielke, a former colonel of King Karl XII.*

RIGHT *Portrait of Nicodemus Tessin the Younger (1723) by Georg Desmarées.*

Swedish architecture in the late seventeenth and early eighteenth centuries evolved during a time of extreme political swings within and hostilities without. Between 1690 and 1730, Sweden progressed from the royal autocracy under King Karl XI, through two decades of war and hardship, to a long-awaited time of peace, followed by the institution of a new political system—the parliamentary regime of the Age of Liberty. Throughout it all, a continuous driving force came from the outstanding architect and conscious ideologue, Nicodemus Tessin the Younger. Together with the court painter, David Klöcker Ehrenstrahl, Tessin gave artistic expression to the importance and authority of the monarchy, with work reflecting more strongly than ever before influences from Europe's leading cultural nations, Italy and France.

Tessin's architecture did not win over the conservative Swedish nobility, however, and aristocrats continued to commission buildings in the traditions of their forebears. The tone is different from earlier work, however—stricter and more austere. The architecture from this period is therefore known as late baroque or (for the kings Karl) late Karolinian. Though the terms are used interchangeably, the restrained simplicity of forms is today most closely associated with the word Karolinian.

NICODEMUS TESSIN THE YOUNGER

No architect in Sweden has ever attained the stature of Nicodemus Tessin the Younger (1654–1728), whose multifaceted career also won him great influence as a politician and courtier to the king. From his youth, his bright prospects distinguished him from his peers. His education began in Sweden, first under his father, Nicodemus the Elder, then at Uppsala University. In 1673, when the young Tessin was just nineteen, he went to Rome to continue his studies. While he was there, former Queen Christina, having abdicated the throne and taken up residence in the Eternal City, took a lively interest in her gifted compatriot and helped to see that his stay in Rome was a productive one.

Tessin was invited to study with the architect Carlo Fontana, through whom he made the acquaintance of the great Gianlorenzo Bernini.

During his six years in Rome and the following two in England and France, Tessin developed the style that would later determine his architecture. Though both Roman antiquity and the Renaissance were important to him, it was the baroque architecture of Bernini that Tessin admired most and that shaped his future work. In Tessin's hands, the heavier Roman baroque of Bernini was complemented by the lighter, more decorated baroque classicism of Louis XIV's France. The surroundings being created by Charles Le Brun at Versailles and at the Louvre, and, in fact, the entire artistic devotion to glorifying the king of France, greatly impressed Tessin. He was drawn to the new principles of palace architecture that he encountered in France, especially to those developed and implemented by the architect Louis Le Vau in his designs for Vaux-le-Vicomte (1658–1661) and to the landscape architecture of André Le Nôtre. Over the years, Tessin compiled a unique and extensive collection of French drawings and engravings, many of which are now preserved at the National Museum of Fine Arts in Stockholm.

Sweden had high expectations for Tessin. Even while still in Rome, he was appointed court architect. Upon his return to Sweden in 1681, he took over the position that his recently deceased father had held as city architect in Stockholm; along with that post, he inherited responsibility for completing Drottningholm Palace for the dowager queen, Hedvig Eleonora.

Throughout several hectic years, Tessin was inundated with projects. He designed palaces, churches, gardens, and grounds, and he orchestrated royal festivities and ceremonies of all kinds. His career was further secured by the crown's desire to centralize artistic administration. In 1697, when Tessin became superintendent of buildings, the goal was to create a position comparable to the French *Surintendent des Bâtiments du Roi*, even though, at first, the title—*överintendent*—was only a prestigious designation for "royal court architect."

Tessin's skill also drew international attention, and in 1693 the Danes commissioned him to submit designs for a new royal palace, Amalienborg, in Copenhagen. His designs, and then a model for Amalienborg, were delivered, but when political relations between the two countries deteriorated, the project was abandoned. The French foreign minister in Stockholm, Count d'Avaux, also commissioned designs from Tessin for the palace outside Paris at Roissy (today the site of Charles de Gaulle airport), but this edifice stood for less than a century before it was demolished during the French Revolution. Later on, Tessin challenged his French colleagues on a large project for the Louvre, suggesting that the rectangular inner courtyard be transformed into a circle; this proposal was presented in 1705 to King Louis, only to be disregarded after customary exchanges of the requisite courtesies.

Through the years, Tessin became increasingly involved in politics. He achieved the highest possible political rank when he was named council of state and marshal of the court, and he was made a count in 1714. He also succeeded in marrying into the old nobility. In 1718, King Karl XII conferred on Tessin a new title, naming him commissioner of public order, a position with a vast array of political responsibilities.

Tessin remained loyal to the absolute monarchy until the very end, even when it must have become apparent that the old order was headed for catastrophe. After the fall of the regime, his loyalties cost him his position as council of state, though he managed to retain the title of superintendent and a seat on the council.

ARCHITECTURE FOR THE MONARCHY

Tessin the Younger is best known today as the architect of the Royal Palace in Stockholm. The old castle, Three Crowns, which still functioned as a royal residence, was outdated and dilapidated. It was composed of a conglomerate of buildings from various periods skirting a central medieval tower. Both Jean de la Vallée and Nicodemus Tessin the Elder had been asked to devise a more modern frame around the historic sections of the castle, but none of their proposals were ever realized. Tessin the Younger, who disapproved of most older Swedish architecture, considered the former castle a disgrace to a superpower such as Sweden. He desired to create a truly regal palace, based on classical ideals, that would measure up to the best in continental Europe.

Tessin's plans were hindered, however, by the modest and frugal King Karl XI, who disapproved of costly new construction for himself. The king could, though, accept a larger renovation of the old royal chapel located in the Three Crowns' north wing. Thus, after returning from a second trip to Paris and Rome (1687–88), Tessin began work on this refurbishment. Two years into this project, it took on a new

This engraving of the north facade of the Royal Palace in Stockholm was made in 1695 by Sébastien Leclerc from an architectural drawing by Nicodemus Tessin the Younger. At first, the engraving showed only the palace's central block, which was the first portion of the palace to be built; when Tessin added the wings some years later, the engraving was modified to include them.

dimension. After a minor fire in the north wing, Tessin was ordered to rebuild the wing entirely, adding two full stories. He persuaded the king to allow him also to modernize the facade. The work began in 1692, which became the official date of the current Royal Palace. Within a few years, the walls were raised, stuccoed, and painted a light brick red, with the stone trim painted white.

Tessin's new northern facade was depicted in a copper engraving after his drawing, by the French artist, Sébastien Leclerc; this image spread throughout Europe's royal courts. It showed a three-story, horizontal building in a strict, Roman, Renaissance-Baroque style, with a large central portico, a recessed mezzanine floor, and a roof line concealed behind a balustrade. The older sections of the castle were cleverly hidden behind the new facade. Tessin's point of departure for the design may have been a proposal that Bernini had presented several decades earlier for a refurbishment of the Louvre.

What happened next is well documented. On May 7, 1697, a violent fire broke out in the castle. A few weeks earlier King Karl XI had become gravely ill and died at just forty-two years of age; his body, lying in state, was among the first things to be saved from the flames. In only a few hours the south, east, and west sections were destroyed, and soon thereafter the tower of the Three Crowns collapsed. The heavy bronze bells broke through the wooden joists and landed with a thunderous crash in the wine cellar. Tessin was among the firefighters. Engulfed in billowing smoke, he tried to save the north wing but was forced to retreat. His newly built walls withstood the fire, but several of the inte-

A drawing (ca. 1704) by Nicodemus Tessin the Younger reveals how the portico in the north wing provided a prominent entrance to the inner courtyard. Visitors to the palace's administrative offices on either side of the entrance would enter through a vestibule. On the top floor, beneath an attic, is King Karl XI's gallery.

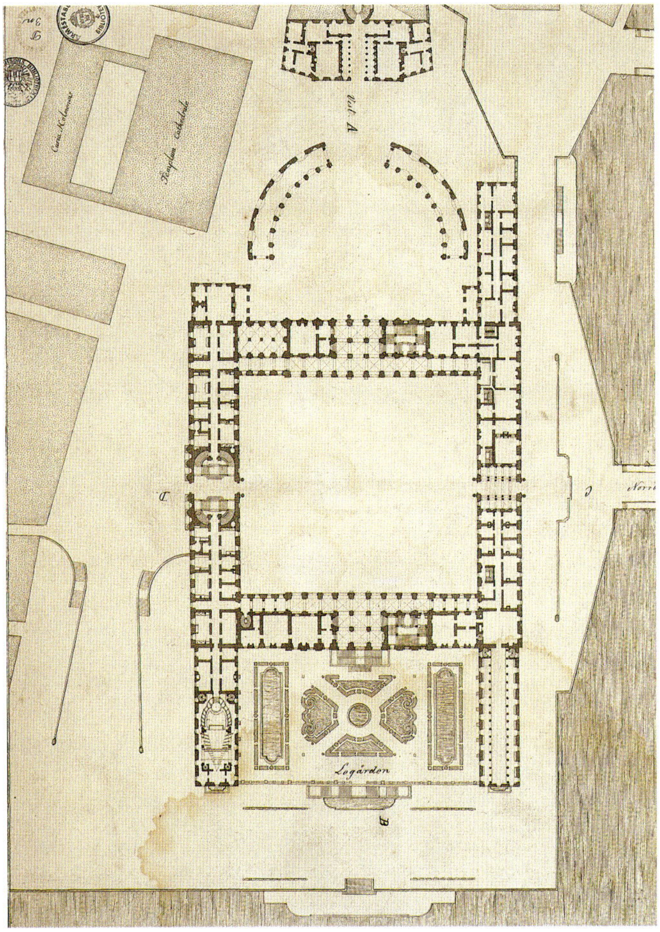

In laying out his plan for the Royal Palace, Tessin used the existing north (right) wing as a guide. To the building's nearly cubical volume he added two stair halls that gave access to eight large royal apartments. This plan was drafted around 1710 by the French artist Claude Haton from Tessin's original drawings.

RIGHT *Evening photo of the Royal Palace from the northeast. The influence on Tessin the Younger of Roman Renaissance and baroque palace design is very apparent in his concept for the Swedish palace.*

FACING PAGE *King Karl XI's gallery in the Royal Palace's north wing was one of the few interior spaces actually completed under the direction of Nicodemus Tessin the Younger. French artisans made the regal furnishings.*

The east wing of the Royal Palace has a festive central core with a rusticated base and colossal pilasters. The symmetrical stairways lead to Logården, *the topiary garden. The insignia of the first Bernadotte king, Karl XIV Johan, appears in the foreground.*

riors perished, including those of the newly consecrated royal chapel. The castle's historical continuity, which until the fire had prevented any radical changes in its appearance, was destroyed.

This left just one way to proceed: rebuilding the entire castle. On the day after the fire, Dowager Queen Hedvig Eleonora and the guardian regency gave Tessin the task of preparing plans for a new palace. Six weeks later, the architect presented a general proposal that included a complete set of drawings for two of the planned three stories—an unparalleled presentation, even though drawings for the facades and the cross-sections were still to come. The design alone won Tessin artistic free rein to plan what remained on the basis of his initial scheme. Construction began that very summer. The sheer size of the new palace greatly complicated the task at hand, and diverse activities—administrative as well as ceremonial—had to be carried out within the walls. In the beginning, Tessin improvised creative ways to solve perplexing problems, but, as time went on, he became more confident with his new responsibilities.

The principal layout comprised a quadrangle enclosing a large, square inner courtyard; the most prominent feature

With its ciffered dome and elaborate stairways, the south archway of the Royal Palace creates a magnificent entrance to the Hall of State and the Royal Chapel.

FACING PAGE *The Royal Palace's south wing, with its ceremonial triumphal arch motif, faces Stockholm's Old Town. Behind this facade are the palace's ceremonial rooms, the Royal Chapel, and the Hall of State. The civic church* Storkyrkan *can be seen in the distance to the left.*

was the architect's addition of two pairs of low wings projecting to the east and the west. The wings imparted vigor to the building and provided opportunities for varied treatments within the general layout. The overall effect surprised even Tessin himself. In a series of detailed drawings prepared in 1704, Tessin had fully worked out the exterior schematics of the palace along with the monumental interiors, which he regarded as his finest work.

Tessin was a decided classicist and unafraid to apply solutions devised by other architects. He repeatedly made use of drawings and measurements from the study tours of his youth, to the Palazzo Farnese and Palazzo Chigi in Rome, and beyond the city, to the Villa Farnese in Caprarola and the Villa Aldobrandini in Frascati. Although he borrowed ideas from the Renaissance and baroque palaces within and outside Rome, his finished products were always completely his own and reflected his unique ability to combine broad ideas and specific details into a truly new and original whole.

He also understood how to take advantage of the environment of a site. The varied surroundings, with water on two sides and the adjacent city on the other two, inspired the architect to give each side of the palace its unique character.

Tessin placed the apartments of both the king and the queen behind the strictly Roman north facade. The rooms were situated on the upper two floors, laid out enfilade, with the state apartments facing the water and the private apartments located toward the inner courtyard. They were reached via two impressive stairways located in the east and west wings. A magnificent room on the third floor, called Karl XI's gallery, linked the two suites. The inspiration for this clearly came from the Hall of Mirrors at Versailles. The open view to the east toward the Saltsjö Sea inspired a graceful, even feminine, form for the palace's eastern facade, behind which the queen would eventually reside. The two lower wings on this side of the palace were to house a theater and a library, as well as two orangeries on the first floor. These indoor gardens faced a small topiary garden (*Logården*) out of doors, from which a staircase provided a path to the sea below.

On the opposite side of the palace, Tessin used a more severe and imposing architectural vocabulary for the exterior of the king's apartments. The western facade's disciplined character fullfilled the outer courtyard's purpose as a site for military drills and exercises. The motif of the first floor, with ribbed Tuscan-style columns, continued in the curved freestanding wings that framed the courtyard; these were originally open porticoes.

The southern facade, looking onto the sloping road, Slottsbacken, and the Old Town, presents the palace's most grandiose aspect. Here, a central triumphal arch motif marks the entrance to a high-domed great stair hall and to the palace's two ceremonial rooms, the Hall of State and the Royal Chapel. The elaborate design of the exterior, with colossal Corinthian columns, elaborately sculpted niches, and inscriptions paying tribute to King Karl XII, distracts attention from the southern exterior's imperfect symmetry—a result of the need to accommodate the civic church, *Storkyrkan*.

In contrast to the exterior facade's great variety, the inner courtyard makes a harmonious and uniform impression. The sheer size of the space is more like that of a public square

than of a palace courtyard. The open arcades around the stairways located in the east and west wings (enclosed during the 1750s), together with the proposed equestrian statue of King Karl XI at the courtyard's center, are good indications that Tessin himself actually regarded the space more as a public square than a palace courtyard.

Tessin's goal to create a palace that met a high international standard imposed heavy demands on his crew. The available pool of Swedish workers was inadequate to carry out Tessin's plan, so—with the help of Sweden's envoy in Paris, Daniel Cronström—the architect enlisted artisans and craftsmen from France, where they had proven their skills during service to King Louis XIV. Their arrival in Stockholm throughout the 1690s brought a new artistic coterie to the palace construction project. Among them was the sculptor Bernard Fouquet, who was entrusted with all the bronze statuary, such as the two lions on the Lion Ramp (*Lejonbacken*), four large groups depicting the feats of Hercules to be placed at the south entrance, and the royal equestrian statue that Tessin had planned for the inner courtyard. The lions were completed in 1704, but the other sculptures never progressed beyond the model stage. Indeed, only a few of the bronzes that the architect had planned were ever completed. During times of war, most of Sweden's bronze ended up at the cannon foundry.

This bronze lion and another facing it, by the French sculptor Bernard Fouquet, guard the Royal Palace's north wing. The palace's very Roman facade was begun in 1692.

Many of the palace's interiors were modeled after French prototypes. The largest artistic endeavors focused on the royal state apartments on the third floor of the north wing, where decoration had begun in 1694. After the fire, the French artists had in large part to begin again. The painter, Jacques Fouquet, son of sculptor Bernard Fouquet, executed a series of ceiling paintings that honored the Swedish crown's triumphs and virtues in full allegorical splendor. In Karl XI's gallery and the adjoining cabinet, the theme celebrates his war against Denmark, while the king's audience room and the state bedchamber were later dedicated to Karl XII's military exploits. René Chauveau was responsible for decorative plasterwork, while Jacques de Meaux embellished the window reveals with delicate grotesques in the spirit of the French artist Jean Berain the Elder. Tessin was well aware that, with these lavish decorations, he was going way beyond the familiar limits. The result, however, was far superior to any earlier artistic achievement in Sweden.

Work on the palace continued at full speed until the Nordic War erupted, financially draining the Swedish economy. In 1700, Karl XII left Stockholm at the head of his army, and soon no further funds were available for palace refurbishment. By nine years later, the project had nearly come to a halt. For almost two decades, boards were left to cover the bare, half-finished walls. Finally, in 1728, work commenced once again. But Nicodemus Tessin the Younger never saw the project completed; he died in the same year. A new generation of architects, artists, and craftsmen finished his Royal Palace.

The Royal Palace was just a fraction of Tessin the Younger's large-scale plans for Stockholm. During the embattled years in the early eighteenth century, the king and the architect had exchanged letters planning radical changes

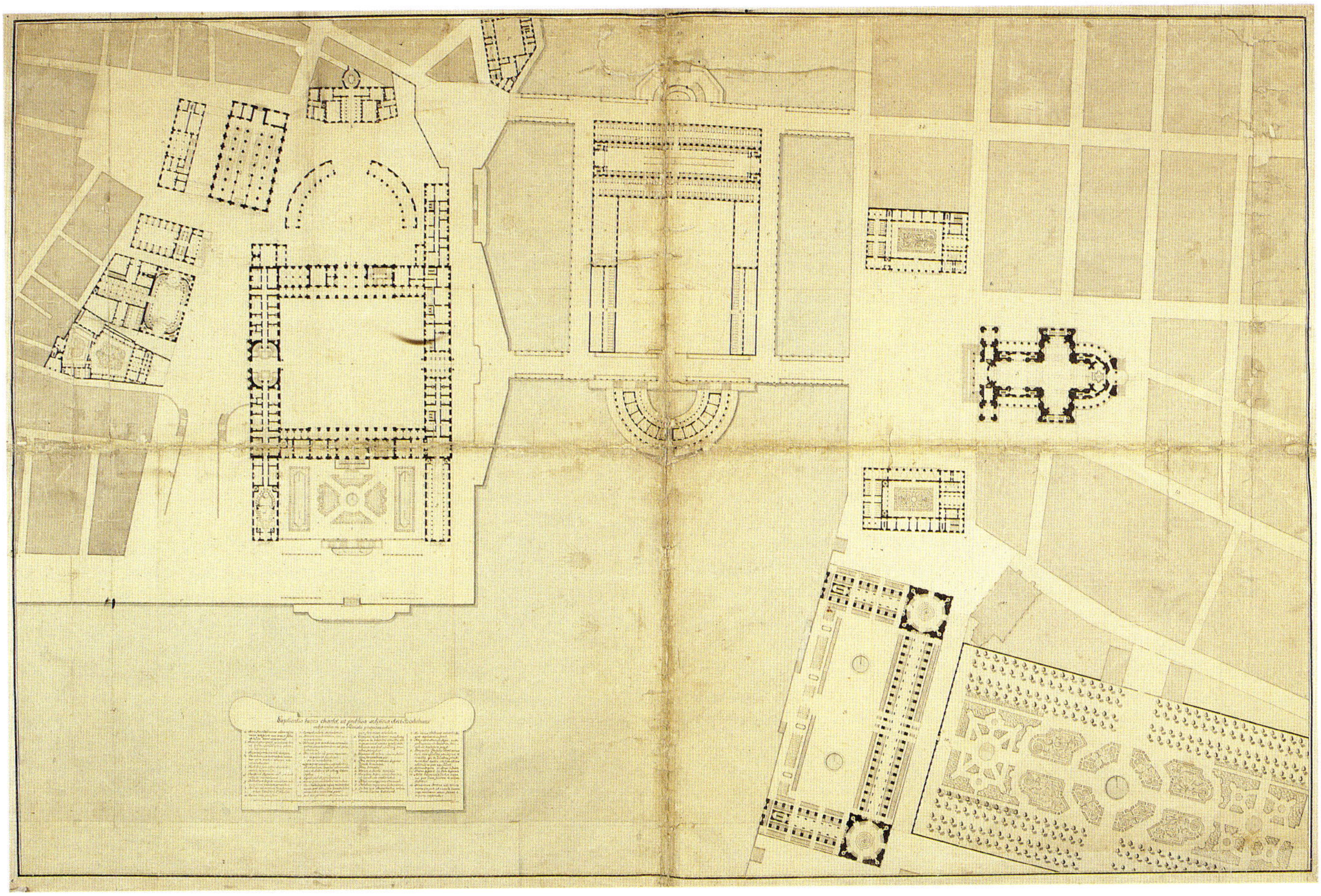

Nicodemus Tessin the Younger's 1712 project of transforming the Royal Palace's surroundings included a series of royal buildings, among them a new stable, a massive arsenal building, and a magnificent baroque church intended to function as a mausoleum for the Swedish kings. None of these plans ever materialized. Based on the Latin cross, the church has its apse pointing north instead of east.

in the urban environment of the palace. The goal was to create a capital city worthy of the absolute monarchy. In reality, however, the plans were more of an escapist's fantasy. This was probably understood by both the architect and the king, who was detained in Turkey after his disastrous defeat at Poltava in 1709. The full scope of the project to glorify Stockholm is known today only through a drawing by Tessin that has been preserved.

The general plan was to form an axis running through the northern waterway to a monumental open square located on the opposite shore, today's Gustav Adolf's Square (*Gustav Adolfs torg*). There, on the far side, Tessin planned a large baroque church with domes and clock towers; this would serve as a royal mausoleum. The square was to be flanked by courtiers' palaces, and between them were to be two fountain sculptures in the form of elephants carrying obelisks—an idea drawn from Bernini's famed *Elefante* in Rome's Piazza Minerva, just steps from the ancient Pantheon. The plans also included new royal stables with a show arena (where the House of Parliament stands today), an arcaded space for an open market, and, in the northeast, an enormous armory to display war trophies.

If Tessin's utopian ideal had become a reality, Stockholm would have been one of Europe's most magnificent capital cities, but plans to complete it collapsed with the fall of the absolute monarchy. Not until the end of the eighteenth century was the project revived, and then it was only partly realized by architects practicing in neoclassical styles.

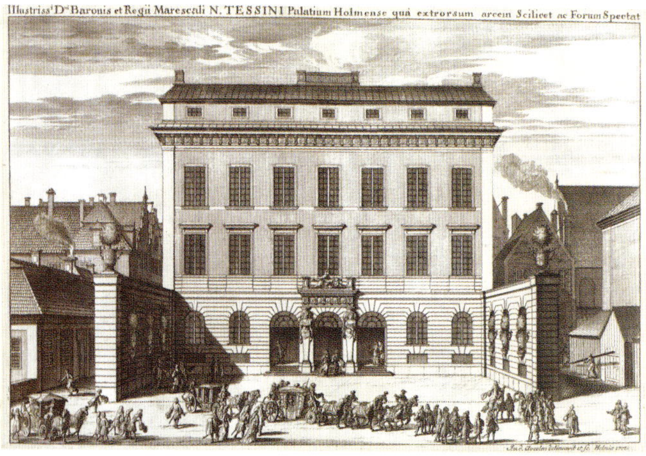

The somber facade of Tessin's palace looks toward the Royal Palace on the opposite side of the sloping road, Slottsbacken. Projecting walls originally framed the forecourt, shielding it from its surroundings. Engraving from Erik Dahlbergh's Suecia antiqua et hodierna.

The foyer through which one passes on entering Tessin's palace looks out on the exquisite formal garden (see also pages 92–93). For the summer months, Tessin intended to leave the three archways open, in effect allowing the interior and the garden to flow together.

ARISTOCRATIC PALACES AND MANOR HOUSES

Tessin's plan for Stockholm included his own palace, erected on a property that he had acquired in 1692 on Slottsbacken, just opposite the south entrance to the Royal Palace. Behind a Roman facade, he masterfully created for himself and his family an ideal dwelling, which he conceived as a stylistic continuation of the Royal Palace. His son, Carl Gustaf Tessin (discussed in Chapter Four), later wrote, "The Stockholm house of my father of blessed memory is by no means a big house, but it can certainly be considered a model." Moderate in size and with a simple, refined exterior, the house is easily distinguishable from the other private palaces that had been built in Stockholm by past generations. For its exterior and general composition Tessin looked at modern palaces in Rome, and like some of his Italian colleagues, he drew inspiration from the noteworthy aristocratic homes of antiquity. The most important rooms are clustered in one main building, with a foyer forming a classical atrium in the middle of the first floor. From the foyer, one can enter a peristyle of

FACING PAGE *The state apartment of Tessin's palace, here seen from the architect's bedchamber, includes an antechamber, a salon, and at the far ends in both directions, cabinets. Since 1772, the architect's palace has been the residence of the Governor General of Stockholm.*

Nicodemus Tessin the Younger had the salon in the state apartment of his palace adorned with views of Italian sites; a smoking Mount Vesuvius adorns the chimneypiece. The central ceiling paintings depict Apollo and the muses, while the figures in the corners represent the Italian masters Bernini and Bramante, two of the Swedish architect's idols.

greenery and a miniature baroque garden, which is considered one of the most exquisite in all Europe. From the outside, the second floor gives the impression of a *piano nobile*, but in fact it housed the family's private apartments. The formal state apartment, containing a salon, antechamber, bedchamber, and a cabinet at each end, was located on the third floor and overlooked the garden.

Tessin left this description of his plans for this apartment: "After much thought on how to decorate it, I decided to paint both ceilings and walls with all sorts of [antique-style] grotesque ornamentation . . . [In these] will be figures and small stories in colors, as well as some mirrors, bronze frames, etc. In the salon, the Fine Arts and Sciences will be the subject; in the antechamber, the satisfaction which comes from the study of Philosophy is depicted." For the rich decorative paintings that dominate the interiors, Tessin enlisted the help of the same French artists who had come to decorate the Royal Palace, including Jacques Fouquet, Jacques de Meaux, and the painter Evrard Chauveau (brother of René Chauveau). Trompe l'oeil paintings in the salon depict southern European harbors and sunny Italian landscapes with ancient ruins, while the bedchamber gives the illusion of continuity into an expansive sculpture gallery. This apartment has been referred to as one of the finest "French" interiors of the 1690s, and ceiling decorations of this quality in particular are rare indeed. Various figures are combined here

Shielded from urban Stockholm, the palace that Nicodemus Tessin the Younger built for himself hides a perfect miniature baroque garden. At the rear stands an elaborately articulated wing, at the center of which on the upper level he incorporated an arch with false perspective that gives the impression of a receding colonnade. Tessin drew his inspiration for this artistic trickery from Borromini's Palazzo Spada in Rome.

with ornamentation in the spirit of Jean Bérain but following a subtle, allegorical program of Tessin's own invention. The salon is dedicated to the god Apollo and the nine muses. The theme of the bedchamber is night, while in the antechamber are depictions of the struggle between Virtue and Vice.

The small, irregular lot that Tessin had acquired he transformed with precision and imagination into a symmetrical, terraced courtyard with a garden shielded by wings on all sides from the city's jagged skyline. Protruding chimneys were once cleverly concealed by sheet metal cutouts faux-painted as trees mounted atop the wings. A pond and a broderie parterre of boxwood, surrounded by marble sculptures of ancient gods and goddesses, made up the front section of the garden. The garden's rear section functioned as a stage, separated from the front section by a pair of freestanding wings. Behind these, Tessin created an illusion of depth by using false perspective with a row of columns gradually diminishing in size like the Italian baroque architect Borromini's false-perspective arcade at the Palazzo Spada in Rome. From the beginning, a garden grotto, birdsongs from aviaries, the babble of trickling water, and the scent of honeysuckle transported the visitor mentally to a southern European idyll. Landscapes painted in the wing's original open arcades enhanced this sensation.

In 1700, Tessin wrote to his good friend Daniel Cronström, "As God is my witness, my house is costing me more than a hundred thousand livres, even without the furniture. God willing, everything is nearly completed and I

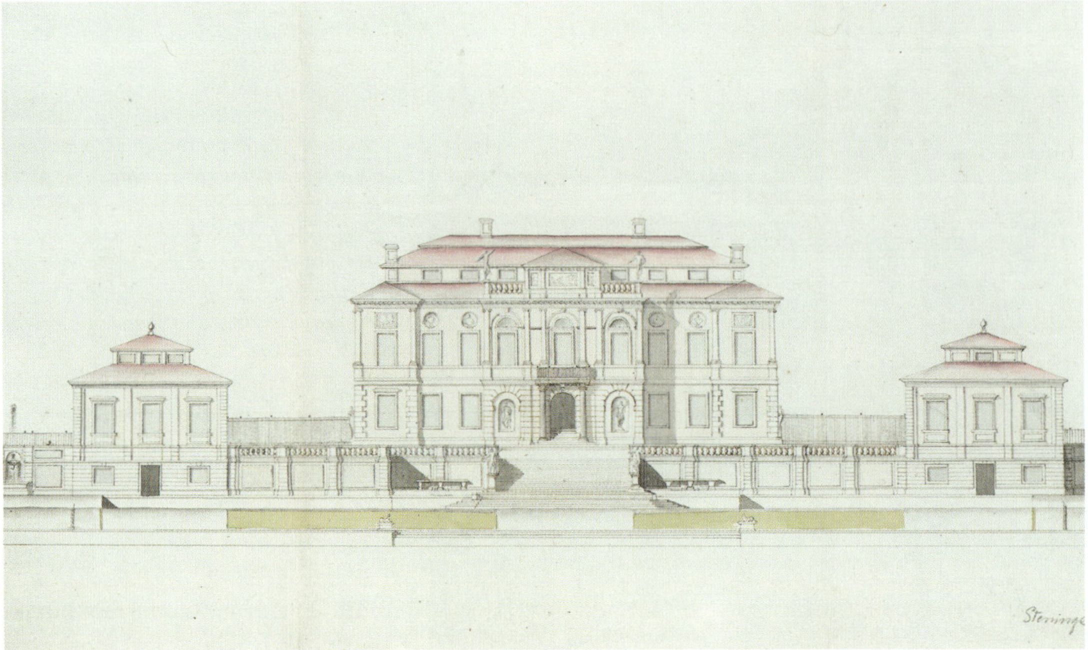

Steninge palace outside Stockholm was Nicodemus Tessin the Younger's first large-scale residential commission. The architect's drawing, from around 1690, clearly shows the influence of Italian Renaissance villa architecture; originally the facade was to be decorated with statues and busts in niches.

This 1690 cross-section drawing of Steninge palace by Nicodemus Tessin the Younger reveals how the architect tailored his plan to the slope of the site.

expect it to be my greatest source of happiness in my remaining days." Tessin proudly had engravings made of his house's architecture, its interiors, and its gardens to make known to the world this ultimate expression of his taste and artistry.

The work on Tessin's own palace drew on experience gained during the early years of his career. As a young man, Tessin the Younger had captured the attention of the highest stratum of Swedish society. In 1681, when he was just twenty-seven and newly returned from travels abroad, he was commissioned by Count Carl Gyllenstierna, the dowager queen's chief administrator and marshal, to design a palace. Situated just outside Stockholm, Gyllenstierna's palace—Steninge—was to be Tessin's first large-scale residential assignment; it gave the architect the opportunity to put to use the considerable knowledge he had garnered in France and Italy. Tessin's design for Steninge manifested the young architect's reaction to the heavy baroque style of his father's buildings erected in recent decades.

At Steninge, the younger Tessin replaced the corner pavilions, high roof, and projecting central bays of, for exam-

RIGHT *Vaux-le-Vicomte by Louis Le Vau, built 1658–61 for Nicolas Fouquet, minister of finance for Louis XIV, Maincy, France.*

BELOW *This Tessin floor plan of Steninge shows how the interior was dominated by grand stairways, an oval hall, and symmetrical suites of rooms flanking the state apartment. Tessin's plan for Steninge closely followed that of Vaux-le-Vicomte.*

BELOW RIGHT *General plan of Vaux-le-Vicomte.*

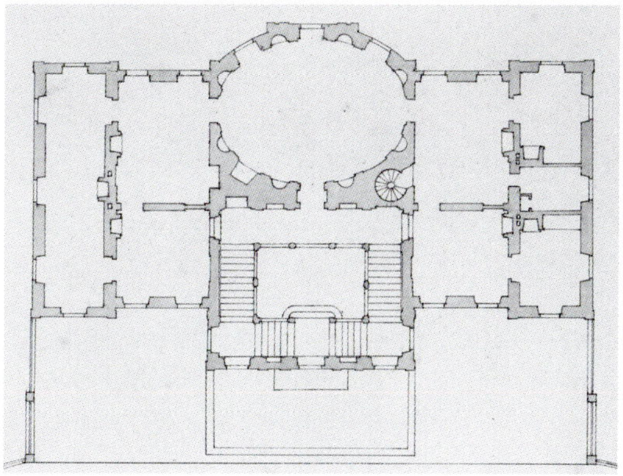

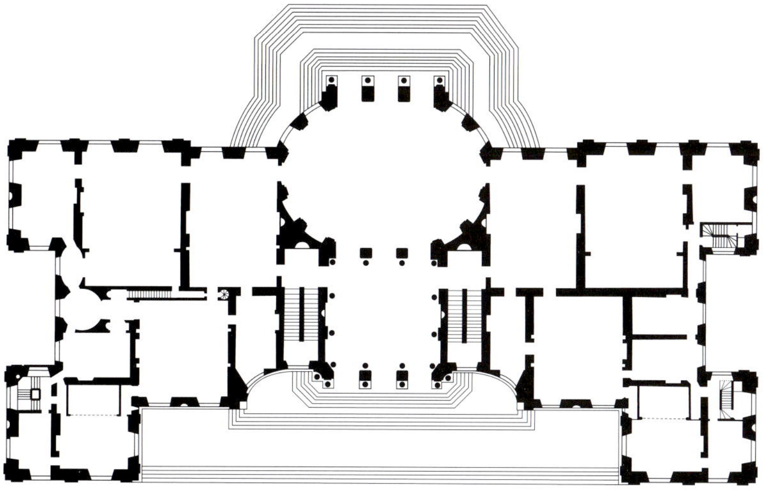

ple, his father's Strömsholm Palace and created something reminiscent of an Italian country house, with a facade adorned with statues in niches. Faithful to his Swedish heritage, however, Tessin replaced the typical Italian lantern roof with a Swedish *säteri* roof. Freestanding wings flanked the main building, and a stairway once led to docks on Lake Mälaren.

The floor plan of Steninge Palace was almost an exact copy of the palace Vaux-le-Vicomte, outside Paris, with its double suite of rooms situated around a high, oval central hall (*salon d'Italienne*). Tessin deviated from his model, however, by placing the main state rooms on the second floor instead of the first. The stairwell has a central role, reaching magnificent proportions as it rises the full height of the house, with symmetrical branches of steps, Corinthian pilasters, and decorative niches. With his design for Steninge Palace, Nicodemus Tessin the Younger felt that he had developed an ideal prototype for country manor and palaces.

Although Steninge stands as one of Sweden's finest architectural accomplishments, it did not in fact have any signif-

FACING PAGE *With the austere tone of its architecture beneath a characteristically Swedish* säteri *roof, Sturefors exemplifies the late baroque country manor house. It was built at the beginning of the eighteenth century for Field Marshal Count Carl Piper, with some assistance, but not a great deal, from Nicodemus Tessin the Younger.*

icant influence on Swedish domestic building traditions. Nor did the superior composition of the imposing Roman facade of the Royal Palace leave a lasting effect. This is perhaps attributable to the fact that construction of the palace languished for almost twenty years and was not completed until after Tessin's death. During the first decades of the eighteenth century, the Swedish high nobility continued to build in the styles of earlier generations, especially those of architects Nicodemus Tessin the Elder and Jean de la Vallée. While pilaster-strips and pediments continued to give palaces and manor houses a classical tone, the exteriors became much stricter and more austere, with hardly any facade decoration.

The first building of significance in which this new aesthetic was fully carried out was Sturefors, a manor house located in the province of Östergötland. The property belonged to Field Marshal Count Carl Piper, a favorite of King Karl XII, who, though away at war, directed the construction project in letters from the army's camp on the far shore of the Baltic Sea. Although documents indicate that Nicodemus Tessin the Younger assisted him, in reality the architect had little influence on the overall appearance of Piper's house, and Tessin's Continental style was hardly evident at Sturefors. The imposing three-story stone building, completed in 1707, had low projecting wings on one side and a Swedish *säteri* roof topped by a massive clock tower. With its vast, spare, stuccoed exterior, Sturefors mostly conveys aristocratic understatement.

In general, the floor plans of Swedish late Karolinian country manor houses followed the French prototype depicted in Augustin-Charles d'Aviler's handbook, *Cours d'architecture* (1691). They could, however, be slightly modified to suit Swedish conditions, traditions, and styles of living. At Sturefors, the state apartments, or reception rooms, are located on the second floor, directly above the family's private suites, and are dominated by a great salon that runs through the full width of the house and extends to the next floor, where the servants' quarters are found. The salon is flanked by two symmetrical suites looking onto the garden, each comprising an antechamber, a bedchamber, a cabinet, and a dressing room. The walls of the salon were originally covered by tapestries, while the white and gold ceiling was (and still is) painted with scenes joined by graceful linear ornamentation in the style of Berain and reminiscent of the decor of the Tessin palace. The symmetry of the floor plan was repeated in the splendid garden, which Tessin designed with a *broderie* parterre, bosks, topiaries, and an orangery serving as a backdrop for the cross axis. Overall, Tessin's garden at Sturefors followed the concept of André Le Nôtre's gardens at Versailles.

Carl Piper never saw his new manor house at Sturefors completed. He died in 1716, a prisoner in Russia, to which he was taken after the battle of Poltava.

The austerity of the facades of Sturefors and Sweden's other late baroque palaces was not necessarily an indication of worsened economic conditions. Rather, it expressed new values and a reaction against the excessive luxuries associated with the Baroque period. Moderation, earlier deemed appropriate solely for public or governmental buildings, was now considered suitable for private properties as well. King Karl XII, who was known for his modest lifestyle, quite possibly influenced the taste of other Swedes commissioning buildings. Whether or not King Karl's abstemious ways were a determining factor, when the troubled times that followed the war reached a peak, and demands for luxuries were considered defiant, it is no coincidence that building commissions showed a certain restraint.

After the death of the king and the end of war, a backlog of building and restoration needs had to be fulfilled. The areas along the Baltic coast that the Russian navy had ravaged (1719–21) had suffered the most. Villages, farms, and factories lay in ashes. In the areas affected, as elsewhere,

FACING PAGE *Tullgarn Palace was built between 1720 and 1727 from drawings by the French fortifications officer Joseph Gabriel Destain. The palace originally had a tall hip roof, but it was replaced at the end of the eighteenth century with the lower, balustraded roof seen here.*

*This 1723 drawing for a city palace (*Hôtel pour un grand seigneur*) by the French Academy pupil Jean Pinard is thought to resemble the facade of Tullgarn Palace.*

Swedes continued to build literally on the past, on the legacies from the Karolinian times. Fire-ravaged houses were repaired, and new ones were built directly on old foundations.

Beyond Tessin the Younger, there was a shortage of trained architects in Sweden. People wanting to commission buildings had to search elsewhere for the skills they sought and often found them in military personnel. An example was Joseph Gabriel Destain, a French fortifications officer who had come to Sweden in 1716. Destain contributed to Swedish architecture through his involvement with three manor houses in the province of Södermanland: Tullgarn, Björksund, and Berghammar.

Tullgarn Palace stands on a peninsula in the archipelago of Södermanland, south of Stockholm. The site was chosen not only for its beauty but also because it offered the ideal connections to the capital via waterways; no matter what the season, these were far superior to the narrow, winding, hilly roads. Despite its exposed location along the coast, Tullgarn escaped the Russian raids. Nevertheless, Tullgarn's owner, Count Magnus Julius De la Gardie (a relative of Magnus Gabriel De la Gardie), still chose to replace the old, outdated palace. The new structure he commissioned, following designs by Destain, was completed in 1727. It is today a three-story building facing a garden, with two lower wings projecting on opposite sides and embracing an imposing courtyard that opens onto the sea.

At the beginning, the palace had a high hip roof, which originally gave greater height to the building than it has today. Under the original roof there was a fourth floor. The facade of Tullgarn was also more articulated than that of the typical Swedish manor house of this period by its rustication and its masonry belt-coursing in a contrasting color. The high, arched French windows were very modern in Sweden and, behind these, on the second floor, the architect unified the state rooms with a private apartment to make one continuous suite. This began a new trend in Sweden, but one that would take some time to gain acceptance.

Tullgarn Palace has sometimes been compared with a drawing for a city palace by a student named Jean Pinnard at the Royal Academy of Architecture in Paris; in 1723 Pinnard had won the coveted *Prix de Rome* for his palace project. The similarities between Tullgarn and Pinnard's drawing show how closely related the Swedish manor house was to contemporary French counterparts. (Late in the eighteenth century, Tullgarn underwent dramatic stylistic modernization, discussed in Chapter Five.)

Among the properties that the Russians ravaged in the attacks of 1719 was Thureholm, situated not far from Tullgarn. The rebuilding of Thureholm began in 1729 by

ABOVE *Thureholm, designed in 1729 by Carl Hårleman, is one of the last Karolinian country palaces. Presented with a complicated, multilevel site, the architect ingeniously solved the problem of connecting the allée to the house by providing a ramp spanning the stables.*

FACING PAGE *According to Carl Hårleman's plan for Thureholm, the two main floors have identical floor plans but represent something radically new with their asymmetry. On the second story, to the left of the large, square salon, is the countess's suite of rooms; opposite it on the right are the count's antechamber and bedchamber.*

Count Thure Gabriel Bielke, one of Karl XII's officers, who had become a leading politician after the war. The new main building at Thureholm echoed the old one, which is evident in the builder's having used the old foundation and portions of the original walls. A possible motive for this reuse may have been the aristocracy's strong loyalty to tradition: The property had been in the Bielke family for centuries and was itself symbolic of the family's influence in the district. With its plain facades, its frontispiece, and its *säteri* roof, the building also conformed to the prevailing late baroque style. Originally, its austerity was reinforced by somber hues—gray for the walls and pitch black for the roof.

Thureholm's architect, Carl Hårleman (discussed further in Chapter Four), would later introduce the French Rococo in Sweden, but none of the characteristics that came to be associated with his style are evident in this, his first residential commission—at least not on the exterior. But Hårleman's floor plan for Thureholm does reveal something novel: The salon on the second and third floors is placed slightly off the central axis, which results in two asymmetrical suites of rooms flanking the axis. Within the combined private apartment and state rooms on the second floor, the countess occupied the larger suite, which lay to the left of the salon; it consisted of an antechamber, bedchamber, cabinet, dressing room, and a room for her chambermaid. The count

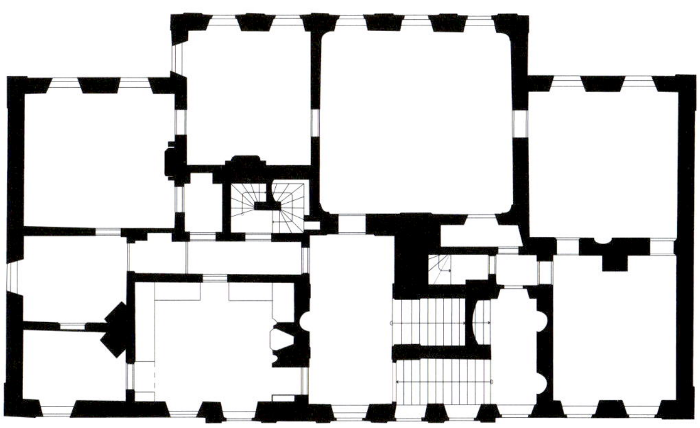

FACING PAGE *The salon on the second floor at Thureholm has coved corners and paneling with circles, a pattern that was a Carl Hårleman trademark. The panels of pine were faux-painted to imitate oak.*

ABOVE *In the vaulted porcelain kitchen at Thureholm (1744–47), Count Thure Gabriel Bielke displayed his collection of Chinese ware. The Asian theme was carried to the walls, doors, and paneling, which were painted with chinoiserie motifs copied from German and Dutch pattern books.*

had to make do with the smaller suite to the right of the salon, but his quarters also included a workroom on a concealed mezzanine floor some steps down. This type of floor plan with asymmetrical suites became common in Sweden during the eighteenth century, especially in the manor houses designed by Hårleman.

The rebuilding of Thureholm coincided with the resumed reconstruction of the Royal Palace, but with Nicodemus Tessin the Younger now dead, completion of the Royal Palace fell to Carl Hårleman. This enabled Count Bielke to use at Thureholm many of the same craftsmen and artisans working on the Royal Palace. For his salon on the second floor, as stipulated in Hårleman's designs, a master carpenter from the Royal Palace executed modern paneling consisting of circular fields and coved corners. The pine paneling was faux-painted to emulate oak, a common practice in Sweden. In this same room, Guillaume Taraval, another artisan from the Royal Palace, executed two allegorical paintings thought to portray Virtue and Courage. These rococo paintings contrasted boldly with the imposing series of royal portraits hanging on the walls. Though Bielke went along with many modern ideas, however, there were limits to how far he would go. This conservative inclination became evident when a sculptor suggested richly embellished plaster details for the ceilings. Count Bielke replied very decidedly, "No." Simple and straightforward suited his taste.

Painted wall coverings were in high demand during the Age of Liberty. Sweden's most comprehensive collection of painted wall coverings adorns the rooms as in this salon on the upper floor at Thureholm.

Thureholm typifies the prevailing trends in interior decoration in wealthy households just before the emergence of full-blown Rococo as Sweden's dominant style. Heavily sculpted and gilt French baroque pieces and colorful faience brought from France were mixed with less precious furniture of Dutch, English, and Swedish manufacture. For his elegant "porcelain kitchen"—a pantry intended explicitly for the display of collections—Bielke combined Swedish faience with Chinese porcelain acquired through the Swedish East India Company. The color schemes of the rooms were refined and the textile decoration mostly uniform. Perhaps the most stunning element of the (still intact) interiors is the painted wall coverings, which extend throughout the third floor. Nowhere else in Sweden is there so fine a collection of these materials. Equally remarkable is the sheer quantity and variety of popular baroque motifs all rendered in one place: chinoiserie, trompe l'oeil statuary, German grotesques, and depictions of heroes from classical myths. Several of the wall coverings were imported from Dresden; others were painted on site by German painters. From this point forward, painted wall coverings replaced varieties of embossed wallpaper, gilt leather, and woven wall coverings in the residences of affluent Swedes. To give the house's architecture an appropriately monumental frame, Hårleman designed a garden influenced mainly by André Le Nôtre, though with features that were uniquely his own invention (discussed in Chapter Four).

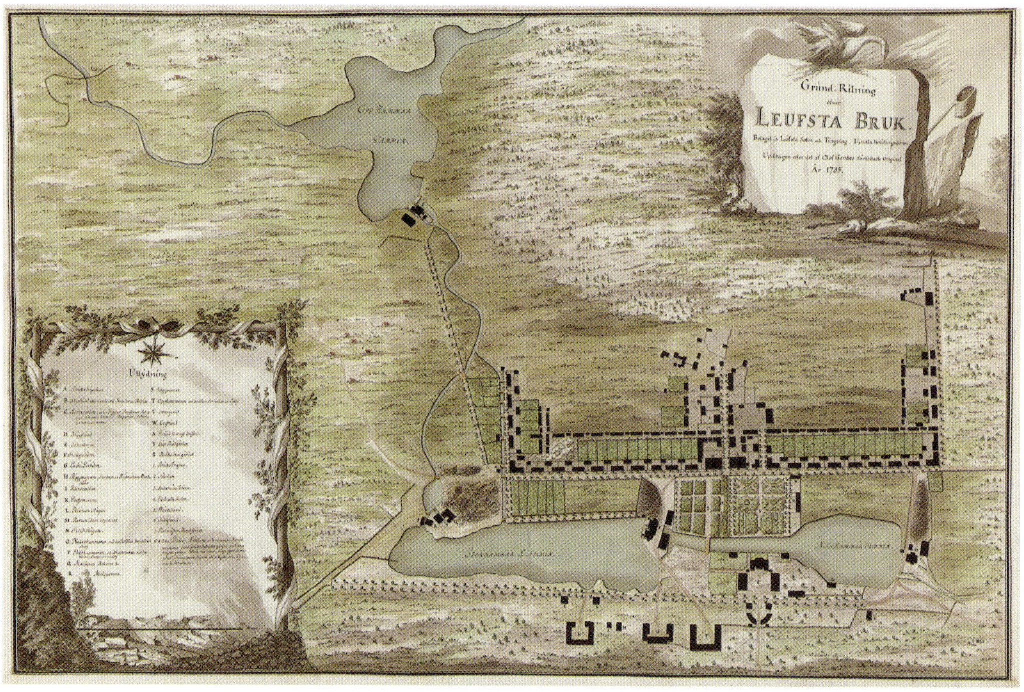

After destruction by Russian invaders, Leufsta ironworks was reconstructed on a strict, regular axis system, which is apparent in this 1735 map. At the lower right is the main building with its wings framing the courtyard.

FACING PAGE *The main house at Leufsta ironworks, seen here with its garden under snow, was built during the 1720s. The name of the architect has been lost.*

THE IRONWORKS VILLAGE, LEUFSTA

Sweden's natural wealth in iron ore, combined with the skills of blacksmiths and furnace builders brought from Wallonia (now southern Belgium), gave rise in the seventeenth century to many Swedish ironworking settlements. The high-quality product produced by the Walloon ironworkers enabled Sweden to exact steep prices in a growing foreign market for her iron bar. Thus, the ironworking communities—the most important being those set up deep in the forests of Uppland province—provided both the financial and material power that drove the engine of Swedish empire building. Thriving on the profits of their coveted product, the ironworking towns in time grew into miniature, self-sustaining communities. By the eighteenth century, some were comparable in scale to small towns.

The corporate ranking in such settlements, mirrored in a social hierarchy, was rigid and clear. At the top was the owner, followed by the bookkeeper, the clerk, the manager, the blacksmiths, and on down to the foundry workers and other day laborers. The types of houses constructed reflected this pyramid: Everything was designed and built according to the wishes of the ironworks owner. The characteristic form that many of these villages took as they grew and, in many cases, were rebuilt, was fully evolved in the course of the eighteenth century. They thus attained a special status in the architecture of the epoch.

Leufsta (or Lövsta), one of Uppland's best-preserved ironworks villages, took shape at a site on which an organized ironworking settlement had already existed in the seventeenth century. After the Russian attack of 1719, the layout remained almost unchanged, but now the buildings were erected in stone masonry rather than wood. A general plan from 1735 shows how the ironworks village was reconstructed, with straight streets and strict symmetry.

Leufsta's new manor house, on the site of the former one, was commissioned (from an architect whose name has been lost) by the owner of the ironworks, Charles De Geer. His dwelling, which still stands, is a grand, two-story masonry house with a stucco facade originally painted yellow. It boasts a projecting salon on one side and short wings on the other, and it is crowned by a stately *säteri* roof.

The interiors of the manor house were redesigned in the 1760s by the architect Jean Eric Rehn (discussed in Chapter Five). Rehn was also responsible for the design of the two small pavilions situated between the main house and a channel next to it. One of these buildings eventually housed the

At Leufsta, a series of identical workers' houses line the main street, a manifestation of the eighteenth-century ideal of standardized architecture.

comprehensive library and natural history collection of entomologist Charles De Geer the Younger.

The courtyard before the main building is framed by long wings, while on the other side of the house an expansive garden was laid out, separated from the rest of the village by walls and iron fences. The main street, placed at an angle from the central axis, ran alongside the garden and was enclosed by high gates. The street was lined with offices, a church, and identical houses for ironsmiths; the manufacturing buildings were erected at the farthest end near two large ponds. The ponds, in turn, are linked by the channel that passes close to the main house. Altogether, this plan creates a design that incorporates nature as an intrinsic part.

THE KAROLINIAN MANOR HOUSE

Only those families in the top ranks of the nobility or industry had the resources to build their country palaces and manor houses in masonry. For the lesser nobility and affluent commoners, a variation of the simple log house—the so-called Karolinian manor house—became the standard throughout the Swedish countryside during the second half of the seventeenth century and well into the eighteenth. Ultimately, it was the House of Nobility in Stockholm that served as the model for these houses. A typical Karolinian house is the early-eighteenth-century Valsta manor house in the province of Västmanland.

In general, the main building of the Karolinian manor

Valsta Manor in Västmanland is a textbook example of a Karolinian manor house, with a red painted exterior and characteristically Swedish säteri *roof.*

had just one story and a *säteri* roof of slate or wooden shingles. The floor plan consisted of little more than a vestibule, a salon, and a pair of chambers on either side. The number of rooms could be increased by an additional pair of chambers placed at either gable end. This very regular design might occasionally be embellished inside by a projecting central salon opening onto a garden. Freestanding wings often bordered the courtyard in front of the main building, providing additional living space and perhaps guest quarters. Because of the high risk of fire, the kitchen was normally located in one of these wings.

As a matter of course, the log exterior was painted red to give the impression of brick, the corners were painted gray to imitate sandstone pilasters, and the pine window frames were faux-painted to look like oak. Indeed, the paint was used less to protect the wood than to give the impression of more expensive building materials. A pediment facing a courtyard might be added.

There was no need for architects for these unpretentious country houses, so there were hardly any drawings. The builder's wallet decided the size of his house; the sizes of his rooms were determined by the length of the logs.

The main building of such estates was just one element in a symmetrical, consistent architectural plan. Separated from the main house and courtyard, which were often surrounded by fencing, were the stables, a carriage house, a granary, and other storage buildings. A garden extended behind the main building, and allées bordered the roads

ABOVE *At the von Echstedt manor house, two grenadiers depicted directly on the wood paneling stand guard before faux-marble blind doors in the vestibule. The interiors were painted in the 1760s.*

RIGHT *The salon of Liljeholmen manor house in Östergötland had landscapes painted on the walls around 1710 in an attempt to emulate the rich wall coverings in the great palaces. The ceilings too were painted in imitation of those in royal dwellings.*

closest to the farm.

The elaborate compositions and rich colors that once marked Karolinian manor house interiors can be seen in the main building at the Liljeholmen estate in the province of Östergötland. Using humble materials and simple techniques, naval captain Erik Ahlfort and his wife sought to create a milieu reminiscent of the rich interiors of the great palaces, with plastered and painted ceilings and lush tapestries. In the vestibule, climbing vines and leaf garlands that spread over the walls and ceiling greet the visitor. A uniformed soldier painted in trompe l'oeil guards the entrance to the salon, where the timber walls are decorated with a painted woodland scene and illusionary architecture framed by borders of flowers. The richly decorated ceiling is embellished at the center with the monograms of the owner and his wife.

Styles and trends were often slower in reaching the country than the city. This was true for the von Echstedt estate situated deep in the woods of Värmland. Though the house was erected as late as 1762–64, much of it still reflects the late baroque style. In the vestibule, the visitor encounters

ABOVE *In the lantern of the von Echstedt manor's privy, the lord and lady of the house were depicted much as they would actually appear in this room, with servants to offer them pieces of linen.*

LEFT *The privy at the von Echstedt manor could accommodate large numbers of people. Five adults and two children could tend to their needs simultaneously.*

two uniformed grenadiers painted directly on the wood paneling. In the main salon, the walls are covered with biblical motifs copied from a venerable illustrated Bible painted on canvas in muted colors. That the images were already outmoded seemed not bother the owner, who allowed the Rococo style to flourish in other rooms.

One of the two small pavilions with conical roofs flanking the main building is furnished as a privy, with five seats for adults and two for children. In the lantern of this room, the owners are shown seated and being assisted by servants handing them small pieces of linen. The need for privacy was not so strong during the eighteenth century as it was to become.

Closely related in form and style to the Karolinian manor

house are the residences built for military personnel. A new army of professional soldiers was created after the defense reorganization by King Karl XI in the 1680s. Each of the men who served the monarchy received a plot of land, a house, and a small stipend. The size of a military residence directly reflected the rank of its owner. During peacetime, these soldiers worked as farmers.

The oldest surviving designs for military quarters were executed by Erik Dahlbergh in 1687. His standard drawings were intended for two groups. The first group comprised enlisted men, military trumpeters, lieutenants, and second lieutenants; the second, captains and cavalry officers. For both groups, the designs involved narrow, one-story houses built of logs with small windows and sod roofs. There were no standard designs for higher-ranking officers' residences. Normally, a colonel or a major was housed on one of the larger farms that the monarchy had regained through its Reduction program (see Chapter One).

In 1730, the city architect of Stockholm, Johan Eberhard Carlberg (1683–1773) introduced a new series of patterns that raised the architectural level. Carlberg's standard model for higher-ranking officers included a main house, which was crowned with a *säteri* roof and flanked by freestanding wings. His proposal did not gain popularity with the commanders, however, who saw it as far too expensive. A year later, the state reverted to models closer to Dahlbergh's designs.

The desire to standardize military residences can be seen as an attempt to improve the quality of housing for people living in the countryside. These residences were to serve as models for other houses in rural communities, creating an essential link between the building traditions of aristocrats and those of commoners.

CHURCH ARCHITECTURE

In 1680, when the city of Karlskrona was established as a royal naval base during the reign of King Karl XI, it was decided that three new churches would be built. One was to serve the city's Swedish congregation, the second was for German congregants, and the third was for naval personnel. The last—the Admiralty Church (*Amiralitetskyrkan*)—was to be built of masonry, but instead, the provisional timber church that was consecrated in 1685 became permanent. Erik Dahlbergh, most likely the architect of this church, attempted to imitate the classical features of contemporary monumental stone architecture by using such ornamental elements as pilasters. The red color of the exterior was

Johan Eberhard Carlberg's design for a colonel's 1730 dwelling is closely related to contemporary manor house architecture. Such residences for military personnel provided a vital link between aristocratic and provincial building traditions.

LEFT *This provisional version of the Admiralty Church in Karlskrona attributed to Erik Dahlbergh was consecrated in 1695. It was constructed entirely of wood but was painted red to imitate masonry construction.*

BELOW *Rational simplicity characterizes the interior of the Admiralty Church, with visible posts and beams that call to mind the masts of a ship.*

intended to resemble masonry.

The central-plan church prototype based on the Greek cross that Jean de la Vallée had introduced in Sweden (see Chapter Two) was an ideal model for the Admiralty Church. It allowed for a large room that could be built at a reasonable cost and with relatively little labor. Carpenters from the shipyards could provide the craftsmanship. The interior was simple and robust, with all structural elements visible, as in ship construction. This resulted in a very light and open space, sparsely decorated only with polychrome epitaphs for deceased seamen, starkly contrasted against the bright whitewashed wood. Large sections of pews and an original double gallery were provided for a spacious room that could accommodate three thousand worshippers, seated according to military rank. The Admiralty Church is still Sweden's largest wooden church.

The two other Karlskrona churches, designed by Nicodemus Tessin the Younger, reflect the architect's wish to base his designs firmly on the classical architecture to which he was so devoted. His aspiration was to create buildings worthy of a royal naval port. By situating the churches on the city's expansive main square, he created one of Sweden's most monumental public spaces.

For the German congregation, Tessin presented draw-

FACING PAGE *The Church of the Holy Trinity in Karlskrona was designed on a central plan with a dome and four projecting arms with pediments. An open portico with Ionic columns serves as the main entrance from the city square.*

The Pantheon, Rome, second century. Drawing by the architect Gustaf af Sillén from his travel journals of 1788–92.

Villa "La Rotonda," Andrea Palladio, Vicenza, 1556–70.

ings of a magnificent eight-sided, central-plan church with four projecting temple pediments and a high cupola crowned by a lantern. The design recalled Rome's ancient, majestic Pantheon, the twin baroque churches in the Piazza del Popolo, and Palladio's Villa Rotonda in Vicenza; all these served as inspiration for this project. Karlskrona's German congregation, however, had other ideas. They preferred a more traditional, oblong church and insisted that the altar be placed at the east end, not in the south arm, as the architect had proposed. But Tessin's ideas were supported by one particularly important parishioner, Admiral Hans Wachtmeister, who had the greatest authority over not only the navy but also the town. Tessin thus had his way, and in 1697 construction began on the Church of the Holy Trinity (*Heliga Trefaldighetskyrkan*), which, though still unfinished, was consecrated in 1709.

Four decades later, the cupola of the Church of the Holy Trinity was finally put into place, but, sadly, it was destroyed by fire in 1790, along with the entire interior of the church. During the rebuilding, Tessin's classicism was successfully

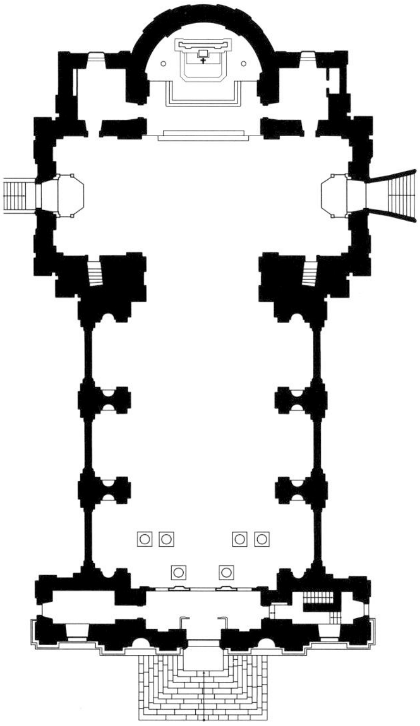

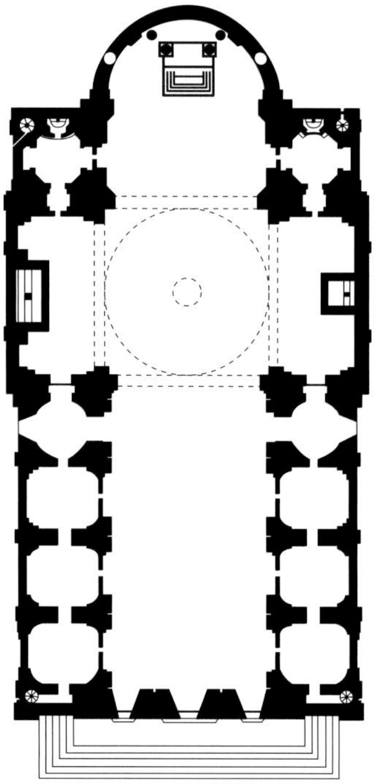

FAR LEFT *The plan of Fredrik's Church derives largely from the Jesuit church Il Gesù in Rome. The wide nave, short cross-arms, and chancel terminating in an apse are all reminiscent of the Roman baroque model.*

LEFT *Plan of the church of Il Gesù, Rome. Giacomo Vignola, 1568.*

FACING PAGE *Consecrated in 1744, the Fredrik's Church in Karlskrona turns its Roman-inspired west facade toward the city's public square. In his ecclesiastical architecture, Nicodemus Tessin the Younger followed his father's monumental style.*

fused with the then-current neo-classical style. A low, round, Pantheon-style dome designed by architect Olof Tempelman (discussed in Chapter Five) replaced the tall, octagonal dome. The facade retained its original character, and the intended open portico facing the square that was planned but not built was finally completed in 1862. The columns and strict pilasters were still considered stylistically acceptable and were therefore retained. There was no interest, however, in completing the interior decorative embellishments that Tessin had planned.

If the Church of the Holy Trinity was based on round Roman temples, Rome's boxlike Constantinian basilicas must have inspired Tessin's largest ecclesiastical project, the Swedish Church. Though the drawings for the Swedish Church were ready by the 1690s, construction did not take place until much later. Like the Church of the Holy Trinity, the Swedish Church, too, was consecrated unfinished, in 1744, by which time it had been given the name it still has today: Fredrik's Church (*Fredrikskyrkan*), for the reigning king.

The imposing west facade facing the square—clad in yellow-painted stucco like the rest of the exterior—is composed of two stories with pilasters in the Doric and Ionic orders, a pediment, and two towers. The entire composition is very restrained, though Tessin had in fact planned some extra decoration, including a sculptural group in the pediment. He also planned for the towers to be crowned by bell-shaped domes. The classical language of the facade was reminiscent of two Roman churches: Trinità dei Monti, overlooking the Piazza di Spagna, and Sant'Atanasio dei Greci.

Inside Fredrik's Church, Tessin copied Giacomo Barozzi da Vignola's design for Rome's Jesuitical Il Gesù by using a wide, barrel-vaulted nave, side chapels, short transept aisles, and a chancel leading to an apse. In Tessin's church, however, the Catholic architect's dim chapel serves instead as a source of light and provides space for pews. In fact, from the arched windows and the openings in the barrel vault, the interior is flooded with daylight. This is a prime example of a Roman Catholic design adapted to a Swedish evangelical Lutheran church, simplified and toned down. No overembellished decor was there to distract the congregation during

FACING PAGE *Tall Ionic pilasters dominate the interior of Fredrik's Church, which otherwise has a minimum of surface decoration.*

ABOVE *At the Turinge church in Södermanland, Erik Dahlbergh erected this mausoleum—his final great work—for himself. The mausoleum was under construction from 1696 to 1699; Dahlbergh lived until 1703.*

its spiritual hour.

The high nobility's use of mausoleums had reached magnificent proportions during the Baroque period. Toward the end of the seventeenth century, the grandeur and pomp of funerary customs began slowly to diminish, however, just as it had in aristocratic and common residential architecture. A more restrained aesthetic expression was now desired.

This is evident in Erik Dahlbergh's last work, his own mausoleum (1696–99), located in Turinge church in the province of Södermanland. The architect used his own gravesite to explore new ideas. The rich vocabulary of baroque architecture expressed, for example, in the Kagg mausoleum here yielded to a more austere and refined style adorned with little more than rustication and engaged columns. The decoration is minimal. On the exterior, the Turinge chapel appears to be an independent structure, but in fact it is a direct continuation of the nave and forms the church's high chancel. The room has relatively spare plasterwork executed by the Italian Giambattista Bretano. On either side of the chancel stand sculptural groups depicting Hope and Faith carved by Nicolaes Millich of Antwerp. The heraldic characteristics of the interior are overshadowed by the religious aura.

One of the last mausoleums of this type to be executed in the manner representative of the Age of Greatness is the De Geer chapel located in Österlövsta church near the Leufsta

Near the Leufsta ironworks, the De Geer mausoleum at Österlövsta church (1730s) gives a monumental impression, with its cool, somber classical tone. A sarcophagus stands at the center of the room.

FACING PAGE *The Karolinian mausoleum at the Riddarholm Church in Stockholm is the work of three of Sweden's greatest architects, father and son Tessin and Carl Hårleman. It was completed in 1743.*

ironworks. This chapel, designed by an architect whose name is not known, was completed in the 1730s. It is generous in size but very stern in its decoration. Inside, cool whitewashed walls, vast openings, and the black-and-white checkered stone floors combine to create a disciplined yet monumental atmosphere. The De Geer mausoleum lacks the customary crypt, and it also deviates from tradition by the obvious use of personal and intimate symbolism. A stone sarcophagus stands in the center of the room.

The kings of the Palatine dynasty—Karl X Gustav, Karl XI, and Karl XII—rest in the Karolinian mausoleum at the Riddarholm Church (*Riddarholmskyrkan*) in Stockholm. This mausoleum can be said to mark the end of the Karolinian epoch. Architecturally, it also signifies the grand finale of a long tradition of mausoleums of this type.

Drawings for the Karolinian mausoleum had been presented by Nicodemus Tessin the Elder in 1671, but construction was delayed. The plan was revived by his son in 1686, but the building was not completed until 1743, by superintendent Carl Hårleman. In his original plans, Tessin the Elder had projected a robust structure with columns crowned by a small, circular temple holding a sculpture representing Rumor. Like the other mausoleums attached to the Riddarholm Church, this too consists of an upper chapel and a subterranean vault for sarcophagi. But Hårleman toned down the building's overall baroque elaborateness, although he retained the high base, the recessed rounded corners, and Tessin's proposed columns. The upper section he completely reinterpreted by adding an attic story above the entablature and a richly embellished dome of gilt copper.

Thus, the creation that we see today is the sum of the several architects' contributions. Despite the significant interval separating the original design and the edifice that was finally executed, a consistency of treatment linking Tessin the Elder's baroque classicism to Hårleman's rococo produces a stylistically unified whole.

CHAPTER FOUR

The Rococo

PRECEDING PAGES *Palatial Svartsjö, the hunting lodge outside Stockholm that Carl Hårleman designed in 1734 for King Fredrik I, manifests the Swedish architect's reliance on French rococo.*

RIGHT *Completed in 1754, one of architect Carl Hårleman's early interiors in the Royal Palace was King Adolf Fredrik's rococo dining room (today called the Hall of Pillars). With its original classical elements, including twelve Ionic columns, the room was easily transformed in the 1780s, under King Gustav III, into a neoclassical milieu. The modernization entailed replacing wall paintings by Antoine-Baptiste Monnoyer, of cornucopias overflowing with abundant fruit, with the mirrors seen here behind a marble figure by sculptor Johan Tobias Sergel,* Venus aux belles fesses.

By the mid-1730s, the French Rococo style had a firm hold in Sweden. Applied primarily in interior decoration, the Rococo was reserved mainly for regal environments such as the Royal Palace in Stockholm, where the style first became evident in newly completed rooms. Not until the middle of the eighteenth century, however, did the Rococo become solidly established and common in Sweden's private houses as well. Though Swedish Rococo is normally considered to encompass the years 1750 to 1770, this discussion begins with the very first signs of the Rococo's arrival in Sweden.

The architect Carl Hårleman, who introduced the Rococo in Sweden and was responsible for forming its Swedish character, had already died by the 1750s. Hårleman is credited with having laid the foundation for the modern Swedish house, although in fact his architecture is based entirely on French prototypes. But the models were not simply copied in Sweden. Rather, they were adapted and modified into more moderate and disciplined forms than appeared in France. The Swedish Rococo has indeed its own, very dis-

tinctive character, and this applies comprehensively to architecture, to interiors, and to the decorative arts of the period. It is sometimes said that the French Rococo cooled down in Sweden's Nordic climate.

ARCHITECTURE FOR THE MONARCHY

The year 1727 is often cited as the starting point of the art and architecture of the Age of Liberty (see Chapter One). It was during this year that the Swedish Parliament decided to resume work on the Royal Palace, which had been at a standstill for two decades. Nicodemus Tessin the Younger, by then elderly, died the very next year, and his son, Carl Gustaf Tessin, inherited the position of superintendent. One of the eighteenth century's most illustrious personalities, Carl Gustaf Tessin made major contributions to the palace and to Sweden's artistic life in general, but he lacked both the training and the ambition to practice architecture. Thus, the leading architectural role went to Carl Hårleman, who assumed artistic responsibility for completion of the palace.

Nicodemus Tessin the Younger himself had hand-picked Carl Hårleman (1700–1753) for the job. The son of the keeper of the royal gardens and grounds, Hårleman possessed talents that had been noticed early on, and in 1721 Tessin arranged for Hårleman to travel to Paris for further studies. After six years abroad, including a study sojourn in Italy, Hårleman was ordered home to Stockholm, with the understanding that he would assist the aging superintendent. Instead, despite his lack of practical experience as an architect, he soon found himself bearing both the title of court architect and full responsibility for the royal building project. Even after he became superintendent in 1741, which gave him license to practice very much as he liked, Hårleman nonetheless adhered closely to Tessin the Younger's vision for the palace.

By the early 1730s, construction of the Royal Palace had progressed to the point of being ready for planning of the interior decoration to begin, especially for the interiors of the royal apartments on the second floor of the north wing (see Chapter Three). As had been the case with artisans and

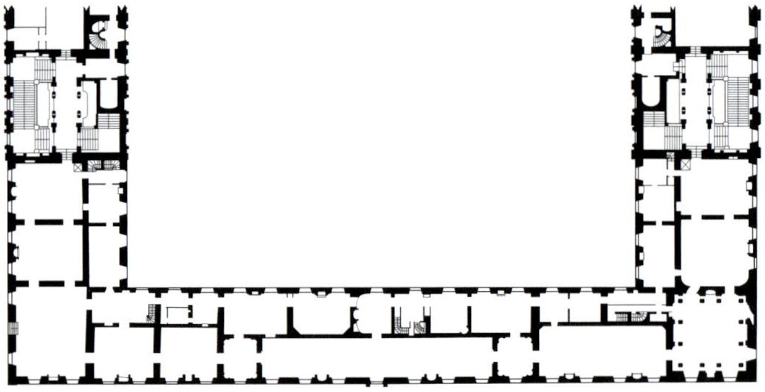

In this floor plan showing parts of the second story of the Royal Palace, the Lower Gallery appears at the center of the north wing, flanked by the two octagonal cabinets. The Hall of Pillars is situated in the right corner.

Detail of Carl Hårleman's rococo ornament of gilt carved wood in the room referred to as the octagonal west cabinet in the Royal Palace.

This proposal by Carl Hårleman for the Lower Gallery at the Royal Palace was carried out in the mid-1730s. Compared to the palace interiors by Nicodemus Tessin the Younger, Hårleman's are distinctly lighter and less formal in tone. (See, for example, page 82.)

craftsmen back in the 1690s, the need for skilled workers for the interior again became acute. So in 1731 Hårleman was sent to Paris to recruit qualified artisans, as well as to bring back drawings and patterns of designs for furniture and textiles. This journey was of vital importance to the entire artistic development of Sweden. Hårleman was able to absorb everything he encountered in the French capital. In letters, he confessed that there were many things that he had overlooked during his earlier travels, adding how the Paris he had encountered just four years before had in the interim changed dramatically.

The Rococo was on the verge of a breakthrough in Paris. During his eight-month stay, Hårleman had plenty of time to study the latest developments in architecture and interior design. He successfully fulfilled his duties to the crown by returning to Sweden with vast knowledge, a portfolio of drawings reflecting the current styles in Paris, and a list of new recruits. During the summer of 1732, the first group—nine French artisans and ornament sculptors—arrived in Stockholm. Other artists followed, including two Italian painters whom Carl Gustaf Tessin had met in Venice. With the influence of these Continental artists and artisans, Sweden quickly became up-to-date with the most current styles. This not only affected the palace project but also influenced the overall artistic development of Sweden.

In the interiors of the palace, Hårleman was free to make contributions reflecting the latest trends. One of the first for which he was responsible was Crown Prince Adolf Fredrik's dining room, also called the Hall of Pillars. Work on this room, in the northwest corner of the palace, began in 1733. Here, Hårleman's regard for classical traditions is evident. Behind twelve Ionic columns, the walls are divided by Ionic pilasters. Providing a strong contrast to the columns' somber effect, large paintings of magnificent cornucopias of fruit by Antoine-Baptiste Monnoyer were set into the wall panels, and matching overdoors carried similar motifs. The system of joists takes the shape of a coved molding with gilt decoration, and the ceiling was (and still is) decorated with a light, playful painting representing the Four Seasons executed by one of the artists brought from Italy, Alessandro Feretti.

As with the Hall of Pillars, many of Hårleman's interiors at the Royal Palace have undergone changes and modernization since the architect's original plan was realized. Moreover, most of Hårleman's drawings have been lost. In fact, the only room in the royal apartments for which an original Hårleman plan exists today is the Lower Gallery (today called the Bernadotte Gallery) located on the second floor of the north wing. Made in the second half of the 1730s, the drawing depicts a windowed wall. The wall panel's large, sculpted framework is held together by pilasters with rich rococo ornament, while the chimneypiece

FACING PAGE *In Crown Prince Gustav's bedchamger at the Royal Palace, the masterful carving of the boiserie panel (c. 1746–47) was executed by French ornament sculptor Adrien Masreliez. It reflects a mature rococo style of genuine French origin, although it was designed by Carl Hårleman. The woodwork was originally painted white and gold, which heightened the visibility of the carving. The overdoor depicts* Diana and Endymion *by Guillaume Taraval, 1740s.*

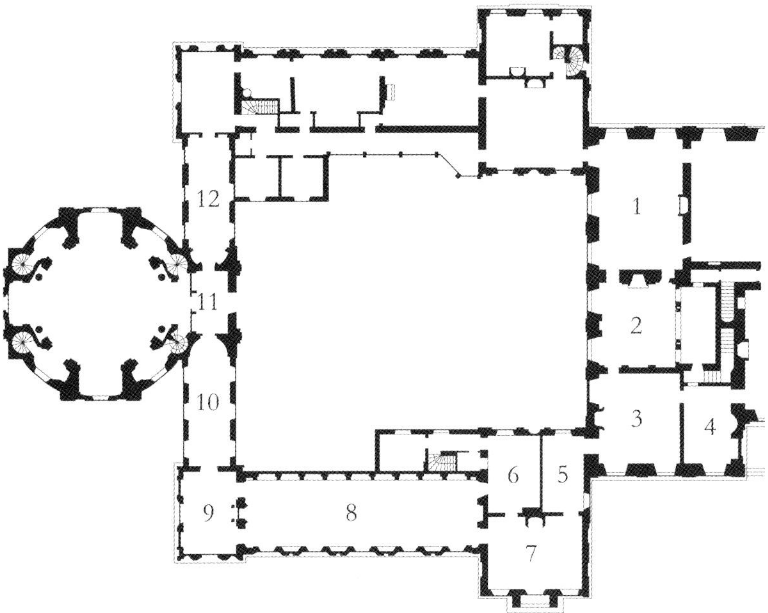

Floor plan of Lovisa Ulrika's apartment on the main floor of Drottningholm

1. Audience Room
2. State Bedchamber
3. Green Cabinet
4. Dressing Room
5. Cabinet
6. Cabinet
7. Blue Cabinet
8. Library (formerly Natural History Cabinet)
9. Marble Cabinet (formerly study library)
10. Coin Cabinet
11. Natural History Cabinet
12. Mineral Cabinet

over the fireplace is embellished with a framed mirror decorated with dragons—one of Hårleman's signature images.

Similarities between this room and the Galerie Dorée in the Hôtel de Toulouse in Paris, designed by the French architect and sculptor François-Antoine Vassé, have often been noted. Vassé, Hårleman's teacher at Paris's Royal Academy of Architecture, and the architects Robert de Cotte and Nicolas Pineau, were the Swedish architect's main sources of inspiration for his work at the Royal Palace. Hårleman's style always remained independent, however. Within the Rococo traditions, his work was considerably more restrained than that of his French colleagues. His designs were simpler and toned down, and he never allowed decoration to overwhelm a room's architectural integrity.

Among the Royal Palace's best-preserved rococo interiors are the two cabinets flanking the Lower Gallery. Tessin the Younger had planned the cabinets to be rectangular, but, in 1737, Hårleman transformed them into octagons with recessed, arched niches. The Frenchman Jean Bourguignon led the carving work and executed the heavily sculpted and gilt doors that were, according to the artist himself, *"d'un gôut tres nouveau"*—of a very new taste. Around 1754 two other Frenchmen, François Menard and Jean Gaspar Caillon, carved the exquisite relief ornamentation that Hårleman designed for six of the room's eight niches; within the reliefs were various rococo motifs such as mosaic patterns, floral garlands, mussels shells, *rocailles*, and *trofée* groups. (*Rocailles*, the source of the term Rococo, refers to elaborate rock work, often using marine motifs and applied in grottos and formal gardens. *Trofée* groups are ornamental compositions made up of spoils, or trophies, of war such as the helmets and shields of the vanquished.) These carvings, gilt and faux-marble painted in diverse tones, are considered one of the finest examples of Swedish Rococo.

A third trip to Paris, in 1744–45, broadened Hårleman's sources of ideas. Among his new guiding spirits was Ange-Jacques Gabriel, under whom Hårleman had worked during an earlier stay in Paris. At Versailles, Gabriel and his coworkers had created *rocailles* with figurative scenes similar to those that eventually appeared in Crown Prince Gustav III's apartment in the Royal Palace. For the designs of this room, Hårleman was assisted by the Frenchman Adrien Masreliez, who in 1748 was put in charge of the ornament workshop at the Royal Palace. Gustav III's apartment exhibits a mature but disciplined Rococo. The pilasters and dado, carved in shallow relief, blend into the walls' oak paneling (which was originally painted), while the individual decorative ornaments, such as cherubs playing, stand out distinctly.

Hårleman died at the height of his career, before completing the crown prince's apartment. Thus, he did not wit-

Drottningholm's Green Cabinet, completed around 1747, offers a fine example of the restrained rococo that characterized Carl Hårleman's work.

ness the royal family's return to the palace in 1754. (In the interim, the Wrangel palace in Stockholm had served as the royal residence; see Chapter Two.) For a long time, the Rococo in Sweden was limited to Hårleman's interiors in the Royal Palace, executed with the assistance of the French master artisans. Rococo interiors of equal distinction were, by and large, never again created in Sweden.

The second largest royal building project during the Rococo period was the rebuilding of Drottningholm Palace for Crown Princess Lovisa Ulrika. When the Prussian princess married Sweden's Crown Prince Adolf Fredrik in 1744, she was given use of the palace as a wedding gift from her father-in-law, King Fredrik I. From the very beginning, Lovisa Ulrika demonstrated exceptional aptitude as a patron, becoming deeply engaged in the remodeling of Drottningholm. Her first concern was an extension of the building that was to provide modern private apartments for her family.

Where to place these apartments was a dilemma that Carl Hårleman ingeniously solved by adding a second floor to the one-story wings that connected the central building of the palace to the two round towers at the north and south ends (see Chapter Two and page 38). These additions (replacing what had earlier been open roof-terraces) integrated well with Nicodemus Tessin the Elder's work, though the overall character of the palace changed slightly. The original, rhythmic counterbalance of the imposing central building, lower wings, and terminating towers was transformed into a single, cohesive composition of even more monumental aspect.

Hårleman's interiors at Drottningholm resemble those he designed for the Royal Palace, even though they were planned for different living conditions. The emphasis at Drottningholm was more on private life than on public duties. From a forthright exchange of ideas among the commissioner, Lovisa Ulrika and, most likely, her personal esthetic advisor, Carl Gustaf Tessin, Hårleman was able to create a more restrained but elegant environment that was equally well-suited to family life, entertaining, and study.

The queen's dressing room, with its painted boiserie *wall coverings, Swedish tile stove, and limestone floor, is one of Drottningholm's best-preserved rococo interiors. The room was completed in the 1750s.*

FACING PAGE *A chimneypiece designed by Carl Hårleman graces the Blue Cabinet, which was refurbished in the 1760s to serve as Queen Lovisa Ulrika's study at Drottningholm. Dragons support the frame around a portrait by the French painter Carle van Loo of his daughter. To the right of the chimneypiece hangs a portrait of Lovisa Ulrika by Alexander Roslin.*

In the treatment of the interiors, decoration was generally concentrated around the windows, doors, and chimneypieces. Otherwise, many of the rooms were given only basic wall treatment, such as a dado with circular and rectangular fields below, and above this, fielded panels (that is, panels framed by a system of raised moldings) of textile. This was the approach in the newly furnished Green Cabinet, in which green silk damask was adorned with portraits of the princess's Prussian family. In this room, a large mirror with a heavily carved and gilt frame was also mounted between the two windows. Crowning the mirror is a still life of a hare and a partridge painted in 1739 by the French artist Jean-Baptiste Oudry.

Originally part of the dowager queen's state apartment, the Green Cabinet as well as her splendid bedchamber and audience room (*Ehrenstrahlsalongen*) now constituted the core of Lovisa Ulrika's private apartment. This was situated in the northern part of the palace's main building and in a second story newly added to the northwest wing. To these three formal rooms, the crown princess also adjoined a suite of more intimate rooms. One—formerly Lovisa Ulrika's dressing room—was embellished throughout with blue *boiserie* panels and garlands. The chandelier and silvered bronze appliqués were purchased in 1754 in Paris. A stove, with blue Swedish tile decoration from the Rörstrand ceramics factory, stood in a niche on the limestone floor.

This proposal drawing from the late 1740s by Carl Hårleman shows the south wall planned for Lovisa Ulrika's first study library at Drottningholm. Double doors flank the fireplace and chimneypiece, and bookcases can be seen at the sides.

FACING PAGE *Lovisa Ulrika's Coin Cabinet at Drottningholm was completed in 1753. The collections were originally kept in eight tall cupboards, probably arranged in the middle of room so as to not obscure the decorated walls. The low work table seen here may have been added in the 1780s.*

Originally intended to house a portrait gallery, the oblong room in the palace's north wing facing the gardens instead became Lovisa Ulrika's Natural History Cabinet; the great botanist Carl Linnaeus helped the princess to organize her collections here during the summer of 1751. From this room, one could reach the northwest corner pavilion, which was fitted out as a *cabinet d'étude* (study library). Though it was completely rebuilt after just a few years, Hårleman's original drawings give an accurate picture of its strict classical appearance, with glass-fronted bookshelves incorporated between pilasters spanned by arches. In a 1748 letter to her sister, Lovisa Ulrika described her favorite room. "Here at my home Drottningholm," she wrote, "I live like a philosopher. If you could see me at this moment, you would find me sitting in my Cabinet which I have commissioned, with all my books on shelves that are built into the wall and equipped with doors of glass, all gilt and carved with ornament. The overdoors depict the attributes of the sciences; there is a mirror over the chimneypiece, and below are bronze sculptures from antiquity. In the center of the room there is a table of a completely new type that has come from France and is fitted out with a hutch that supports a clock. It is at this very table that I now write to you; a barometer is hanging by one window and by the other is a sundial. A lovely chair completes my description and it is sitting in this chair that I make these observations."

Next to the library, in the section that connects the palace's northwest and northeast wings, is the Coin Cabinet, which Carl Hårleman designed to house the large coin and medal collection that Lovisa Ulrika had acquired from Carl Gustav Tessin in 1746. The cabinet walls were paneled and faux-painted as walnut and embellished with carved, gilt rococo ornaments, *trofée* groups, and portrait medallions. Similar motifs were repeated on the bronze hardware on the eight tall, walnut cupboards in which the collections were stored. Prototypes for this interior could be found in Germany in the library at Sanssouci, the country palace in Potsdam of Lovisa Ulrika's brother, King Frederick II (*i.e.*, the Great), as well as in the royal palace in Turin, Italy. The Coin Cabinet at Drottningholm was the first in a suite of display rooms that Lovisa Ulrika ordered to use for scholarly purposes. The others were completed later by Hårleman's successors.

One of Adolf Fredrik's and Lovisa Ulrika's primary contributions to Drottningholm is the Chinese Pavilion, constructed in a wooded area adjacent to the baroque garden. In the eighteenth century, a fascination with East Asia spread through Europe, and it is reflected in this pavilion. The

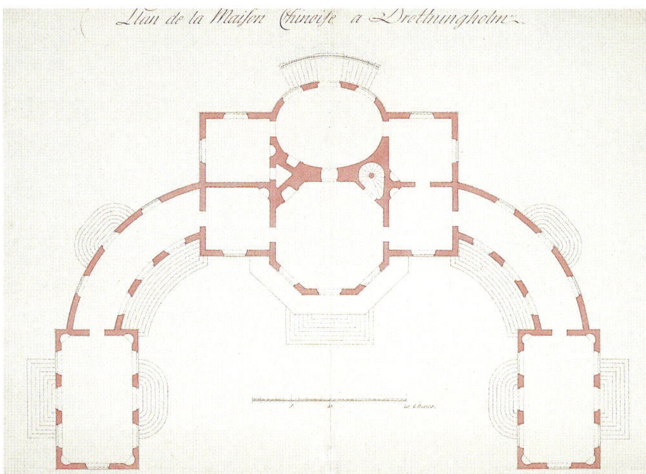

ABOVE *Drawing by Carl Fredrik Adelcrantz (ca. 1763) of the later and more durable version of King Adolf Fredriks and Queen Lovisa Ulrika's Chinese Pavilion at Drottningholm.*

LEFT *A floor plan by Carl Fredrik Adelcrantz of the Chinese Pavilion displays the central block as consisting of an octagonal vestibule before an oval salon, with flanking pairs of cabinets. Curved galleries link the central block to the Blue and Green salons located in the two pavilions; beyond these were two freestanding wings. The stairway leading to Lovisa Ulrika's private apartment was discreetly recessed into the wall and hidden behind a door.*

FACING PAGE *The Chinese Pavilion at Drottningholm, which began as a wooden structure in 1753, was made more permanent a decade later by architect Carl Fredrik Adelcrantz. Though designed to evoke East Asian styles, the pavilion took shape as Sweden's most elaborate rococo milieu.*

Swedish royal couple associated themselves with other European rulers who showed this interest by erecting special buildings *à la chinoise*—in the Chinese style. Again, counterparts are to be found elsewhere in Europe. Closely related to the Drottningholm Chinese pavilion was the now-lost *Maison sans Gêne* at Schloss Augustburg outside Cologne. Another German prototype was erected at Schloss Wilhelmsthal by the count of Hessen-Kassel. In France, meanwhile, Jossigny-en-Brie was built outside Paris in 1743; this example has especially close similarities to the Drottningholm pavilion in both construction and decor. Soon after Jossigny, still another Chinese pavilion went up, this one at Sanssouci. During the 1750s, when King Frederick was planning his Chinese teahouse, he and his sister Lovisa Ulrika were regularly exchanging letters.

The Chinese Pavilion to be seen today at Drottningholm replaced a smaller version that was given to Queen Lovisa Ulrika on July 24, 1753, as a birthday present from her husband. The king's gift was a wood frame structure made in Stockholm and shipped on barges to Drottningholm, where it was secretly assembled in an overgrown area just south of the formal gardens. The pavilion comprised five rooms, and its facades were painted to imitate woven reeds. Its roof was covered with pleated cloth and hung with tassels and

lanterns. The main building was flanked by smaller wings. Several days after the dedication, the queen wrote in delight to her mother, Sofia Dorothea of Prussia, "Everything is distinguished with the magnificence and good taste of the one who presented the gift." The new superintendent, Carl Johan Cronstedt, is believed to have been the last architect involved with the pavilion's construction, although he based his design on that of his predecessor, Carl Hårleman.

Plans to expand and beautify the site around the pavilion came under consideration early on. The natural environment complemented the desired informal character and closeness to nature, but the royal couple also yearned for something more lasting. After only a few years, they had the site expanded to include two additional pavilions. One was the king's pavilion, which Adolf Fredrik used for a woodworking shop with a lathe; the other, called *Confidencen* from the French *confidence*, functioned as an intimate dining room. By means of an ingenious rig of ropes and pulleys, the dining table—already set—could be raised from the basement and presented to the assembled guests. With these additions, the architectural standard rose.

In the damp of its woodland setting, however, the original pavilion was vulnerable to mold and decay, and it was torn down in 1763 to make way for the current masonry

building. The architect responsible for the new drawings was Carl Fredrik Adelcrantz (1717–1796).

In Adelcrantz's plan, the new *corps de logis* consisted of a two-story main building connected to a pair of lower pavilions by curved galleries augmented by two freestanding wings; the whole assemblage enclosed a courtyard. On the outside, the new structure was to blend with the king's pavilion and *Confidencen*. These in turn were stylistically anchored to the first main building, which allowed many original elements to be carried over into the new construction. The roof, of sheet metal bent in an undulating tent-like pattern, was painted green and appears to be supported by pilasters resembling the trunks of palm trees. Yellow dragons brace the balcony over the main entrance, and urns crown the chimneys on the roof. On the stucco facade, Adelcrantz replaced the wall panels' woven-reed pattern with solid red panels decorated with lighter meander borders and spatter-painted, marbleized frames. The red panels were varnished to achieve a glossy surface to resemble Chinese lacquer. For all its exotic motifs, though, the facade has also been compared to rococo interiors, with its wall panels of glossy silk surrounded by faux-marble panels.

Responsibility for designing the interiors fell to Jean Eric Rehn, whose ideas for colorful, richly varied furnishings came from many sources. A collection of engravings called *Designs of Chinese Buildings*, compiled by the Swedish/English architect William Chambers and published in 1757, is often thought to have provided much of the inspiration. The collection was said to derive from Chambers's own interpretation of buildings in Canton, but it also shows clear traces of European classicism. While Sir William's patterns were used for the decor in some of the rooms, engravings by the French artist François Boucher inspired the wall paintings that Johan Pasch did in a few of the other rooms, such as the Blue and Green salons in the pavilions at each end of the curved galleries. The strong colors, as well as the inclusion of East Asian objects and materials such as lacquer, silk, and porcelain, contributed to the "Chinese" character of the rooms; some of these were newly acquired, others were already in the royal collections. Otherwise, it is the connection to French interior decoration that is most obvious—for example, in the disciplined vestibule, the marble hall with its polished stucco walls painted different colors, and the oval drawing room, with its large framed panels and restrained white and gold decor.

That the Chinese Pavilion is more characteristic of Europe than of Asia was clear at least to one eighteenth-cen-

FACING PAGE *The Red Salon at the Chinese Pavilion has paneled walls embellished above with black and gold Chinese lacquer panels and below with raised gold circles and bands on a painted red field. Below the ceiling, a Greek key runs around the entire room. The design for this ornamentation came from Sir William Chambers's pattern books.*

BELOW *Engravings such as these, in Sir William Chambers's 1757 pattern book,* Designs of Chinese Buildings, *inspired Jean Eric Rehn's designs for the interiors of the Chinese Pavilion.*

Jean Eric Rehn was responsible for the Chinese Pavilion's interiors. The Blue Salon's figurative scenes à la Chinoise *are painted on canvas by the court painter Johan Pasch and copied from engravings by François Boucher. The salon's present wood floor replaces the original one in limestone.*

tury visitor, Nathaniel Wraxall, who had spent time in Canton as a cargo merchant on an English ship. The pavilion, he wrote, is built "in that taste which we usually call the Chinese; though, unless a few [costumed] Mandarins and Vases from China form this style, of which we really know scarce anything, it may just as well be called a European structure, where whimsy and caprice form the predominant character and spread a grotesque air through the whole." Even if the exotic mood at Drottningholm was only superficial, it still helped to keep the dream of the Far East alive.

Carl Fredrik Adelcrantz had been discouraged from becoming an architect by his father, Göran Josuæ Adelcrantz, the former city architect in Stockholm and a colleague of Nicodemus Tessin the Younger. Nonetheless, Adelcrantz attended lectures at the Royal Drawing Academy (*Kungliga ritareakademien*) while working for the government as a clerk. After his father's death, Adelcrantz was free to depart Sweden for a long study tour to France and Italy (1739–43). Later, while working with Carl Hårleman at the Royal Palace, he made other trips as well. In 1757, he was made superintendent, a position he held for almost forty years.

While Adelcrantz was completing his drawings for the Chinese Pavilion, Queen Lovisa Ulrika asked him also to construct a new court theater at Drottningholm, the older one having burned down in 1762. This was not Adelcrantz's first experience with the special design challenges of theaters. Less than a decade before, when a French theater company arrived in Stockholm, he had been called upon to contrive a small stage at Ulriksdal Palace on short notice. Expectations for the theater at Drottningholm, however, were higher.

The Drottningholm theater, here seen from the south, was designed by Carl Fredrik Adelcrantz and inaugurated in 1766. Flanking it are the Court Marshal's wing and the Hunting Pavilion. To the west side of the theater one can see a glimpse of the déjeuner *salon added in 1791 on a design by Louis Jean Desprez.*

The drawings and plans for the Drottningholm theater occupied Adelcrantz until 1764, when preparations for construction finally got under way. Despite the risk of fire, the new theater was built of wood and finished with plaster. The southern half of the length of the building houses the theater salon with suites of rooms arranged around it; the northern half was the stage area, with performers' and stage crews' accommodations and studios. The style of the exterior is a restrained classicism, while the interiors consist of a series of charming rococo reception rooms with hand-painted wallpaper. The salon, with its stalls, can be characterized as a form of rococo classicism. The room is held together by sixteen Corinthian pilasters and a robust entablature that leads to the proscenium. The marbleized wall decoration, in pale pink, yellow, and gray, is painted on fabric. And the console brackets seeming to support the balcony boxes are constructed of papier-mâché. The ornament sculptor, Adrien Masreliez, renowned from the Royal Palace project, was responsible for the refined interior ornamentation.

After its dedication in July 1766, the theater held a central position in court life. It was filled not only with actors—who performed, ate, and slept there—but also with members of the court who lived there. As superintendent and project supervisor for the French theater troupe, Adelcrantz had the use of a suite located to the right of the main entrance and consisting of an antechamber, bedchamber, and servants' room.

Drottningholm's court theater is one of very few eighteenth-century playhouses in the world that are still intact and operating today. All the more remarkable is that more than thirty of the original stage sets survive. Moreover, the ingenious original stage equipment, such as ropes and pul-

The actors and stage crew working at Drottningholm theater found exceptionally elegant accommodations, such as this dressing room.

RIGHT *The interior of the Drottningholm Theater should be experienced in the evening by candlelight since the wall decoration is only painted on canvas and made partly of papier-mâché.*

Inspired by contemporary French architecture, Carl Hårleman gave the projecting central room at Svartsjö the form of a salon à l'Italienne *two stories in high. The walls' stucco decor was originally painted to imitate marble. The original stone floor was replaced in the 1770s by the wooden floor seen here.*

leys can still, to an audience's amazement, evoke thunder, whistling winds, and crashing waves.

While both the Royal Palace in Stockholm and Drottningholm Palace prepared the way for the breakthrough of Rococo in Sweden, the country's civil architecture was extensively influenced by another royal building: Svartsjö, on the southwest outskirts of Stockholm. Designed by Carl Hårleman in 1734, Svartsjö manor house—actually a hunting lodge—was built for King Fredrik I; construction began in 1735. Much of Svartsjö's exterior still survives, but at the end of the eighteenth century, it was enlarged by Carl Fredrik Adelcrantz.

Svartsjö is clearly different from the civilian architecture discussed thus far: a two-story, stucco building with arched windows, and with flat and rusticated surfaces subtly interacting. The main living quarters are situated on the ground floor, with a three-cornered projecting salon flanked by symmetrical suites of rooms. The basic schematics for Svartsjö can be found in a 1728 pattern book by French architect Charles-Étienne Briseaux, *Architecture moderne ou l'art de bien bâtir* (Modern Architecture, or the Art of Building Well). The exact model, however, seems to be the *Chateau de Champs* by the architect Pierre Bullet, who had been Hårleman's teacher in Paris.

In France's rococo palaces, both upper and lower residential apartments were more or less equal in height. Hårleman, however, invariably gives the upper floor less headroom than the one below, resulting in a building of elegant proportions.

Carl Hårleman's manor houses, typified by Svartsjö, normally had mansard roofs and interplay between the plain stucco facades and rusticated pilaster-strips. The side of Svartsjö shown in this original drawing was to face the garden.

FACING PAGE *Inspired by contemporary French architecture, Carl Hårleman gave the projecting central room at Svartsjö the form of a salon à* l'Italienne *two stories high. The stucco decor of the walls was originally painted to imitate marble. The original stone floor was replaced in the 1770s by the wooden floor seen here.*

FACING PAGE BOTTOM *Carl Hårleman's manor houses, typified by Svartsjö, normally had mansard roofs and interplay between the plain stucco facades and rusticated pilaster-strips. The side of Svartsjö shown in this original drawing was to face the garden.*

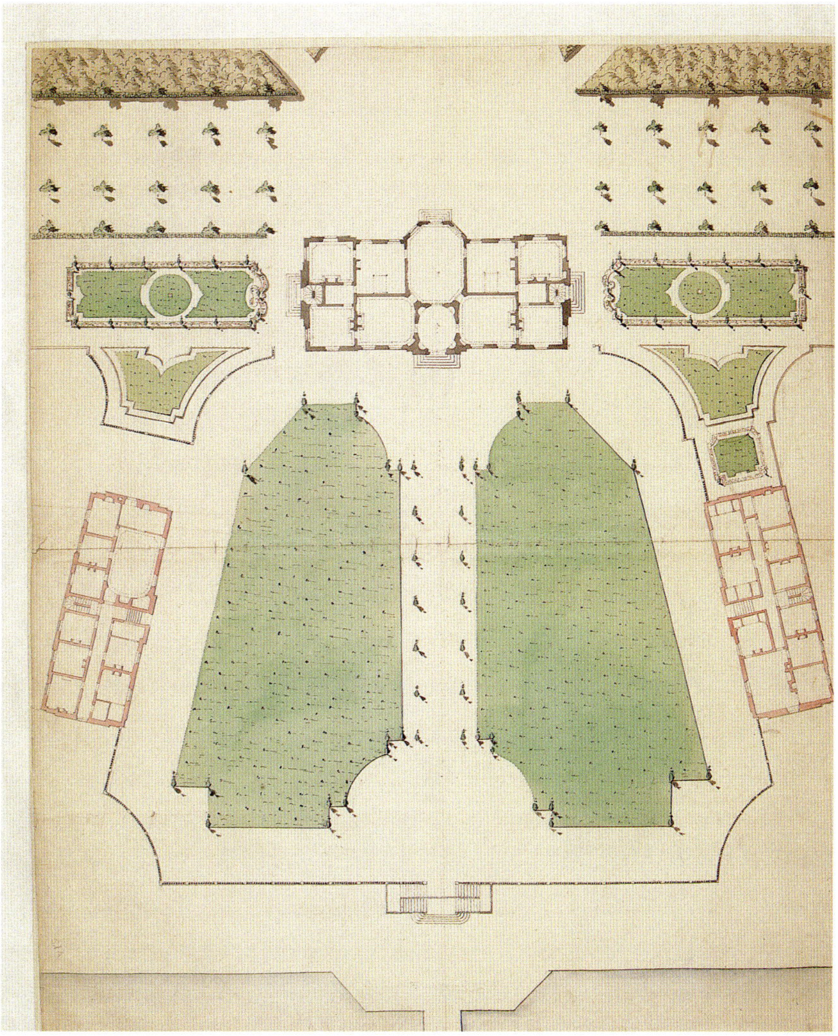

Carl Hårleman's overall plan for Svartsjö includes a floor plan of the main building, the wings, and the garden facing the sea. In Hårleman's manor houses, the main salon was either at the center or slightly offset, as at Thureholm.

In addition, he made the divided French mansard roof lower and more gently shaped than the French prototypes. Hårleman's adaptation of the mansard became the most common roof form during the Swedish Rococo. The use of pale yellow on the facade, a color similar to that of the sandstone used by French architects, became a Hårleman trademark.

Gardens continued to be influenced during the eighteenth century by the elaborate French baroque style, but in Sweden—as was the case in many other aspects of design—there was a clear inclination toward simplicity. Contoured lawns replaced costly *broderie* parterres, while ponds and fountains were filled in or just neglected. Thrift and practicality became the guiding principles for both the design and the content of gardens.

Trained in landscape architecture while in Paris in the 1720s, Carl Hårleman was Sweden's leader in the field, and his general plan for Svartsjö (though it was never carried out) provides a fine example of his approach. The parterre in front of the main building was to take the form of a flat lawn framed by individual yew trees. A rhythmic interplay of concave and convex shapes supplanted the focus on surface decoration. In addition, bosks and newly planted trees, intersected by straight paths, gave the main building a serene sylvan setting. A new element (one also encountered at Thureholm) would have been enclosure of the kitchen garden by the formal garden—a radical deviation from Le Nôtre's style, in which purely esthetic and utilitarian gardens were strictly segregated.

Svindersvik was constructed in the 1740s as a simplified and smaller version of Svartsjö. The main building appears to have only one story, but there is space beneath the mansard roof for a full second story.

RESIDENTIAL ARCHITECTURE

With Svartsjö, Hårleman established the stylistic base for Sweden's domestic architecture for the rest of the eighteenth century. In contrast to earlier architecture, his houses blended the meeting of practical, daily needs with comfort and coziness. His style attracted a new group of well-to-do civil servants and merchants who emerged during the Age of Liberty wishing to commission buildings. These new clients desired pleasant and comfortable houses that were moderate in scale—houses suitable for living rather than for formal functions.

An important contribution to the warmth of houses was the improvement of the Swedish tile stove by architect Carl Johan Cronstedt and General Fabian Wrede in the 1760s. By passing heated gases through a system of internal pipes, this device efficiently provided a continuously comfortable room temperature. The tile stove soon became a standard feature in eighteenth-century houses. Other changes also contributed to domestic comfort: Wooden floors of such materials as oak parquet or scrubbed plank replaced cold stone floors; ceilings were smoothly plastered and painted white; and walls were fitted out with window-high dadoes. Above the dado paneling, linen canvases painted in pale colors gave the rooms a warm, home-like atmosphere. Interiors were furnished in a relaxed manner, with light, practical furniture.

At Svindersvik, which Hårleman created outside Stockholm in the 1740s as a summer house for the wealthy merchant Claes Grill, one finds an environment that is completely characteristic of the new ideal. Here the architect is

Carl Hårleman's interiors are characteristically bright and airy. In this antechamber at Svindersvik, colorful Chinese rice paper wall coverings contrast both in color and style against the blue-and-white Swedish rococo tile stove.

FACING PAGE *The vestibule at Svindersvik shows a refined simplicity typical of Hårleman. Light enters through an oval opening overhead, and curved doors and arches complement the oval and each other.*

thought to have been inspired by Charles-Étienne Briseaux's 1743 volume, *L'art de bâtir des maisons de campagne* (The Art of Building Country Houses). The main building, with smooth stucco external walls, rusticated pilaster-strips, and quoins, was painted yellow and given green shutters under a mansard roof. At the center of the house was, and is, an octagonal dining room, austerely decorated with cool gray walls and brown door frames. The room is furnished simply with a gray gateleg table and eighteen chairs. The original floor was white marble. To the right of the dining room are a bedchamber and a cabinet. Opposite the dining room, an antechamber is decorated with a gray dado, above which is Chinese rice paper brightly painted with birds among bamboo and exotic plants. As director of the Swedish East India Company, the commissioner of Svindersvik had both financial and practical means to acquire luxuries from the East.

A guest often seen at Svindersvik was Carl Gustaf Tessin, who expressed his appreciation in his diary: "A glorious view facing the vast fairway, a change of scenery to the shady dale and the steepest mountains, pleasant walkways, nice neighbors (the city excluded), a house based on Svartsjö, splendidly executed, neatly furnished, a fruit-bearing garden, a diverse library, paintings, coppers, accommodations. With one word, nature's play, Mr. Grill's purse and taste, plus my friend Baron Hårleman's art have made of Svindersvik a joy for man that few can equal in scenery and order."

Carl Gustaf Tessin also commissioned work from his friend, colleague, and political ally, Carl Hårleman. In 1749, Hårleman designed Åkerö manor, situated near a lake in the province of Södermanland, for Tessin. An older house on the site was torn down to make way for a new one, the result of intimate collaboration between architect and patron. It was completed and ready to furnish in 1756.

Hårleman's house for Tessin was somewhat different from his typical manor-house design and does not have the usual central axis with the entrance, vestibule, and salon. Rather, the main entrance is to the right, and only a solitary, round attic dormer indicates the center. On the back side of the house, a wide rusticated frontispiece creates a monumental facade that is visible from the lake. The walls are painted light yellow, complemented by pink decorative sections.

Tessin had plenty of his own ideas for the house and sketched many versions of the floor plan. Instead of two symmetrical suites of rooms flanking a salon (see page 170), there are two parallel suites, one for himself looking onto the courtyard and one for his wife looking onto the lake. The rooms he had placed to the left of the stairway consisted of the Yellow Cabinet, the Mineral Cabinet, a bedchamber, the Red Cabinet, and his personal attendant's chamber. Directly in front of the stairway was the large salon, followed by the countess's suite, consisting of an antechamber, a bedchamber, a cabinet, and her chambermaid's room.

According to the French pattern, Hårleman experimented at Åkerö by planning no cellar beneath the main apartments on the ground floor, a design that proved ill-suited to Sweden; snow and cold left the ground floor chilly and damp through much of the year. During the winters, Tessin retreated to one of the freestanding wings where he kept his library. His wife, however, bravely stayed in the main house, where she is to be seen, in a watercolor by Olof Fridsberg, working at a magnificent rococo desk in her tastefully decorated cabinet. The walls of the room are covered with hand-painted Chinese silk and are adorned with paintings from Tessin's famous collection. A fireplace stands in one corner; in the other is a built-in corner cabinet painted in trompe l'oeil to imitate Chinese lacquer. Sten Åke Nilsson, a leading expert on Swedish eighteenth-century art, remarks that the owner of Åkerö freely and self-confidently mixed styles: the foreign with the domestic, the lofty with the humble, the formal with the relaxed. This artful blending is immediately noticeable in the vestibule, where guests encountered a prized marble sculpture by Giovanni da Bologna together with a painting of an unusually large pumpkin that had been grown on the estate.

FACING PAGE *Åkerö manor house was designed by Carl Hårleman for Count Carl Gustav Tessin. The simple, direct facade toward the sea is articulated by a broad central frontispiece and windows that vary subtly in shape and size.*

BELOW *In this well-known 1763 watercolor by Olof Fridsberg of a Swedish rococo interior, Countess Tessin, wife of Carl Gustav, sits at the richly gilt desk in her study at Åkerö. Fridsberg painted in trompe l'oeil the corner cupboard with a child and a cupid at play; his models were engravings by François Boucher and Antoine Coypel, and a French art dealer's business card. High over a glass-fronted cupboard hangs a portrait of the count.*

LEFT *The unusually complete architectural composition of Övedskloster in Skåne comprises a* corps de logis, *park land, plus wings and walls framing a stone-paved forecourt. Carl Hårleman designed Övedskloster in 1750, but it was not built until 1768–76.*

BELOW *The floorplan of Övedskloster (somewhat changed from Hårleman's original design) shows the characteristic eighteenth-century use of a meticulously balanced but asymmetrical interior within a perfectly regular exterior.*

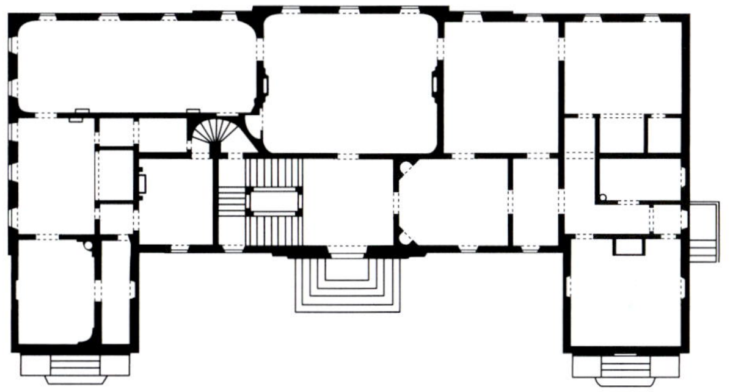

Late in life, Carl Hårleman made a general plan for Övedskloster manor house in Sweden's most southerly province, Skåne, for his brother-in-law, Baron Hans Ramel. Using long allées, Hårleman connected the surrounding landscape with the architecture and created one of Sweden's most monumental country environments. A long allée leads to the main, open portico located within a high wall surrounding the inner courtyard, or *cour d'honneur*. Separate from this is the lower courtyard, with a series of detached utilitarian wings. The composition of the layout has an unmistakably French character. The noble cobblestone courtyard, framed by wings and connecting walls, lies before the imposing, two-story main house representing a far more disciplined and classical style than Hårleman's earlier works. Constructed on a gentle slope, Övedskloster manor has three stories on the garden side, allowing for an arcaded loggia within the base. The facade is of pale pink stucco, with linear rustication and other decorative details made in local red sandstone. The building is crowned with a mansard roof.

Hårleman died before work actually began on Övedskloster. As a result, Carl Fredrik Adelcrantz and Jean Eric Rehn carried the project to completion. Their collaboration resulted in so dignified a milieu that it was comparable to

689 444 137 324
689 444 137 324

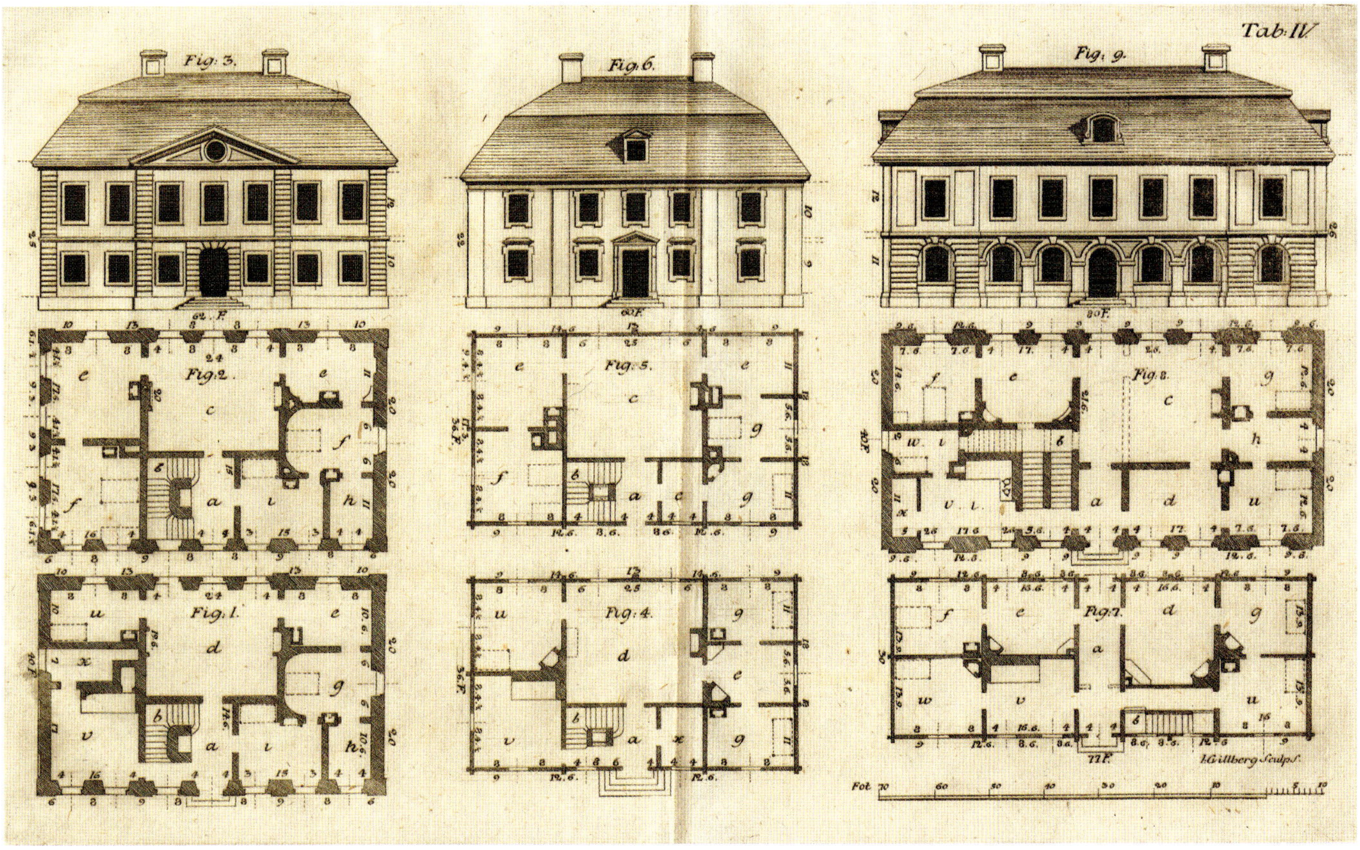

FACING PAGE *The interior of Carl Hårleman's Öved church is reduced to the most refined and elegant simplicity.*

ABOVE *Elevations and floor plans from Carl Wijnblad's 1755 work on country houses in stone and wood.*

Stockholm's royal residences. This was all too obvious to King Gustav III, who, during a visit, remarked with some irritation that Övedskloster was "too royal for a commoner."

In view at the end of a long allée is the small village church designed by Hårleman, which also functions as a family chapel. Its west facade presented a stylized screen before a tall nave separated from lower side aisles connected by volutes. Details in red sandstone contrast starkly against the white walls. One can see a reflection of Italian and French baroque churches in this unusual Swedish church facade, but the interior is more characteristically Swedish, with whitewashed walls, mirrored arches, and a gently coved chancel. Baron Ramel and his farm workers worshipped together in a space with a beauty that only utter simplicity can create.

Completed some twenty years after Hårleman's death, Övedskloster confirmed that the authority of his architecture long outlived him. Among the men most responsible for spreading his style was the fortification officer Carl Wijnblad. In 1755, Wijnblad published a great many designs for manor houses in a work titled *Ritningar på fyrtio wåningshus af sten och trettio af träd samt åtskilliga lusthus m.m.* (Drawings for Forty Houses of Stone and Thirty of Wood, as Well as Various Pavilions, etc.) More designs followed in 1756. Wijnblad drew on two traditions: Karolinian buildings and those of Hårleman, most often combining the two. His work was devoted largely to private commissions and was widespread. Although his publications surely were of use here and there, however, there are no known examples of manor houses constructed entirely from his designs.

Another way in which Hårleman's style spread was through carpenters and masons, who were familiar with his work and applied this knowledge to projects of their own. One example is Värmlands Säby (1772–74) situated by lake Vänern in Värmland province and built by the master car-

LEFT *Värmlands Säby (1772–74) is one of many Swedish manor houses that display the posthumous influence of architect Carl Hårleman.*

ABOVE *The 1766 Skottberg House, in the city of Karlshamn, illustrates how provincial architecture using wood was treated to emulate masonry.*

penter Johan Georg Reincke for Colonel Carl Linroth. Värmlands Säby is a two-story structure with a pale stucco exterior, simple facade decoration, and a mansard roof. The floor plan is typical of Hårleman's manor houses, with the most important rooms laid out in a row and looking onto the garden.

Värmlands Säby was one of the few manor houses in this region built of masonry. Hårleman had strongly advocated masonry constructions, but provincial Swedes did not always heed this caution and instead often used wood. But to imitate the more elaborate city houses in stone and brick, wooden timbers were covered by flat painted panels, pilasters, and quoins.

This was most evident in rural towns, where wood construction continued to dominate well into the next century. The Skottberg House in Karlshamn was built of wood shortly after a devastating fire in 1763, which had left large portions of this southern mercantile town in ashes. The two-story merchant's house is erected on a tarred base and has a tall, hip roof. Wooden pilasters articulate the facade, with the center of the building accentuated only by an attic dormer. Like the larger manor houses that served as prototypes, the double entrance stairway has elegant wrought-iron railings. The

heavily contoured cornice, as well as the proportions for the house, were based on Wijnblad's suggestions.

Stora Wäsby manor house, attributed to Jean Eric Rehn and built in 1750, has been described as rococo architecture with classical features. The builder was Court Marshal Charles De Geer, proprietor of the Leufsta ironworks. Stora Wäsby's main building had a low, pitched, saddleback roof, and a richly articulated facade composed of pilasters supporting a central pediment and decorated with festoons, laurel swags, and console brackets. The facade was originally painted pale pink with decorative elements and pilasters in gray.

Some architectural historians attribute Stora Wäsby's exterior to Carl Hårleman, although there is a distinct difference between its stylistic vocabulary and that of the other Hårleman houses discussed so far. The question of attribution is revealing about the close link between Hårleman's manor houses and those built in the neoclassical style during the late-eighteenth century. While Jean Eric Rehn's designs differed from Hårleman's and represent a new style, there is an unbroken link between Hårleman's architecture and the Gustavian style. Rehn worked under Hårleman for many years at the Royal Palace and so was well-versed in the Rococo.

When traveling to France and Italy in 1755–56, however, Rehn encountered other artistic stimuli. The interiors at Stora Wäsby, which Rehn clearly mentions having decorated himself, represent two stylistic tendencies. In the more intimate rooms, one encounters distinctly rococo furnishings: The wife's antechamber—one of the finest rococo decors in Sweden—is embellished with colorful wall coverings painted with birds in flight surrounded by plump arabesques and *rocailles*. In rooms for which a stricter appearance was appropriate, one finds a style more influenced by the neoclassical. An example is the salon, a completely paneled, pearl gray room that faces the garden through three arched French windows. The shape of the windows is repeated in the grayish-red marbleized frames, which form bold arches over the double doors. The overdoors are painted to give the illusion of coffers, blue skies, and cherubs in brown and gold. What gives the room its strict classical atmosphere most of all, however, is the framed, painted canvas hung to counterbalance the fireplace. This work depicts a large, theatrically composed landscape of temple ruins, solitary columns, and ancient statues. It was probably painted by Rehn's traveling companion, court-painter Johan Pasch, and is one of the earliest expressions of Swedish admiration for antiquity, a trend that was growing in Continental Europe at this time.

FACING PAGE *The manor house Stora Wäsby was built during the latter half of the 1750s, probably after drawings by Jean Eric Rehn, in a style that points toward that of the Gustavian period.*

ABOVE *The painted wall canvases in the lady's drawing room at Stora Wäsby express a fully developed rococo style.*

A painting, probably by Johan Pasch, adds a classical reminiscence to Jean Eric Rehn's early Gustavian interior at Stora Wäsby. The painter's fantasy landscape includes Roman architectural ruins and statuary.

CIVIC ARCHITECTURE

Carl Hårleman was more than just the architect who introduced the Rococo into Sweden; he was also an active member of the Hat Party (see Chapter One), who involved himself in all kinds of issues, including manufacturing, ironwork, and agriculture. He was thus a true son of the Age of Liberty. In 1748, he was granted the title of baron. As superintendent from 1741, he lobbied actively for increased responsibilities and authority in this position. Indeed Hårleman sought to expand the office of superintendent into a central authority with jurisdiction over all civic, ecclesiastical and other public building financed by the crown. His aim was to raise architectural standards by establishing a uniform building tradition in Sweden, which often had him revising other architects' drawing.

About twenty-five of Hårleman's projects appeared as engravings by Jean Eric Rehn, published under the title *Plans et elevations des bâtiments de Suede* (Plans and Elevations of Swedish Buildings). This collection of engravings can be seen as the Swedish equivalent of contemporary French work by Charles-Étienne Briseaux and Jacques-François Blondel. Differing from most previous architectural books focused primarily on analyzing classical architecture, this Swedish collection, like its French contemporaries, presents different types of plans and designs for buildings of various uses.

Hårleman's collection presents diverse designs for state residences. The building proposed for a governor's two-story mansion is typical of the architect's simple but functional public architecture. The ground floor housed office space, while the governor's private apartments were located on the upper floor. But no such governor's residence was ever built. Instead of following Hårleman's designs, simpler houses of wood were erected.

Carl Hårleman's patterns for various types of buildings represent his attempts to standardize Swedish architecture. This 1746 engraving depicts his proposal for a provincial governor's residence.

Erik Palmstedt's drawing for the Stockholm Exchange was approved by King Gustav III in 1773.

A major building project during the Age of Liberty and one of the few in which Hårleman was not involved was the exchange house in Stockholm. In affluent trading cities, the town halls and exchange buildings have commonly been manifestations of local wealth and power. This was not the case in Stockholm, however. Lacking the usual array of offices, the city's various administrative bodies were squeezed together in a jumble of outdated office buildings near Stortorget in the Old Town. Merchants had no public trading facilities at all, which meant that they had to conduct business under the open sky.

The construction of a new exchange house became a drawn-out project that continued throughout the entire Age of Liberty. In 1728–29, the city architect Johan Eberhard Carlberg presented two different suggestions for an exchange building. The first proposal was based on restoring the existing city hall complex, providing more room for commerce; the other plan called for replacing the existing complex with a new, monumental building that would accommodate both the city hall and the exchange building. Neither of the proposals was accepted, however, and the point became moot when, in 1730, the city purchased the Bonde Palace (see Chapter Two) to house the administrative offices. The move from the square and Stortorget solved the problem of location and meant that the exchange could lay sole claim to the building contemplated.

Year after year, Carlberg's initial suggestions were followed by new ones, both by himself and by superintendent

The main entrance of the Stockholm Exchange faces Stortorget *(the Great Square) in Old Town.*

Carl Johan Cronstedt. One of Cronstedt's designs was finally approved by the king in 1768. The year before, however, a young man in the city architect's office by the name of Erik Palmstedt (discussed in Chapter Five) presented his ideas for the building's appearance based partly on earlier drawings by Cronstedt. The city administration granted Palmstedt the task of continuing to develop the plans, which resulted in his proposal's being accepted by King Gustav III in 1773. The building was completed three years later.

The new exchange building, in the form of a two-story trapezoid with coved corners and a flat, baluster-rimmed roof, took up an entire block on the north side of Stortorget. Its rusticated ground floor opens into generous arcades that face the square; the upper floor is enclosed. The building prompts associations with a French rococo private palace, but emphasizes its public status through an accentuated central section with engaged columns, a pediment, and a clock-tower lantern crowning the top (the latter being a remnant from the baroque). In the large second-floor reception room, which today houses the Swedish Academy (*Svenska Akademien*), Palmstedt created an austere interior in white and gold with colossal Ionic pilasters and a robust joist system.

The Stockholm exchange was the first building of monumental scale that Gustav III approved during his reign. It was soon followed by many prestigious projects within Stockholm's center in which both Carl Fredrik Adelcrantz and Erik Palmstedt were involved. With these, however, Sweden entered a new epoch: the Gustavian.

CHAPTER FIVE

Neoclassicism

PRECEDING PAGES *An engraving (1806–7) by Johan Fredrik Martin shows Gustav Adolf's Square before the razing in 1891 of Gustav III's opera house, which appears at the left. On the right is Sophia Albertina's Palace; the Royal Palace is in the background. An equestrian statue of King Gustav II Adolf by Pierre Hubert L'Archevêque adorns the square.*

LEFT *The salon at Åkerö manor house with painted wall decoration after designs by Louis-Joseph Le Lorrain (1753).*

FACING PAGE *During his 1755–56 journey in Italy, Jean Eric Rehn sketched everything he saw. Here he captured his traveling companions and several other visitors at the entrance to the Posillipo grotto near Naples.*

In 1753, the French Count of Caylus, one of Europe's greatest advocates of neoclassicism, persuaded the Swedish Count Carl Gustav Tessin to commission avant-garde artist Louis-Joseph Le Lorrain to prepare proposals for the wall decoration in the salon at Tessin's country house, Åkerö. With its illusionistic arrangement of painted columns, ancient statues, urns, and fountain motifs, this salon has been considered by some observers to be the first neoclassical interior in Europe. As noteworthy as this room may have been historically, however, the sudden appearance of this new style had no great effect on the development of Swedish art.

In fact, neoclassicism was slow to penetrate Sweden. Precursors of the new style were evident during the 1760s, but not until King Gustav III's reign (1771–92) was the Rococo entirely supplanted by the classicism of the Gustavian style. Like its French counterpart, the Louis XVI style, the Gustavian began as a soft and somber adaptation of the art and architecture of Greco-Roman antiquity. Later, after King Gustav's journey to Italy in 1783–84, it shifted into a more strict and severe neoclassicism similar to the one that emerged throughout Europe. This, the late Gustavian style, was to last well into the 1800s.

ROYAL ARCHITECTURE BEFORE GUSTAV III'S JOURNEY TO ITALY

Creation of the Gustavian style was to a great extent the work of the renowned and versatile Jean Eric Rehn (1717–1795). In 1756 Rehn returned from a year-long study tour that he, court painter Johan Pasch (1706–1769), and a master builder, Georg Fröman, had embarked on together. As a designer at the Swedish Manufacturing Office, Rehn had been dispatched to gather information about silk design and production in Paris and Lyon. The three friends continued on to Rome and then Naples, where they were the first Swedes ever to study the excavations at Pompeii and Herculaneum. Rehn zealously sketched the finds: architecture—sometimes just fragments—as well as sculptures, household goods, and the furniture depicted in wall paint-

LEFT *A soft classicism is evident in this Jean Eric Rehn drawing from the 1760s for the treatment of a new library for Lovisa Ulrika at Drottningholm.*

FACING PAGE *At the center of Lovisa Ulrika's library at Drottningholm, the long table topped with white Carrara marble is one of the original furnishings from the 1760s. The alabaster figurines were added later by Gustav III.*

ings. Indeed, the enthusiastic travelers reported having sensed at the ruins the aromas of ancient herbs, grains, and balsam—a vivid and very personal experience of the ancient world. Then, en route back to Sweden, Rehn encountered France's great enthusiasm for antiquity and its influence on the new and prevalent Louis XVI style.

Rehn's travels initiated a new period in Swedish art history. His exposure to the ancient world and to its echoes in contemporary work definitely shaped not only his own personal artistic development but also that of Sweden. Already before his journey Jean Eric Rehn had assisted Carl Hårleman with the interiors of the Royal Palace in Stockholm. Rehn's contributions there obviously pleased Queen Lovisa Ulrika, who soon thereafter engaged him as her personal interior designer. He also was named Court Architect and a professor at the Royal Academy of Fine Arts.

One of Rehn's main commissions was the interiors and furnishings at Drottningholm Palace, which had been left uncompleted after Carl Hårleman's death. The suite of furnishings that Rehn designed here during the 1760s marked a breakthrough for the early Gustavian style in Sweden. His first project at Drottningholm was a new library for the queen's growing collection of books; this was to occupy the oblong room in the northwest wing that until now had functioned as Lovisa Ulrika's Natural History Cabinet. In a succession of proposals, the architect tested an increasingly radical neoclassical style. In the end, the drawing that the queen accepted and that was eventually followed showed a moderate and soft form of classicism. Observers often note that a major source of Rehn's inspiration was the great neoclassical work, *Receuil élémentaire d'architecture* (Elementary Collection of Architecture) of 1757–72 by the French architect-engraver, Jean-François de Neufforge; but Rehn's interior appointments still had distinct rococo characteristics. This was actually typical for Rehn, whose work often resulted in a blend of classical and rococo elements—a combination that, under his direction, had a particular and unique elegance and refinement.

The library at Drottningholm is considered one of Sweden's most beautiful interiors. One side of the room is made up of a series of French windows with views toward the baroque garden; the opposite side consists of built-in bookshelves separated by Corinthian pilasters. Below the ceiling, everything is held together by friezelike panels bearing Queen Lovisa Ulrika's monogram alternating with the three crowns of the lesser national coat-of-arms and a cornice of festoons with Latin inscriptions and images of ancient philosophers in medallions. The repetition of forms and the interplay between cool and warm colors—pearl gray and gold against cedar wood and the brown leather of book bindings—give the room a pleasing harmony. Crowning the doors and windows are lunettes with plaster reliefs of female allegorical figures most likely modeled in the studio of the French-born sculptor Pierre Hubert L'Archevêque. The craftsmanship in the library is of the highest quality; Rehn had been assisted by such leading Swedish artisans as master

ABOVE *In the 1760s, Jean Eric Rehn transformed Carl Hårleman's rococo design (see page 136) for Queen Lovisa Ulrika's study library at Drottningholm into a neoclassical style similar to what the French termed* le Goût grec*—the Greek taste. At the same time, the library acquired a new name: the Marble Cabinet.*

RIGHT *The Natural History Cabinet belongs to the suite of rooms at Drottningholm that Lovisa Ulrika furnished to safeguard and display her several collections. The door leads to the queen's mineral, coin, and marble cabinets.*

carpenter Lorentz Nordin and ornament sculptor Adrien Masreliez.

After the new library was completed, the space in the northwest corner pavilion that had earlier served as the queen's workroom and study library needed to be modernized and adapted for a new use. The Marble Cabinet (*Marmorkabinettet*) as it later came to be called still retains the original decor based on Rehn's drawings from 1765.

The point of departure for Rehn's redecoration of this room was a pair of antique green marble columns in the queen's collection. Using these, Rehn created a heavy Ionic

Gustav III's state bedchamber was decorated (1772–79) according to plans by Jean Eric Rehn, with carvings by Jean Baptiste Masreliez. This was the first interior in the Stockholm Royal Palace to be executed in the new Gustavian style.

aedicule and placed in it a bronze urn—a decorative element commonly used in neoclassicism—designed after an antique model. Contrasting with this severe creation, which in fact disguised a tile stove, were the smooth, marbleized, painted walls of the room in pale colors. Two tall built-in bookshelves and a desk made for the queen in 1770 by Georg Haupt, Sweden's foremost cabinetmaker and marquetry craftsman, confirm that the room retained its use as a workroom well after the new library was completed.

The Marble Cabinet conveys a more severe tone than is normally seen in Rehn's designs. The two connecting rooms in the north cross wing, the Mineral Cabinet (*Mineraliekabinettet*) and the new Natural History Cabinet (*Naturaliekabinettet*) that were fitted out to house Lovisa Ulrika's collections are more characteristic of Rehn's early Gustavian style. Both rooms have marbleized paneling with precise rectangular fields. The Natural History Cabinet, with its glass-fronted display cabinets, is adorned with friezes of laurel garlands and portrait medallions, by Sweden's prominent sculptor Johan Tobias Sergel, of famous contemporary Swedish scientists (including, of course, the botanist Carl Linnaeus). The Mineral Cabinet has imposing overdoors made in 1768 by sculptor Johan Ljung who ornamented them with seashells, corals, coins, and medallions—in other words, examples of the types of objects in Lovisa Ulrika's museum rooms.

During the 1760s, Jean Eric Rehn was also a major artistic force at the Royal Palace, where he became responsible for the first room to be executed in pure Gustavian style: King Gustav III's state bedchamber, furnished in 1772–78. The king's and queen's state bedchambers in the Royal Palace were Jean Eric Rehn's most prestigious commission.

Greatly impressed by what he had encountered in Paris and Versailles, the newly crowned king immediately decided to transform Karl XI's former audience room into a worthy bedchamber for himself. Here, the king could assert his power with a theatrical zeal comparable to that of his ideal model, King Louis XVI of France, by holding *lever du Roi* (the king's arising) ceremonies; more than a few of his foreign guests found this outdated practice strange. To realize

To the fortress-like structure of Gripsholm Castle, King Gustav III added what came to be called the Courtiers' Wing (1780–82), seen here in the center.

the room's maximum grandeur, he retained portions of Tessin's original decor, such as the magnificent baroque ceiling, cornices, window reveals, and doors. The connection with the country's honored past can be seen as a direct parallel to early French neoclassicism, in which prototypes were readily taken from *l'ancien régime* (i.e., that of Louis XIV). Since the basis for the new decoration of the bedchamber was preserved architectural elements, Rehn's goal was to connect the various components esthetically, giving the room a new unity. He moved the inner wall back to make space for a bed alcove, which he separated from the rest of the room with a pair of columns and a balustrade. The walls he treated with a heavy, imposing neoclassicism in the style of Louis XVI, with Ionic pilasters in white and gold. Laurel wreaths and swags, as well as vertical rectangular fields filled with a mosaic pattern, adorned the paneling.

Following his father's path, Jean Baptiste Masreliez, son of Adrien Masreliez, was the primary ornament sculptor; the precocious young artist had just returned from studies in Paris with sufficient knowledge to carry out the architect's intentions. Jean Baptiste Masreliez was personally responsible for two heavily sculpted and gilt console tables made for the room.

In 1775, Rehn began work on the state bedchamber of King Gustav's consort, Queen Sophia Magdalena. The room was situated as a counterpart to the king's bedchamber, on the opposite side of Karl XI's gallery, and it followed basically the same plan as the king's, with the exception of the alcove, which in the queen's room was flanked by four columns and a balustrade. Here, the architect once again took advantage of existing architectural elements such as the ceiling, cornices, and doors. The treatment of the walls of the queen's room is distinctly feminine; instead of being divided by pilasters, they have richly decorated panels framed in the stylish French *bouclé* motif of repeated overlapping loops, and high vertical fields of mosaic pattern. Where the king's room has laurel wreaths and swags, the queen's has roses.

During the first decade of his regency, Gustav III often stayed at the old Vasa castle, Gripsholm, beside Lake Mälaren. Just as the Renaissance palace Fontainbleau functioned as a romantic and historic setting for the French

court, the sixteenth-century milieu of Gripsholm offered an evocative stage for the Swedish monarch's dreams. At Gripsholm, he could feel an almost physical connection to his forebears, with the blood of the venerable Vasa dynasty pulsating in his veins. After being uninhabited for more than a half-century, the castle at Gripsholm was refurbished and made to shine again.

Immediately after taking the throne, Gustav III recruited the best architects to make the old castle habitable. Along with the new furnishings at Gripsholm, one of the first priorities was to install a theater, since the king wished to pursue a lifelong passion: writing and acting in his own dramatic productions.

In 1772, the architect Carl Fredrik Adelcrantz had fitted out one of Gripsholm's towers with a preliminary private theater for the royal family. Here, amateur performances were conducted for a limited audience. But the arrival in Sweden during the summer of 1781 of a French theater troupe, led by the actor Jacques Marie Boutet de Monvel, called for something on a grander scale. This time it was the architect Erik Palmstedt (1741–1803) who was charged with the task of preparing drawings for a new theater. Palmstedt had just returned from studies in Paris and Rome as a committed classicist.

Palmstedt's design is an early example of Swedish architecture carried out in the full neoclassical manner. Inspired by ancient amphitheaters and by Andrea Palladio's amphitheater-like *Teatro Olimpico* in Vicenza, Palmstedt incorporated the auditorium into the upper story of one of the castle's round towers. In it he had semicircular bench seating placed on an incline. The thick walls of the tower housed access stairs and corridors. Palmstedt ingeniously solved the problem of uniting a classical semicircular auditorium with a baroque deep-perspective stage by placing half of the theater in the round tower and carving the other half out of the adjacent Queen's Wing, to which he had three floors added for this purpose.

Palmstedt's original plans called for an open colonnade, but this was hindered by limited space. Instead, the auditorium is encircled by monumental Ionic half-columns mounted against mirrored panels, creating the appearance of whole, freestanding columns. (The source of this idea is thought to have been the Palais Bourbon, which the architect had visited during his stay in Paris.) To reinforce this illusion, Palmstedt had crystal half-chandeliers mounted on mirrored backgrounds. The room is crowned by a half-dome that is faux-painted with coffers, from which servants could view

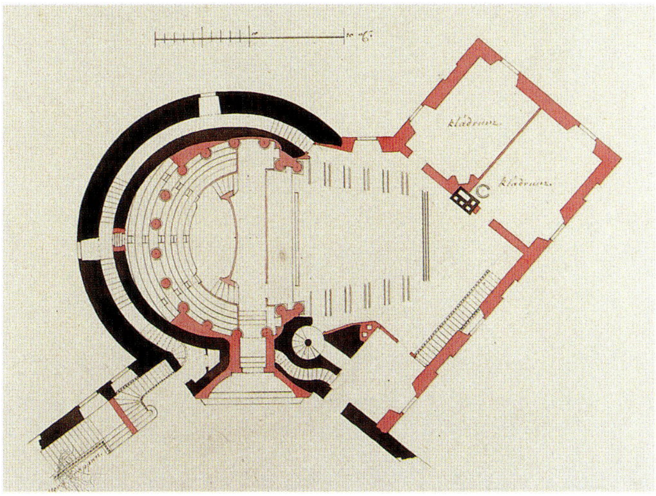

FACING PAGE *The court theater at Gripsholm, designed by Erik Palmstedt in 1781, is one of Europe's most remarkable eighteenth-century playhouses. Half-columns and half-chandeliers mounted against mirrors give the tiny auditorium the impression of an expansive space.*

ABOVE *This drawing, copied from a 1781 original by Erik Palmstedt, shows how the auditorium of the Gripsholm theater was fitted out in the old tower, which had two wings with the stage and two dressing rooms.*

the performances without being seen by simply opening the lower row of "coffers." With Sergel's marble statues of the Greek muses of theater, Thalia and Melpomene, in niches flanking the stage, the interior was complete. It was used for the first time in May 1782, although it was not finished until a year later.

Despite major renovations within the castle, not enough sleeping quarters were available when the entire court visited Gripsholm, and guests complained about the lack of comfort and poor conditions. The king therefore asked court architect Fredrik Cronstedt (1744–1829), the son of architect Carl Johan Cronstedt, to add an extra wing to the castle, the Courtiers' Wing (*Kavaljersflygeln*). Though the addition appears from the outside to be a two-story structure, it actually has four stories, which house twenty-eight sets of rooms—sixteen for men and twelve for women; rooms for married couples were arranged in pairs with connecting doors. Each guest room was given a vestibule and a small room for a servant with a window overlooking the whitewashed walls of the long corridor that runs alongside the series of the rooms. The interiors are identical, and each room has simple furnishings including a tile stove, a bed, a pair of chairs, and a desk, along with a bowl and pitcher for

The simple guest rooms in Gripsholm's Courtiers' Wing offer an informative glimpse of a basic Gustavian-style domestic setting in the late eighteenth century.

FACING PAGE *The design and position of Princess Sophia Albertina's palace (1783–1794) on Gustav Adolf's Square in Stockholm provided a counterbalance for King Gustav III's opera house; the palace's architect was Erik Palmstedt.*

washing. The Courtiers' Wing at Gripsholm illustrates the most typical style of the Swedish late-eighteenth-century decoration, and, still in pristine condition, it offers a rare glimpse of everyday life in the upper ranks of society during the Gustavian period.

The Courtiers' Wing ceased to be used only a few years after its completion in 1782, however. Gustav III's ideals dramatically changed after his trip to Italy (discussed later in this chapter). Upon his return, he turned his attention to other, higher, artistic aspirations.

PUBLIC ARCHITECTURE

Like Jean Eric Rehn, the architect Carl Fredrik Adelcrantz was at the height of his career during the transitional period between the Rococo and the Gustavian style. Even more than his Chinese pavilion at Drottningholm (see Chapter Four), Adelcrantz's greatest professional challenge came with Gustav III's commission for a royal opera house in Stockholm (1774–82). This would become the most prominent Gustavian building in Sweden (and, after seven decades, the setting of Giuseppe Verdi's opera, *The Masked Ball*).

The opera house was just one feature in the grand plans of Gustav III and his superintendent. The project was based on Nicodemus Tessin the Younger's earlier drawing for the area surrounding the Royal Palace. These plans, which had only recently been rediscovered, agreed with the contemporary desire to create a space comparable to the monumental public spaces that imparted majesty to many Continental cities.

Erected on the east side of the square, the new opera house provided a main element in the architectural setting of the palace. (In 1891, Gustav III's opera house was razed to make way for the current Royal Opera House, *Kungliga operan*.) Nothing on its exterior revealed the building's function. On a rusticated base with windows and entrances framed by blind arcades, colossal Corinthian pilasters contrasting with the smooth facade stretched two full stories. A central colonnade crowned by an attic story marked the entrance toward the square.

Stylistically, the opera house derived completely from

SOPHIA·ALBERTINA
ÆDIFICAVIT.

The customs house in Stockholm, seen here in Erik Palmstedt's original 1783 drawing, foreshadowed the strict neoclassicism that would soon permeate Swedish architecture.

French classicism. It was also to France that Adelcrantz turned for inspiration for the stage and auditorium. The interior resembled the theater designed by Germain Soufflots in Lyon, with its horseshoe-shaped auditorium, long rows of box seats, and raked stage. Adelcrantz's design was likely based on the French prototype, since engravings of Soufflots's theater were publicized the same year, 1773, that Adelcrantz completed his drawings for the opera house. The furnishings in the auditorium and foyer were in red, white, and gold with sculpted decoration of urns, laurel swags, and musical instruments all in the spirit of the older Louis XVI style. Jean Baptiste Masreliez was responsible for a large portion of this graceful ornamentation.

A companion structure on the opposite side of the square, another palace—also designed by Erik Palmstedt—was erected in 1783–94 for Gustav III's sister, Princess Sophia Albertina. With money inherited from their mother, Sophia Albertina had purchased the property in 1782; on it had stood a seventeenth-century palace. Having offered to pay to construct his sister's new palace, King Gustav gave the architect orders to copy the opera house's facade. The palace was furnished with a number of exquisite interiors by Louis Masreliez. Thus, Sophia Albertina's palace, which is still standing, gives a quite accurate reflection of Gustav III's original opera house. The building currently houses the Swedish Foreign Ministry (*Utrikesdepartementet*).

The new square just opposite the Royal Palace provided an ideal site for the equestrian statue of Gustav II Adolf, which was commissioned from the sculptor Pierre Hubert L'Archevêque in 1755 but not inaugurated until 1796. In Paris, many of the public spaces created during the eighteenth century survived the French Revolution intact, while all the effigies of monarchs perished. In Stockholm, the opposite occurred: The architectural framework surrounding the statue was truncated, but the king was allowed to remain in the saddle.

Not far from Gustav Adolf's Square, work began in 1783

on the customs house (*Tullpackhuset*), which consisted of a warehouse and offices. This project afforded Erik Palmstedt an opportunity to carry out on Swedish soil more ideas shaped by his foreign travels. Palmstedt's customs house is firmly anchored in the Italian Renaissance; it has a severe, uncompromising, rusticated facade in stucco but imitating Italy's stone, classically shaped window casements, and a portal with heavy banded columns. The building foreshadows the stern neoclassicism that would soon permeate Swedish design. In 1784, Gustav III returned from Italy a strong advocate of a strict, austere neoclassicism. This radically affected the style of public architecture, since the king's personal tastes were decisive in the esthetics of all new projects. Though drawings for public buildings were submitted first to the superintendent, the king of Sweden exercised his right to approve or deny all designs. This king often made changes to proposals with his own pen. When reviewing a suggestion for an inflated, baroque-style bell tower for the Kartulla church in Finland (then a part of Sweden), the monarch quickly transformed the drawing to a simplified clock turret composed just of four Doric columns.

King Gustav III's 1784 drawing for the bell tower of Kartulla church in Finland, which was then part of Sweden.

From this moment, Jean Eric Rehn and Carl Fredrik Adelcrantz—the proponents of the earlier, much softer classicism—lost their tight grip on esthetics in Sweden. Though they retained their influential positions as court architect and superintendent, the king now marshaled fresh creative forces that could better meet his new demands and stylistic ideals.

The Royal Mint (*Kungliga mynthuset*) in Stockholm illustrates this development. In 1783, Carl Fredrik Adelcrantz began plans for a new Royal Mint to be located just west of the Royal Palace. While the new opera house magnificently displayed the architect's skills, it also exposed his limits with regard to classicism. Just weeks after his return from abroad, Gustav III approved a new proposal, submitted by a younger architect named Olof Tempelman (1745–1816) for the mint house. Tempelman, who in 1779 had been appointed Sweden's first professor of civil architecture at the Royal Academy of Fine Arts, had also recently returned from Italy; he therefore had a clear understanding of what the king wanted. His drawings depict a building with very pronounced rustication and a temple portico with four robust Doric columns. In the last phase of construction, however, Adelcrantz did rework the facade slightly. On direct orders from the king, the rustication was removed, and the portico was given even greater emphasis by extending the height of the columns. The Doric temple facade of the Royal Mint became the first manifestation in Sweden of this new style.

In 1778, the king declared the town of Härnösand in northern Sweden a provincial capital because of the town's promise to build a residence for the provincial governor. When at first no progress had been made despite much prodding directly from the top, Tempelman, whose work on the Royal Mint had won him the king's favor, was assigned to complete the task.

Tempelman radically reworked a two-year-old design that had been rejected by the governor, who had frowned on the proposal of a wooden structure. The drawing was transformed into a two-story masonry building with a saddleback roof and an attic story just below the roof line. The facade is dominated by colossal Doric pilasters indicating the building's center and corners, and it is consciously formed with definition and plasticity that recall the work of Palladio. The simplicity and robustness of the governor's residence in Härnösand, which is still in use, established a model for late

FACING PAGE *Columns of the size and height of those that architect Olof Tempelman placed at the imposing entrance to the Royal Mint in Stockholm (1784) had never before been seen in Sweden.*

RIGHT *The governor's residence in Härnösand, designed by Olof Tempelman in 1784, became a prototype for many Swedish manor houses during the late eighteenth century.*

Olof Tempelman's 1784 drawing for the Gymnasiet *(school) in Härnösand (1784). The building serves today as a town hall.*

Gustavian manor houses.

Tempelman was soon called on for another project in Härnösand. This time it was to rework a local architect's proposal for a new school building that the superintendent's office in Stockholm had rejected. The basic schematics for the school were the same as for the governor's residence: a simple rectangular structure with smooth stucco exterior walls and a saddleback roof. Directly below the roof runs a continuous frieze with inscriptions from the *Epistles* of Horace. To add character to the building, the architect inserted a new element—a rotunda half-recessed into the building, with twelve imposing Doric columns. The rotunda marks the main entrance and divides the spaces within the floor plan. The functional and the symbolic were of equal importance. In a Parisian project by the French architect Claude-Nicolas Ledoux, the Hôtel de Saint-Germain, a rotunda is similarly joined to a rectangular, block-shaped building. Tempelman's ideas were consequently altogether in keeping with current styles; that the open portico was perhaps inappropriate for the Nordic winter climate was not of great concern.

Tempelman's architectural contributions are associated to a great extent with the Doric revival movement, which was inspired most of all by the Greek temples at Paestum and expressed the virility associated with the Doric order. The Doric order was an important feature in Swedish neoclassical architecture during the last decade of Gustav III's reign.

The favor of the king, however, soon veered away from

In 1787, King Gustav III asked Olof Tempelman to design a building, the Linneanum, for Uppsala University to provide a new home for the department of botany. But it was Tempelman's French-born rival, Louis Jean Desprez, who delivered the designs that were used.

Tempelman to a new architect, Frenchman Louis Jean Desprez (1743–1804), whom the king had met in Italy. While on an academic stipend in Rome in 1784, Desprez was enticed by the Swedish monarch to come to Stockholm to work on royal theaters, providing them with up-to-date stage sets. Temperamental and creative, and as brilliant with a paintbrush as with a pen, Desprez raised the temperature of art in Sweden. For three years, he was engaged with theater design and decoration. But his encounters with antiquity in Italy equipped Desprez to go much farther: They enabled him to transform Gustav III's more important ideas into reality, preparing him at the same time to begin to take over building projects begun by Tempelman. In 1788, Desprez was officially named the king's First Architect.

In the spirit of the Enlightenment, projects that furthered scientific and scholarly objectives had particular importance. In 1787, King Gustav III decided to finance a new building for the university in Uppsala. The building he envisioned would not only house the university's department, or institute, of botany (*Botaniska institutionen*), but also would provide a grand memorial hall dedicated to the great Carl Linnaeus, a longtime associate of the university. The site of the building had been the garden of the old Uppsala castle (rebuilt in the 1740s by Carl Hårleman as a governor's residence); it was now given to the university to serve as a botanical garden.

In designing the botany building, Olof Tempelman confronted the delicate task of accommodating the needs and spirit of a scientific enterprise in an edifice fashioned after a Greco-Roman temple. His design consisted of a rectangular block with two long wings projecting at the rear, one to house a greenhouse, the other for teaching facilities and offices. At the front he placed a broad Doric temple portico with eight columns, which provides a splendid view from the castle. For the facade, Tempelman proposed heavy rustication interrupted only by openings for windows. The portico opens onto the magnificent Linnaeus Hall, with its high-vaulted, coffered ceiling, and an apse with a statue of the

famous scientist.

At a stage of the project when Tempelman was weighing different solutions for the greenhouse wing, the king suddenly chose a proposal by Desprez. Before long, the Frenchman had full responsibility for the project. He simplified and reduced the forms even further than Tempelman had, which resulted in, among other things, a still more impressive appearance for the portico. Typical of Desprez was the desire, rooted in his native France's neo-Greek movement, for elementary geometrical shapes and monumental mass.

His most inventive contribution to the building can be seen at the north wing. Here he created an entrance framed by an arch that, by its seemingly truncated appearance, reflects the ancient world as it was seen by eighteenth-century eyes. Specifically, Desprez's composition evokes the triumphal arches of imperial Rome, still half-buried in the ancient soil with only their upper portions revealed to the world.

Surprisingly, it was not a trained architect but a military officer, Admiral Carl August Ehrensvärd (1745–1800), who contributed the most radical and severe form of neoclassicism. As a philosopher of art and self-taught architect, Ehrensvärd had put his entire military future at risk in 1780 when he requested permission to interrupt his career for travels in Italy. Once on his way, he did not stop in Rome but continued south to Paestum and then to Sicily. The Greek and Roman ruins that he encountered became a defining influence in his search for simplification and spareness. Not only was Ehrensvärd passionate about antiquity, but also he was convinced of the South's superiority over the North in all respects: art, architecture, climate, and people. The decline began, he believed, as one proceeded north via Rome, and it grew worse the farther one went. When Ehrensvärd reached

FACING PAGE *Ehrensvärd was among those who most eagerly promoted use of columns in Sweden. In drawings such as this one, he showed how columns could fit into the Swedish landscape.*

RIGHT *In this sketch Johan Tobias Sergel has depicted his friend Carl August Ehrensvärd on his way home from Italy, with examples of the classical architecture he so admired in the background. Dark Nordic pine forests await the traveler.*

Milan, he burst out in despair: "Farewell strength and health, reason for beauty and taste, farewell lovely nature! The North is approaching, welcome disorder!" According to Ehrensvärd, Sweden was beyond hope. He published these views in his 1786 book, *De fria konsternas philosophi* (The Philosophy of the Free Arts) as well as in his travel descriptions in *Resa till Italien* (Trip to Italy) of the same year.

A colleague and good friend to Ehrensvärd was Fredrik Henrik af Chapman, a son of English immigrants. A shipbuilder of international reputation, af Chapman served as an admiral in Karlskrona during several intense years in the 1780s. Gustav III gave to af Chapman the task of building up a naval base and supplying the shipyard with new warehouses. The shipbuilder's proposal—which included three large storage buildings each housing masts, sails, ropes, and other equipment to outfit twelve warships—had won royal favor with the practicality of the construction and despite the facade, which the king considered outdated.

When Ehrensvärd was once again on Swedish soil in 1782, he looked up his old friend af Chapman and became involved in the shipyard project. Ehrensvärd immediately reconfigured the proposal in the direction of Greco-Roman antiquity. A drawing by his hand shows a four-story, rusticated building with a temple-like portico, a flat roof, and uniform window casements. Ehrensvärd simplified the proposal even further, however, by eliminating the portico because it would have impeded the building of an adjacent dock; in addition, the rustication disappeared, and the building was given a saddleback roof. The inventory chamber completed in 1786 (only one was built, not three as planned) is a very long, austere creation with few repeated architectural elements, small windows encased by blocks of stone, and twenty identical doors with pediments. The walls are smooth and topped by a heavy cornice. This was a more

For the naval warehouse at Karlskrona (1782–86), Carl August Ehrensvärd took the purity of neoclassical architecture in Sweden to its extreme.

severe and uncompromising architecture than had ever been seen in Sweden.

ROYAL ARCHITECTURE AFTER GUSTAV III'S ITALIAN JOURNEY

Even as crown prince, Gustav III had dreamed about making a grand tour to Italy. When he finally made the journey as king, it was for reasons of diplomacy. The monarch sought to divert attention from his secret military rearmament for a war against Russia and Denmark; at the same time, he hoped to gather the support of potential allies for his planned military actions. The officially stated purpose of the trip to Italy in 1783–84, however, was rejuvenation in the thermal baths of a spa outside Pisa.

The king traveled incognito, though with an entourage of nearly twenty followers, he could hardly have gone unnoticed. The sculptor Johan Tobias Sergel served as the king's guide. After a few dreary weeks at the baths, the Swedish entourage moved on to Florence in November, where Gustav III for the first time encountered antiquity on classical soil.

On Christmas Eve, the entourage arrived in Rome, just in time to attend Christmas Mass at St. Peter's basilica with Emperor Joseph II of the Holy Roman Empire. To escape the chilly weather in Rome, the group traveled south to Naples, where they could take excursions to the many historic sites such as Herculaneum, Pompeii, and the temples in Paestum. Returning to Rome, the restless monarch continued to visit churches, monuments, and art collections. He also took the opportunity to assemble a private collection, and, from Pope Pius VI, he received gifts of mosaics, tapestries, and a complete, extravagantly bound set of the engravings of Giovanni Battista Piranesi. Totally entranced by everything that he had seen of Roman antiquity and the Italian Renaissance, Gustav III began immediately after his return home to translate his foreign impressions into new building projects.

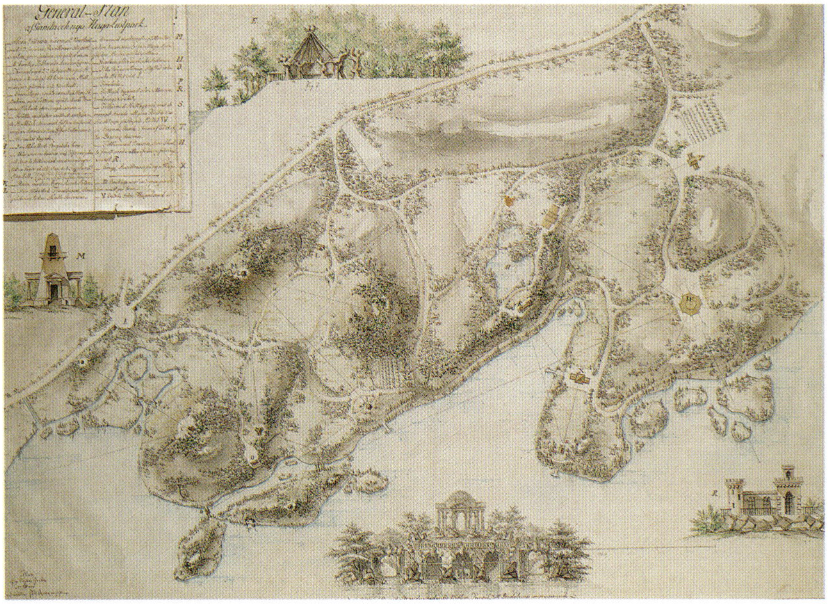

LEFT *Fredrik Magnus Piper's general plan for the English park at King Gustav III's beloved retreat, Haga (1781–86).*

BELOW *Louis Jean Desprez's proposal for a new palace at Haga (ca. 1791) reflected a grand vision, but it was never realized. On the left is the planned large palace and on the right, near the water, Gustav III's pavilion.*

His attention turned to Haga, his favorite place, situated in an untamed natural setting near the waters of Brunnsviken north of Stockholm. Haga served as his private retreat away from the capital to a calmer atmosphere. The first royal residence at the site was a simple wooden house that is still extant, but the king had more ambitious plans for the surroundings. The architect Fredrik Magnus Piper (1746–1824), who had returned in 1780 from landscape architecture studies in England, was asked to create a general plan for the area (it was Piper's designs for the royal parks at Drottningholm and Haga that established the English park in Sweden). At Haga, Piper made clever use of the many possibilities offered by the natural surroundings to create romantic follies—a Temple of Neptune, a hermit's lair, a ruined medieval castle, a pyramid, and more. They appeared in his general plan for the park, which entailed the gentle interplay between expansive lawns, tightly grown vegetation, and water. The several architectural whimsies he planned were to be linked by an elaborate system of sightlines and curving pathways. But only one of Piper's proposals became a reality, the Turkish Kiosk (*Turkiska kiosken*).

Gustav III soon commissioned Olof Tempelman to design a palace that would resemble Andrea Palladio's Villa Rotonda, with four colonnaded porticos and a domed center. The cornerstones were laid in 1786, but the king decided to expand the project dramatically, creating a palace with magnificent galleries for his newly acquired collection of classical sculptures. Once again, Tempelman was bidden to step aside for Desprez. The Frenchman's 1791 proposal had everything: a rotunda, columns, temple pediments, and niches for statues. The new designs doubled the length of the building and surrounded it with a Corinthian peristyle.

The king and his French architect now strived for grandeur charged with a political purpose: to laud the honor of Gustav III and that of his predecessors on the throne. A magnificent watercolor of the site offers an evocative image of Desprez's vision for the palace's environs. Within the grandeur of the scene, the silhouette of the capital city peeks out in the distance, a reminder of reality.

Though for the most part he had been pushed aside, Tempelman still had some responsibility at Haga. In 1787, he had been asked to design a quite small building at the site, the King's Pavilion (*Kungens paviljong*), which was to function as a provisional residence before completion of the grand palace. The pavilion was the most important of Tempelman's royal commissions, and it came to be one of the most beautiful examples of the late Gustavian style. Gustav III had personally made a drawing for a cross-section of the building that he asked the architect to follow.

The core of the pavilion consisted of the original, nearly cubical, stone house, which was to be heightened and extended with a pair of low wings. The roof was to be flat and embellished with a balustrade. The central block was to house the Grand Salon, a library, and the king's bedchamber; one wing housed an antechamber and the dining room, and the other, the Blue Salon and the Mirrored Hall. The latter opened up toward the water through a glass-enclosed colonnade that gave the feeling of no boundaries between the interior and surrounding nature. The windows were otherwise the same as those of the Royal Palace, which the king had pointed out in a letter to Tempelman. It was apparently his idea to link the pavilion to the great work of Tessin, which was symbolic of the absolute monarchy. The pavilion was

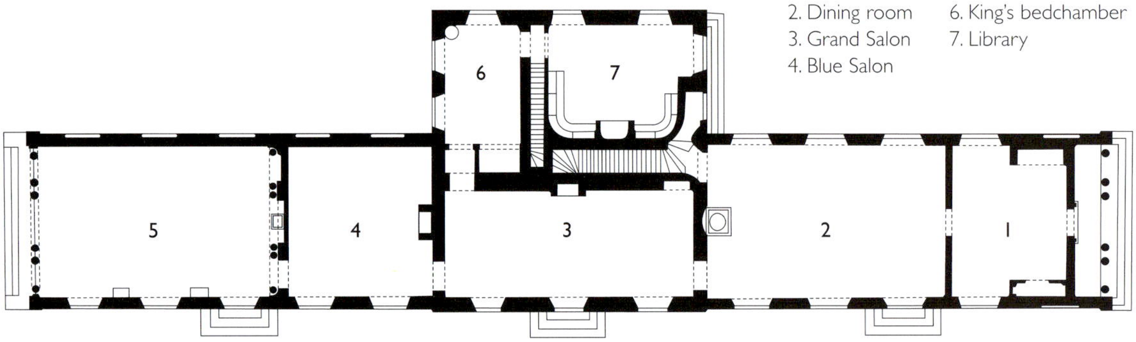

The King's Pavilion at Haga, ground-floor plan.

FACING PAGE *King Gustav III's pavilion at Haga, designed by Olof Tempelman and constructed in 1788–93.*

BELOW *The light entering the water side of the king's pavilion at Gustav III's Haga is multiplied many times over by the mirrors for which this room is named.*

The Divan Room on the second floor of the Haga Pavilion—a beautiful example of the fully developed late Gustavian style—was used as a council chamber.

complete and ready for use in December 1790.

The severity expressed by the exterior is not reflected in the interiors. The principal rooms were adorned by the gifted Louis Masreliez (1748–1810), whose artistic skill lay in his solid knowledge of classical art and literature; his brother Jean Baptiste Masreliez (1753–1801) carried out the work using his drawings. The wall panels were divided into fields with gilt moldings, covered with silks or painted in the elegant arabesque style that Louis Masreliez had learned in Italy. An example of this is apparent in the Divan Room, a council chamber located on the second floor, where the king would sit like a sultan on a Turkish divan sofa directly under the image of the Greek god Apollo, protector of the arts, with whom Gustav III identified himself.

The most exquisite decor in the pavilion is Louis Masreliez's Grand Salon designs, inspired by Raphael's interpretation of ancient Roman mural painting in the Vatican loggia. A very comprehensive allegorical program composed by the king and his philosopher-painter was created around the four ancient divinities, Apollo, Jupiter, Juno, and Minerva. Inspired by classical examples, Masreliez also designed the furniture for the room, including the Klismos

Executed by Louis Masreliez, the elegant interior of the Grand Salon at Haga is decorated with motifs from ancient mythology. The furniture includes a pair of Klismos chairs.

chairs, with their deep concave backs and saber-shaped legs. Since space was limited, Masreliez planned the pavilion to make the most efficient use of each room. The crown prince's bedroom on the upper floor is no larger than a servant's room at the Royal Palace.

Gustav III was not able to enjoy the intimate, exquisite milieu at Haga for more than eighteen months, and his larger palace was never realized. A deadly shot at the Royal Opera in 1792 brought all the king's elaborate plans to an abrupt halt, and with them, Desprez's career as well. Throughout the last few years of the king's life, Desprez had been given free rein in his architecture, but at the expense of his Swedish colleagues. When his royal patron fell, no others came forward. He lived out his last twelve years in sickness and penury. Tempelman, meanwhile, went back to routine tasks at the superintendent's office.

For the brothers Masreliez, new projects were on the horizon—in particular, Tullgarn Palace, the residence of Gustav III's youngest brother, Prince Fredrik Adolf. The Parliament purchased the Tullgarn Palace in 1772 as a summer residence for the prince, and here he created for himself a milieu reminiscent of Haga. Politically, the prince was

LEFT *The Red Antechamber at Tullgarn Palace still has its original furnishings, including the columnar tile stove on a plinth and three console tables (1793) with Swedish porphyry tops. The walls are covered with mid-nineteenth-century silk damask copied from an eighteenth-century original.*

ABOVE *The grand bedchamber at Tullgarn is one of the finest neoclassical interiors designed by the brothers Louis and Jean Baptiste Masreliez.*

rather withdrawn, but as a member of the Royal Academy of Fine Arts, he was quite active. His interest in art was genuine and, like his monarch brother, he was endowed with a developed esthetic sense. This was confirmed by Johan Tobias Sergel, who served as guide on Fredrik Adolf's grand tour in Italy in the 1770s, just as he did a decade later for Gustav III.

While in Rome, Prince Fredrik Adolf also came into contact with Louis Masreliez, and it was he and his brother Jean Baptiste who would come to lead the transformation of Tullgarn's interiors some years later. The exact division of the work between the two is unclear. Jean Baptiste, a newly appointed professor at the Royal Academy of Fine Arts, is thought to have provided the main creative force behind the work at Tullgarn. In 1790, a second phase of interior work began on the palace (the first had been carried out between 1780 and 1785). Fredrik Adolf found his finances limited, yet his taste was refined and very particular, and his attitude toward money carefree, all of which contributed to the slow pace of the project.

FACING PAGE *The walls of Prince Fredrik Adolf's Blue Antechamber at Tullgarn have engravings of Roman motifs by Giovanni Volpatos and Abraham-Louis-Rodolphe Ducros directly affixed to them. The canvas floor covering was painted to imitate a Roman mosaic and is the only example of this practice preserved in Sweden. The chest of drawers is the work of the foremost cabinetmaker, George Haupt.*

In modernizing the late-baroque palace, Fredrik Adolf replaced the tall hip roof with a lower flat roof encircled by a balustrade, and he raised the height of the lower wings facing the water with an additional story. Inside the palace, the floor plan was redistributed to make way for a suite of rooms in the state apartment that faced the gardens. The Red Antechamber, the Grand Bedchamber, as well as the Blue Antechamber were part of this suite and were furnished in 1790–94. The prince's private apartment faced the sea.

A feature that runs throughout the entire state apartment is the Roman-Pompeian style of ornament embellishing the paneling, doors, overdoors, and window reveals. Urns, cornucopias, figures of Mercury, and other forms common in classical imagery were piled on top of one another in what is called a candelabra motif. Pehr Ljung and Ernst Filip Thoman were responsible for the sculpted ornament, while the painted decoration was executed by the prince's personal court painter, Anders Hultgren. The motifs were taken from pattern books from Fredrik Adolf's private library, most especially from the 1777 *Recueil d'ornements* (Collection of Ornaments) by the Frenchman Gille-Paul Cauvet.

Themes based on Roman antiquity were expressed in other forms as well. As a conversation piece, the center of the richly inlaid parquet floor of the Red Antechamber depicted the popular neoclassical scene, "The Cupid Seller," based on an ancient fresco at Herculaneum rendered in the 1757–92 volumes, *Antichità di Ercolano* (Antiquities of Herculaneum). In the Blue Antechamber, the prince created what was literally a print room by gluing engravings from Rome by Volpato and Ducros—souvenirs from his grand tour—directly onto the walls. The floor of the room was made of canvas and painted to imitate an ancient Roman floor mosaic.

As the prince's faux-mosaic floor attests, the Swedes often used humble materials to achieve the visual effect of more precious ones. This is also the case with the very modern Wedgwood-style frieze depicting dancing girls based on a 1785 engraving by Giacondo Albertolli that is found in several rooms at the prince's palace. Instead of porcelain, plaster painted in the classical Wedgwood colors—blue, green, and pink with white—was used.

In 1794, work at Tullgarn halted once again and was not resumed until 1800. As the prince remained unmarried despite numerous affairs, it was his sister Princess Sophia Albertina who completed the interiors at Tullgarn after Fredrik Adolf's death.

CIVIC ARCHITECTURE

Throughout much of the Gustavian period, Carl Hårleman's style left its distinct mark on Swedish manor house architecture; so subtle a change in taste is often recognizable only in details. New forms and ideals were eventually expressed by Jean Eric Rehn, who in the 1760s was involved in several residential projects. Although Rehn raised domestic architecture to new heights, he was never able to create a model house that was so widely adopted as Hårleman's. On the contrary, his designs for interior furnishings are, to a great degree, characteristic for what we associate today with the Gustavian style.

Two of Rehn's early projects for commoners concerned an ironworks in the province of Uppland. In 1763, at Gimo, one of the region's most prominent ironworks, Rehn designed a manor house unlike anything the Swedes had ever seen. The architect joined a two-story main building with a pair of lower wings to produce a building of considerable length. The central section boasts a smooth plaster facade and a low saddleback roof with a lantern. A projecting forepart with a balcony and pediment marks the entrance, while, on the opposite side, a three-sided projection, also crowned by a pediment adorned with festoons and urns, faces

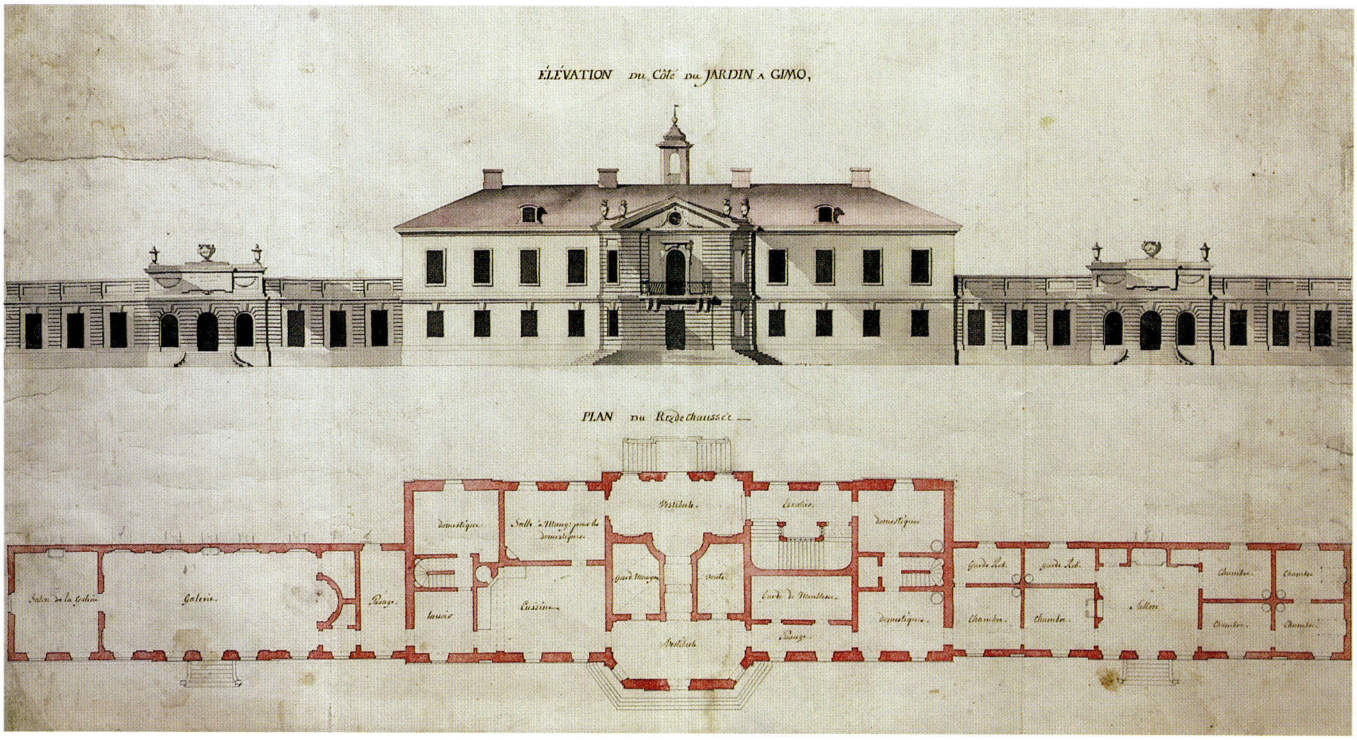

Gimo Manor (1763) was one of the sites at which architect Jean Eric Rehn introduced the neoclassical style of architecture to Sweden. Included with a floor plan, the elevation pictured here shows the facade on the garden side of the house.

Constructed between 1765 and 1774, the manor house in the ironworking town of Forsmark followed Jean Eric Rehn's designs. The house, with its austere facade, stands at one end of the long manufacturing street. The forecourt and gateway are framed by rectangular white fence posts.

the garden. The wings have linear rustication, flat roofs, and frontispieces ornamented with decorative balustrades topped by classical urns. This particular house model, with its strong emphasis on horizontal lines, was not yet accepted in Sweden. It had a future, though; it pointed toward early-nineteenth-century architecture.

Rehn had also made a general plan for the entire area, in which he had double allées of deciduous trees cut through a dense evergreen forest to emerge into open spaces. A demilune space was intended as a workers' square surrounded by residences; another was to form an approach to the main house. Though these ambitious ideas were never fully carried out, Rehn had a second opportunity to realize such plans for the ironworks at nearby Forsmark.

The Russians had destroyed Forsmark in 1719. A simple two-story building had replaced the fire-ravaged *corps de logis*, but the owner, Court Marshall John Jennings, was not satisfied with it. He therefore turned to Rehn, whom he asked not only to redesign a new main building but also to propose a general plan for the entire site. The architect presented at least two proposals for the main house. The first paraphrased Gimo, but it was the other that appealed most to his patron. The design that was accepted depicts a two-story building with a simple, smooth exterior finish; it had a low, peaked, saddleback roof, and short projecting wings with rusticated corners. By 1765, when construction was actually in progress, a third floor for guest quarters was added, giving the building a powerful appearance almost reminiscent of Karolinian architecture. But this cost the house its original, fine proportions.

Rehn planned the schematics of the environment on a strict axis. The manor house, with its wide gravel forecourt, is located at one end of a perfectly straight street, which is lined with almost identical ironsmiths' dwellings. At the opposite end of the street stands the church, an austere neoclassical creation begun in 1794 and based on the designs of Olof Tempelman.

Alongside the manor house, Rehn placed a small topiary garden in the French style. Late in the century, the natural surroundings were were tamed by the creation of a romantic English park with meandering pathways, a primitive temple clad in bark, a hermit's dwelling, and an obelisk represent-

Blacksmiths' residences line the main manufacturing street at Forsmark, one end of which reaches a somber neoclassical church designed in 1796 by Olof Tempelman, around 1790.

The houses built for the families of laborers in the ironworks provided a higher standard of living than was available to city workers.

During the 1790s, an English park was added to Forsmark, one of the best-preserved and most elaborate examples in Sweden. Here one can still find a bark-covered temple and an obelisk traditionally identified as marking the grave of the great Byzantine general Belisarius.

LEFT *The idyllic English park at Forsmark was designed to appear more natural than nature itself. These wetlands, which actually provided water for use in the ironworks, were channelled to twist and bend like meandering woodland brooks.*

The main building at Erstavik was built during the 1760s according to Jean Eric Rehn's designs.

ing the grave of the great Byzantine general, Belisarius, who had become popular through a novel by the French writer Jean François Marmontel. The park at Forsmark is one of the best preserved of its genre in Sweden.

A more pronounced example of the return to the Karolinian style is Erstavik, situated just south of Stockholm. Commissioned in 1763 by an influential merchant named Herman Petersen, Rehn designed Erstavik as a large, three-story house with a high mansard roof. The facade clearly emphasizes the second floor as the main living space, with the rooms for social occasions nobly furnished in latest fashion. The general impression of Erstavik is reminiscent of older Swedish customs, though the floor plan is taken directly from a French pattern book by Jacques-François Blondel.

Erstavik's interiors illustrate clearly the transition from the Rococo to the Gustavian style. The paneling in Erstavik's Blue Salon has the same system of stiles and rails as at Drottningholm, while the medallion-shaped overdoors, with their plump cherubs framed by laurel garlands, still show much of the Rococo. The walls are covered with painted

FACING PAGE *For the Blue Salon at Erstavik, Rehn specified meander borders to frame the linen wall panels. The overdoors are executed in blue cameo-style painting, and the room is furnished in Gustavian style.*

RIGHT *This drawing by Rehn shows the opposite wall of the Blue Salon at Erstavik with similar simple wood paneling, double doors, and paintings. The fireplace and chimneypiece were replaced by a tile stove.*

linen canvas with a blue meander border, floral swags, and birds in flight. The interiors are light, but the entire rococo color scale has been substantially toned down.

Through the 1770s, Rehn's interior decoration became increasingly uniform and austere, and the Gustavian style fully developed, the finest example of it being Carl Hårleman's Övedskloster manor house (which was completed long after it was designed). Nearly everything is preserved intact in the gallery, Övedskloster's most splendid room. The colors are white and gold, with small wall panels and large fields covered with red silk damask, a textile that reappears in the upholstery of the Gustavian furnishings. The sparse decoration of the paneling consists of classical motifs such as laurel wreaths, and carved overdoors depict smoking urns, or *cul-de-lamps*. Between the four windows on the wall that backs on the garden are gilt mirrors over three magnificent, matching gilt console tables probably designed by Rehn himself. The adjacent salon offers a completely paneled interior with double doors in Rehn's style. The lunette overdoors consist of grisaille paintings of scenes from ancient mythology. A white marble chimneypiece enhances the room's very cool and stately character. Today, just as two centuries ago, a portrait of the original builder's father, Malte Ramel, which was painted by the renowned Swedish artist, Carl Gustav Pilo, hangs over the chimneypiece.

Though Carl Fredrik Adelcrantz had only limited involvement with Övedskloster and contributed little to its general composition, his list of achievements includes one of Sweden's most beautiful and best-preserved Gustavian country houses, Sturehov. The property, south of Stockholm, was acquired in 1778 by Gustav III's finance minister, Baron Johan Liljencrantz, who, soon after being named to that post, commissioned from the superintendent designs for a new residence. Liljencrantz's house, completed in 1781, consisted of a two-story building with a rusticated ground floor and mansard roof. On the forecourt side, the central part of the house forms a projecting *avant-corps*, while, on the garden side, a rounded pediment before an ornamental balustrade and windows in the roof create an aura of grandeur. The building generally draws on the style of Hårleman's manor-house architecture except for the placement of the family and state apartments on the second floor. The ground floor has a rather old-fashioned plan with a vestibule extending the entire depth of the house and crossed by a long corridor. Here Adelcrantz planned to place the kitchen quarters to the left of the entrance and living quarters for the house staff to the right.

At the center of the state apartment lies the octagonal

The gallery at Övedskloster was probably furnished according to drawings by Jean Eric Rehn. On the inner wall, silk-covered panels frame two Marieberg tile stoves. The console tables on the opposite side were probably designed by Jean Eric Rehn.

The salon at Övedskloster retains most of its original furnishings. The white marble chimneypiece shows a strict classical composition. Above this hangs a portrait by Carl Gustav Pilo depicting the father of the original builder, Malte Ramel.

The main building at Sturehov was completed in 1781. The wings flanking the courtyard are older, but to match the main building they were repainted a pale shade and given roofs similar to that of the main building.

Carl Fredrik Adelcrantz's original drawings for Johan Liljencrantz's Sturehov manor house (1778) are still preserved. This example depicts the garden facade.

salon, which occupies the projecting *avant-corps* and connects the two flanking suites. The salon is completely paneled in wood and faux-painted to imitate rarer materials. The austere marbleized gray panels decorated with sculpted laurel garlands, Vitruvian scrolls, gilt ribbons, and medallions are reminiscent of Rehn's interiors, although Jean Baptiste Masreliez was most likely responsible for the design of the room.

The flanking suites of rooms do not reflect the strict, neoclassical character of the salon. In several rooms, the walls above the dadoes are decorated with canvases painted with playful floral vines and garlands enclosed by perfectly aligned rectangular borders. The quality of the wall paintings indicates that they were carried out by Lars Bolander, the foremost decoration painter of the Gustavian period. Baron Liljencrantz's yellow bedchamber has pale wall paintings that have faded over time; these contrast starkly with the still-vibrant colors and elaborate decoration of the

Marieberg tile stove that forms a centerpiece for the room. On their own a subject of great interest, the remarkable tile stoves, produced at the Marieberg ceramics factory, were deservedly as famous for their elegant shapes and tiles of beautiful colors on pure white backgrounds as for their capacity to heat a space. Because Baron Liljencrantz was the largest shareholder in the Marieberg firm, Sweden's largest collection of Marieberg tile stoves was assembled at Sturehov.

One of the wealthiest men in Sweden during the Gustavian epoch was John Hall, a prominent merchant in the important commercial and shipping city of Göteborg (in English, called Gothenburg). In 1785, Hall began construction of Gunnebo, a large country villa south of Göteborg. The Göteborg city architect Carl Wilhelm Carlberg was responsible for the designs. The patron's origins—an English father and a Swedish mother—as well as the architect's studies in England, may explain the villa's reflection of English

The octagonal salon on the second floor—Sturehov's most neoclassical room—was warmed by a columnar stove. The painting of the paneled walls imitates marble.

Panels of graceful floral motifs painted by the eminent Gustavian artist Lars Bolander cover the walls of Lady Liljencrantz's bedchamber at Sturehov. The furniture too is Gustavian.

The yellow antechamber at Sturehov, originally furnished as the baron's bedchamber, boasts the finest of all Marieberg tile stoves. Its rich, colorful decoration includes the Liljencrantz coat-of-arms.

Gunnebo mansion (1784–96), here seen from the garden, was designed by Carl Wilhelm Carlberg for the Anglo-Swedish merchant John Hall.

classicism, which, in turn, derives from architecture of Palladio.

The entrance to Gunnebo is dominated by a pair of colossal Ionic columns with dentils before a recessed central section. Above the columns are an elegant frieze and a cornice. The garden facade's dominating feature is its accentuated frontispiece, including a leaded relief depicting the work and pleasures of country life; this rises above a series of large Palladian-style windows and a double staircase that leads to the garden below. The entire house gives the impression of being built of stone, but it was actually constructed of wood, perhaps because the patron had access to unlimited timber through his business.

The interiors at Gunnebo far exceed any others in Sweden outside royal circles. The architect's working materials, including two hundred drawings, are still preserved at the Röhsska Museum in Göteborg. These include designs for everything from park benches and garden urns to dining room chairs and tile stoves. The interior's cool classicism is reminiscent of English interiors, especially those by the contemporary Briton Robert Adam, but there are also connections to the French Louis XVI style. The walls of the salon are rhythmically articulated by tall Ionic pilasters, between which are fields of arched panels. White neoclassical reliefs by the Italian sculptor Gioacchino Frulli fill the overdoors, and cherubs carrying drapery swags that fall in softly folded arcs embellish the deeply coved ceiling. The perfect execution of every detail enhances the room's overall harmony.

In 1801, Johan Tobias Sergel visited Gunnebo. In a letter to his friend Pehr Tham, the sculptor wrote: "Carlberg, a man of merit, has transported a beautiful mountainous site from Italy and placed it at Gunnebo. . . . I believed myself to be in the environs of Rome, at Tivoli, Frascati, Marino, or Genzano. The house is charming in all respects. Carlberg has benefited from a most clever owner; he has made a magnificent staircase next to the garden, which in my view produces an admirable effect."

The design of the country house Skärva, probably by a collaboration of the owner Fredrik Henrik af Chapman and

The grand salon at Gunnebo, situated in the center of the house, opens onto the terrace and a magnificent garden. The walls are articulated by pilasters, and the stuccoed ceiling is decorated by fourteen cherubs carrying drapery, which falls in swags around the room. All Gunnebo's plasterwork is by the Italian sculptor Gioacchino Frulli. In the corners stand statues depicting the four seasons, a popular motif in country villas.

The cool classicism that characterizes Carl Wilhelm Carlberg's interiors at Gunnebo includes an abundance of white plaster reliefs and statuary. The standing figure personifies Autumn; in an overdoor niche reposes a figure representing livestock farming. Beyond this salon is the dining room. The blue-and-white textile of the chairs, which were also designed by Carlberg, is typically Swedish.

Skärva still stands as one of Sweden's boldest eighteenth-century structures, despite nineteenth-century changes that softened its appearance. Red timbers and a sod-covered roof were originally prominent features at Skärva.

Carl August Ehrensvärd, manifested a different Swedish idealization of southern Europe. Since the daring interruption of his military career to visit Italy in 1780, Ehrensvärd had nurtured dreams of the temples at Paestum. But merely to embrace and copy Greco-Roman antiquity, without incorporating it into one's own esthetic context, was not the goal he sought. Rather, Ehrensvärd's objective was to seek a classical simplicity in his own, Swedish national character.

These ideals were best realized at af Chapman's Skärva, outside the naval city of Karlskrona. Here, in a wooded area, Nordic and classical forms met on equal terms and mingled happily. It might have been Ehrensvärd's idea to furnish what he regarded as a "primitive" Nordic house—a basic red log cabin with a sod roof—with a light Greek temple portico. The unabashed combination of temple and cabin, columns and sod roof, must have satisfied the admiral's ideals while also intriguing visitors. And when guests entered the house, they were probably even more surprised. The portico leads to a large octagonal room with a dome and a lantern, its walls adorned with portraits of Roman emperors. With the skills of carpenters from the docks and crafts-

FACING PAGE *The first room that greets a visitor to Skärva is an octagonal salon with light entering through a lantern overhead that recalls the oculus of Rome's Pantheon.*

RIGHT *In Fredrik Henrik af Chapman's study at Skärva, the shipbuilder's work desk stands beneath a wide window. Through a tiny side window he could see the sea route to Karlskrona.*

men from Stockholm, af Chapman was able to put his gifts as a shipbuilder to new and unexpected uses, composing a series of tasteful rooms with a personal character adjacent to the Pantheon-inspired central salon.

The owner transformed the dense landscape around the house into a romantic park with a Gothic tower, a small wooden temple painted in Pompeian hues—a gift from Ehrensvärd—and antique Greek urns placed side by side with blocks of ancient Nordic stone.

CHURCH ARCHITECTURE

In contrast to Sweden's ecclesiastical architecture of the Rococo period, which mainly involved rebuilding and adding to existing churches, the Gustavian period contributed several major church construction projects. The most important of these was Carl Fredrik Adelcrantz's Adolf Fredrik's Church (*Adolf Fredriks kyrka*) in Stockholm. The architect received this commission in 1767, taking on the project after Carl Hårleman died.

One of the commission's complications was the congregation's demand to allow an existing chapel to remain standing until completion of the new church. Adelcrantz solved the problem by building the new church around the old one. This bound his design to the earlier chapel's central-plan design. Adelcrantz's first proposal, based on the Rococo style, was closely related to Hårleman's design for a new, but never completed Admiralty Church in Karlskrona. The plans consisted of a cruciform church with a central tower, but the final results departed from these original plans. The severe two-story facade consists, on the lower level, of paired Ionic columns and a window flanked above by blind bays. A tall octagonal structure capped by a copper dome with a lantern rests on the building's central quadrant, a late-baroque form anchored in the great domes of late-seventeenth-century churches that Adelcrantz had studied during his trips to France and Italy.

The interiors exhibit a robust classicism composed of tall pilasters, reliefs, and shallow vaults with transverse arches. The entire room is whitewashed. Over the altar is a plaster relief by Johan Tobias Sergel of the Resurrection. The same sculptor also designed for Adolf Fredrik's Church a monument to René Descartes, who was buried in the old churchyard; the great French philosopher had been invited to Stockholm to tutor Queen Christina but contracted pneumonia there and died in 1650.

LEFT *Adolf Fredrik's Church in Stockholm—which became the model for many other Swedish churches—was built between 1767 and 1774 after designs by Carl Fredrik Adelcrantz; its tower was completed in 1783.*

BELOW *The interior of Adolf Fredrik's Church with an altar decoration in high relief by the sculptor Johan Tobias Sergel (1785).*

FACING PAGE *The church at Skellefteå was designed by Jacob Rijf, who was inspired by Adelcrantz's church in Stockholm.*

Many of the finest examples of Swedish ecclesiastical neoclassicism are found far from the capital city, in the provincial countryside. Though Swedes during the late eighteenth century were not alone in their desire to add columns to buildings, foreign visitors could nevertheless be astounded by an unexpected meeting of the South and the North such as Doric columns in a snowy landscape. This was the case in 1799, when an English traveler, Edward Clarke, passed through the small northern town of Skellefteå and stumbled upon "a Grecian temple on the borders of Lappland."

The architect of the church at Skellefteå was Jacob Rijf, a master carpenter from northern Finland, who had studied at the Royal Academy of Fine Arts in Stockholm, where he had learned the esthetic principles of antiquity. The church he designed in 1793, which was evaluated and approved in Stockholm, was firmly based upon the same model as Adolf

Fredrik's Church: a Greek cross with a tower above the central axis. To this general plan, a muscular Doric temple pediment with four columns was added, inspired by Adelcrantz's sketches of a similar (though never executed) addition to Adolf Fredrik's Church.

Contemporary with Rijf's work in Skellefteå, a rotunda-style church based on the Pantheon in Rome was erected in Tavastehus in Finland. It had been designed by Louis Jean Desprez back in 1788 and forced on the congregation by King Gustav III, who had harbored a dream since his visit to Rome in 1783 of a Pantheon-shaped church in Stockholm. During the 1790s, various young architects at the superintendent's office had been sketching Pantheon-inspired temples, but reality was now quite changed. Gustav III was dead, and with him, all the royal support necessary to carry out such projects. In the 1780s, the prevailing desire was for functional, oblong churches that met practical demands, without excessive decoration and adapted to accommodate the village's entire population.

Attaining this new ideal was the church that Olof Tempelman designed in 1793 for Forsmark's ironworks (shown on page 205). It is a rectangular, barrel-vaulted church patterned on the Roman basilica plan, with a tower at the west end and an apse at the east. Occasionally this standard model could be fitted out with a few strong classical accents, as in the case of his church at Konungsund (1795), for which Tempelman provided a tower with four pediments under a pyramidal roof, and on the south facade, a Doric portico. If the period for grand neoclassical extravagances was over, Swedish architecture had now been imbued with order, regularity, and clarity. Within these ideals lay the foundation for the next generation of classicists.

CHAPTER SIX

The Empire Style

PAGES 226–227 *A great porphyry vessel was placed in the garden of Rosendal Palace, 1825. Some critics have said that the vessel was too big for the palace; or, instead, that the palace was too small for the vessel.*

LEFT *On the shore of Stockholm's Lake Mälaren, Rosersberg Palace was built in the 1630s and modernized in the mid-1700s by architect Jean Eric Rehn. In the early nineteenth century, Gustav af Sillén made further alterations to Rosersberg at the behest of Prince Karl, brother of Gustav III.*

FACING PAGE *From Princess Hedvig Elisabet Charlotta's bedchamber one can see a row of rooms, each with a different overdoor. The nearest was painted by the artist Fredrik Westin,* The Day with Apollo Driving his Chariot *(1813).*

The Empire style in Sweden is strongly associated with Jean Baptiste Bernadotte, the French field marshal who first set foot in 1810 on the land he had been chosen to rule. Elected Sweden's crown prince and given the name Karl Johan, Bernadotte was adopted at age forty-seven by the childless King Karl XIII. It was the French crown prince who gave the Empire style its Swedish name, the Karl-Johan style.

The Empire is not so much a new style as a continuation of European neoclassicism, and it is more conspicuous in interior design and the decorative arts than in architecture. Inspired by antiquity, mostly by Roman Imperial style, rooms were painted in faux-marble or draped with textiles to give the impression of military tents. Furniture of dark mahogany, gilt ormolu bronzes, and fabrics in vibrant colors were most prevalent. All this is evident at Rosendal, the royal summer palace in Stockholm, which is considered the most harmonious and best-preserved Empire environment in Sweden.

In less aristocratic settings, the influences of the French Empire style were modified and took on a more distinctly Swedish character. Though the terms Empire and Karl-Johan style are almost interchangeable, the Swedish version usually indicates lighter and simpler elements than those of the French counterpart. This difference became especially evident during the 1830s, when Swedish decorative arts and interior design became gradually more influenced by the German Biedermeier style, a bourgeois adaptation of the Empire. Native blond woods such as birch and elm replaced dark mahogany, furniture became more delicate, and interiors became more intimate.

ARCHITECTURE FOR THE MONARCHY

Though Crown Prince Karl Johan was strongly influential in imposing French traits on Swedish design in the early nineteenth century, the transformation from Gustavian to Empire actually occurred before Bernadotte's arrival in Sweden. The royal palace Rosersberg illustrates how the decorative arts gradually took on the new style.

Decorations in the interior of the Hogland Hall at Rosersberg Palace commemorate Sweden's 1789 victory over the Russian navy near the Island of Hogland. The walls are adorned with trofée *groups carved in wood, with portrait medallions of naval heroes above. The medallions on the entrance wall shown here were sculpted by Johan Tobias Sergel.*

Rosersberg Palace, on the shore of Lake Mälaren, was originally built during the 1630s by Count Gabriel Oxenstierna, a cousin of Chancellor of the Realm Axel Oxenstierna (see Chapter Two). Fifty years later, the count's son commissioned Nicodemus Tessin the Younger to rebuild the palace as an elaborate baroque edifice inspired by buildings in both Italy and France and set in one of Sweden's most lavish and admired gardens. In 1757, the state purchased the palace and, five years later, offered it as a country residence to King Gustav III's brother, Prince Karl. With his bride, the intelligent and witty Princess Hedvig Elisabet Charlotta of Oldenburg, the prince, who was also Duke of Södermanland, lived there from 1774.

Several of the palace's interiors had been redecorated during the 1750s under the direction of court architect Jean Eric Rehn. After taking charge, Prince Karl decided to allow Rehn to continue his work. With modest resources, Rehn nonetheless managed to eliminate the baroque character of the palace and to change the tone to conform more closely with the fashionable modern style. At the same time a series of private rooms was furnished for the royal couple, along with Hedvig Elisabet Charlotta's private state apartment. When the project came to the prince's state apartment, however, the money was pretty much gone.

Not until Prince Karl became regent of Sweden, after Gustav III's death in 1792, did work on the palace resume. By this time, the interiors at Rosersberg were completely outdated—especially compared to those of Karl's brother's Tullgarn Palace and his sister Sophia Albertina's palace in Stockholm—so plans for new interiors, as well as for an extension to the building, began at once. Olof Tempelman was the first architect enlisted, but instead, Prince Karl soon chose to employ a younger architect, Gustav af Sillén (1762–1825). Just home from a seven-year study sojourn in Italy, af Sillén had been named court architect. In 1797, the prince put him in charge of Rosersberg.

Gustaf af Sillén designed Princess Hedvig Elisabet Charlotta's dressing room at Rosersberg in 1810. With a comfortable divan sofa placed in an apse-shaped alcove, the room actually came to serve for socializing.

Princess Hedvig Elisabet Charlotta's bedchamber at Rosersberg was decorated (1809–10) under the direction of Carl Christoffer Gjörwell; a section of the inner wall is shown here.

The extensive alterations and rebuilding in af Sillén's plans included a domed rotunda addition to house a large salon. In the end, however, the project was kept to a more moderate scale and was confined mainly to the interiors; both suites of apartments on the second and third floors were redecorated. The restrained neoclassicism expressed in the new interiors was clearly influenced by the French Directoire style, which had preceded the Empire. Compared with the elaborate neoclassical interiors at Tullgarn Palace, Rosersberg's are quite spare. The moldings are smooth and undecorated, and the ornament chosen is precise and discreet.

The interiors at Rosersberg are representative not only of the period's style and tastes but also of the personality of Prince Karl himself. They reveal his strong ties with the secretive Masonic Order, in which he was Grand Master, and the rooms are filled with familiar Masonic symbols such as the red cross, the hexagram, and the lightning bolt of Jupiter. Other decorative elements in the interiors probably carried significance as well but were understood only by the initiated.

In room after room, the observer is further reminded of Karl's high rank as Admiral of the Swedish Navy. A maritime theme especially dominates the Hogland Hall, located on Rosersberg's upper floor and designed by Gustav af Sillén in 1801; the room honors Prince Karl's naval exploits during the Swedish-Russian War of 1788–89. One wall is almost completely covered by Louis Jean Desprez's large painting depicting the Battle of Hogland, which took place just off the Finnish coast; in the painting the Prince is heralded as

In the King's bedchamber at Rosersberg (ca. 1823), furnished by Fredrik Blom, pleated taffeta covers the walls and windows, and carpet loomed in England covers the floor. The two columnar Swedish tile stoves that heated the room were prominently placed near the Ionic columns flanking the entrance to the sleeping alcove.

victor by his fellow officers and troops. The walls, of glossy scagliola plaster, carry life-size *trofée* groups composed of Roman armor and weapons painted yellow and dark brown. Each suit of armor indicates the officer it belonged to—Prince Karl, Gustav III, Carl August Ehrensvärd, and so on—and above each, a medallion frames a depiction of the man. Along the ceiling runs a grisaille frieze with motifs taken from ancient battles at sea. The curtain arrangement, with the blue and yellow Swedish flag, may seem an unconventional feature, but it is a quite effective one to stir nationalistic feelings in the visitors gathered here.

A new period in Rosersberg's furnishings began after the forced abdication of Gustav III's son, Gustav IV Adolf, and Prince Karl's ascent to the throne in 1809. The start of the new king's reign occasioned great demands for official presentations and environments. During the years leading up to 1813, a series of splendid interiors was created at Rosersberg. For the prestigious commission of decorating the queen's bedchamber, Gustav af Sillén was asked to step aside for Carl Christoffer Gjörwell (1766–1836), the city architect of Stockholm. The bedchamber was completely paneled with carved wood painted white, pilasters with gilt ornamentation, and painted overdoors; as was often the case, the royal bed was sequestered in an alcove.

Gjörwell's inspiration for the decor and ornament came directly from French engravings, especially those in the 1801 book, *Recueil de decorations interieures* (Collection of Interior Decorations) by the French architects Charles

FACING PAGE *On a hillock overlooking a field used for military exercises, the pavilion Borgen was built (ca. 1810) for King Karl XIV Johan by Fredrik Blom. The building standing today is a reconstruction of the original, which was destroyed by fire in 1977.*

Percier and Pierre-François-Léonard Fontaine. Gustav af Sillén also used Jean Charles Krafft and Nicolas Rasonett's 1802 work, *Plans, coupes et elevations des plus belles maisons* (Plans, Cross-Sections, and Elevations of the Most Beautiful Houses). The pilasters decorated with circles and palmettes were novel in Sweden, as were the ceiling's torch frieze, the laurel wreaths, as well as the sparsely spaced star motif on the doorframe. In fact, the room is the best example in Sweden of the so-called Consular style, which was fashionable in France around 1800.

Gjörwell's appearance as guest architect at Rosersberg did not mean the end for Gustav af Sillén at the palace. Gustav af Sillén was given the task of completing an addition to the second floor, which housed a pair of other rooms for Princess Hedvig Elisabet Charlotta, a writing cabinet, and a dressing room; the latter actually functioned as a drawing room and was elaborately decorated in the Pompeian style, with a divan sofa in an apse-shaped alcove. Gustav af Sillén's contribution to Rosersberg received high praise during the nineteenth century, and indeed it was among his best work.

During King Karl Johan's reign, Rosersberg experienced a golden age, especially after 1823, when his wife Désirée (once engaged to Napoleon Bonaparte) decided to join him in Sweden. Surely the couple must have felt at home in the French-influenced interiors. Karl Johan's architect for Rosersberg was Fredrik Blom (1781–1853), who, like many members of the regent's inner circle, was a military man. With roots in the naval city of Karlskrona, Blom quickly advanced to colonel in the Navy's engineering division. As early as 1805 with his first large-scale project, the barracks for the Royal Equestrian Guard in Stockholm, Blom had demonstrated his skills in designing buildings with a pronounced formal simplification. His technical competence as well as his great artistic talents earned him a professorship at the Royal Academy of Fine Arts. He became the period's leading architect, and, as important, the favorite architect of the king.

Among the contributions the royal couple made to Rosersberg, the most important was Karl Johan's bedchamber, which Fredrik Blom designed around 1823. The room was given an extravagant decor of textiles, with its walls and windows draped with pleated green and cream-colored silk taffeta and its floor covered with English floral carpet. The opening of the alcove in which the bed stood is shaped as a Serlian (an element resembling a triumphal arch and named for the Italian Renaissance architect Sebastiano Serlio) and is flanked by two columnar tile stoves.

Karl Johan increasingly dominated architecture after his coronation. With the royal summer palace, Rosendal, in Stockholm, the monarch could also step forward as a patron commissioning an environment for his personal use.

With verdant areas, water, and tranquility, Rosendal had everything one could want in a natural setting for a summer palace. At the same time, its proximity to Ladugårdsgärdet, a field used for military exercises, was probably the deciding factor in Karl Johan's purchase of the property in 1817. The building, called Borgen (literally, the Castle), had three arched windows surrounded by war trophies and goddesses of victory carved in high relief—motifs derived from the triumphal arches of antiquity. From the beginning, Borgen was crowned by a tent; adorned with Roman field symbols, it was the general's command post overlooking the camp.

Blom assumed responsibility for Rosendal after the fire of 1819, which destroyed a first structure that Karl Johan

FACING PAGE *The royal summer palace, Rosendal, followed designs by Fredrik Blom (1823–25); this view shows the central portion of the entrance facade.*

RIGHT *The four columns at the entrance of Rosendal, carved of marble from Kolmården in Sweden, show the architect's knowledge of the classical vocabulary of architectural decoration—for example, the rows of egg-and-dart and bead-and-reel between the volutes of the Ionic capitals. Swedish pig-iron was used to build the railing of the upper-story balcony.*

had built. Blom carried out his duties like an army engineer designing and constructing a portable bridge or laying railroad tracks. He had, in fact, developed a system of prefabricated wooden structures that won him international recognition and that came into use at Rosendal. Blom's innovative technology enabled the construction of sections of ready-made wall to be transported to the site, where they were put together, covered with bricks, and then plastered. The design followed the technique: a two-story building, harmoniously divided into a central forepart with side projections. The tone is low key and the decor spare. Only the laurel wreaths in the pediments and helmets over the center windows reveal that this is a dwelling of a military commander. The structure was completed in 1825; the interiors, two years later.

Aside from a few private rooms for the king, Rosendal has only public rooms; bedchambers were considered unnecessary. The dining room was planned at first to be inside the main palace, but in the final design it was situated instead in an adjacent, one-story wing. The room was furnished as though for an emperor, with the most fashionable materials of the period: polished mahogany, gleaming porphyry,

LEFT *The dining room at Rosendal is furnished as a military tent, with walls and ceiling covered with woven cotton. The fabric seen here is modern replica of the original.*

BELOW *The two floors at Rosendal have identical floor plans with the exception of the adjacent wing, which houses the dining room to the left of the ground floor.*

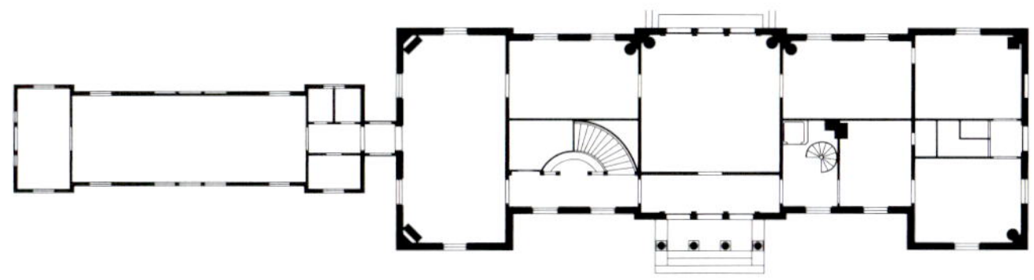

vibrant textiles, bronze ormolu, artistically arranged draperies, and lush carpet. Inspiration for the decor came directly from a new, expanded edition of Percier and Fontaine's *Recueil de decoration interiueres*.

The interiors at Rosendal represent a later style than do those at Rosersberg. The Roman Empire provided a great source of inspiration, although the overall tone is more martial. The dining room, for example, recalls a military tent, with its walls and ceiling covered with gold and white cotton and its slender pilasters representing posts. In another room visitors can almost imagine they hear the clatter of the weapons and armor painted on the walls (similar to those in Rosersberg), which again refer to the king's career and accomplishments.

The painted decoration is the work of the artist Emanuel Limnell, who was employed in the set-making studio of the Royal Theater. In Rosendal's Grand Salon on the second floor, Limnell decorated the ceiling, walls, and overdoors with personifications of the Four Seasons, Day and Night, and motifs from the amorous legend of Cupid and Psyche. The room—considered one of the finest Swedish Empire interiors—admits light through a large, windowed opening in the ceiling, and is therefore called *Lanterninen*.

The room decors at Rosendal convey a clear propaganda message of Karl Johan and his life, from French marshal to king of Sweden and founder of a new dynasty. This is most apparent in the Red Salon on the second floor. In the frieze that encircles the room are scenes from Nordic mythology.

FACING PAGE *The Lantern Room at Rosendal, with its painted decor by artist Emanuel Limnell, is one of the best-preserved Empire interiors in all Sweden. At the center stands a table of painted Sèvres porcelain, a gift from the French King Louis-Philippe to Karl Johan.*

RIGHT *In Rosendal's Red Salon, with its pleated-taffeta wall coverings, everything revolves around the personage of Karl Johan. His portrait (1832), by Olof Södermark, hangs in the center of the wall; above it, in full allegorical splendor in a frieze, he is greeted as the savior of the people over whom he reigned.*

At the center, Oden is welcomed to the North as a savior by the Svea's old king, Gylfe. The message is inescapable.

Parallel with everything French, Karl Johan's patriotism and commitment to development of Swedish commerce is also evident at Rosendal. The king used the fortune that he brought from France to acquire and support domestic Swedish companies. The columns in the portico are of domestic green marble, and the paneling in the vestibule is the most Swedish of all woods: birch. The lawn on the north side of the palace is adorned with an enormous vessel of Swedish porphyry fashioned after a prototype found at Herculaneum. The source of King Karl Johan's porphyry was Älvdalen, where the highly prized stone was quarried. Porphyry, which was so admired during the Empire period, was associated with the purple stone with which Roman emperors surrounded themselves in both life and death. In this case, the symbolic stone was cut and polished to its noble form by peasants from the province of Dalarna, "the roughest of all imaginable beings," as an English visitor described them in 1831.

Houses built near the palace emulated Fredrik Blom's architecture at Rosendal. These simple, elegant wooden structures with pink facades, light gray trim, and yellow decorative ornament formed a kind of bourgeois Empire style that left a clear mark on Stockholm.

ABOVE *The entrance portico at Sperlingsholm manor with its four granite Doric columns and entablature with portraits and inscriptions.*

RIGHT *Following a design by Gustav af Sillén, Sperlingsholm was constructed 1810–20 using forms that became characteristic of Swedish Empire architecture. A rotunda with a shallow dome projects toward the garden; the ground-floor loggia was added later.*

RESIDENTIAL ARCHITECTURE

Though the distinction between Late Gustavian and Empire architecture is not always clear, cubic compositions, restrained and precise forms, and a concentration of decoration around an entrance often characterize the latter. These traits greet the visitor to the manor house at Sperlingsholm in southwestern Sweden. The house was designed by Gustav af Sillén and is often considered one of his finest projects.

In 1800, Baron Carl Adam Wrangel (a distant relative of Carl Gustav Wrangel, discussed in Chapter Two) commissioned af Sillén to design a new main house at Sperlingsholm. Construction did not commence, however, until 1810, when the baron's son Henning Wrangel married the seventeen-year-old countess Hedda Lewenhaupt and, in conjunction with the wedding, took over the estate from his father. Completed another ten years later, the building took a pure rectangular form, consisting of two stories under a shallow saddleback roof. Two lower wings project from the

FACING PAGE *The rotunda, or music room, at Sperlingsholm was one of the earliest monumental creations of Sweden's Empire period, with marbleized walls and a coffered dome ceiling.*

RIGHT *Interior of the Pantheon, Rome, as seen from the portico. Engraving by G. Fontana.*

main building, a configuration most likely drawn from the Royal Palace in Stockholm (this model, by Nicodemus Tessin the Younger, had many imitations during the early nineteenth century). An imposing colonnaded portico stands at Sperlingsholm's entrance, with a wide stairway with four Doric columns of granite supporting the entablature and a balcony. Two bronze medallions adorn the entablature with portraits of the young couple by Johan Niclas Byström, a pupil of the sculptor Johan Tobias Sergel. Between the medallions is an inscription: *Derute ett fädernesland. Här inne en vän. MDCCCXX* (Out there the Fatherland. In here a friend. 1820).

At Sperlingsholm, af Sillén was able to use a central rotunda like the one designed (though not built) for Rosersberg. Beautifully composed with a well-proportioned dome, the rotunda projects from the facade toward the park. More than any other site, Sperlingsholm's domed salon reflects af Sillén's Italian sojourn and his skills as a classical architect. The salon is the Roman Pantheon in miniature, with marbleized interior walls of lustrous stucco painted pale green graduating to white and a coffered ceiling painted marble white. At the dome's apex, the architect installed a window to emulate the Pantheon's oculus that opens to the heavens.

Swedish architects could interpret Italian and ancient Roman design in many ways. In the rural landscape some one hundred kilometers (sixty miles) south of Stockholm and surrounded by forest stands Elghammar, a house based on a Palladian translation of antiquity. The drawings for Elghammar were the work of the Italian-born architect Giacomo Quarenghi (1744–1817), who had made his career in Russia working for the royal court, the state, and the church. It was in St. Petersburg that the Swedish ambassador, General Curt von Stedingk, met Quarenghi. The cultivated general had bought Elghammar in 1804 as a place for his retirement. Ten years later, in 1814, work began at the estate to expand a small eighteenth-century manor house into what has come to be regarded as the finest "Palladian" house in Sweden.

ABOVE *The main building at Elghammar (1814–20), by Italian-born architect Giacomo Quarenghi, is beautifully situated on a peninsula on Lake Lockvatten in Södermanland province.*

LEFT *Elghammar's majestic frontispiece, with its six engaged Ionic columns and inscription,* More Parentum. *Two bronze lions cast at the nearby foundry Åkers Styckebruk guard the entrance.*

The architect's drawings for Elghammar were published in 1821 in *Fabbriche e disegni di Giacomo Quarenghi* (The Constructions and Drawings of Giacomo Quarenghi). As depicted in the volume, Elghammar resembles a royal institution in St. Petersburg more than it does a Swedish manor house. During the construction, some changes in the original plans were made, probably by Fredrik Blom, who had accompanied the count to the Russian capital and who saw the work at Elghammar to completion in 1820. Elghammar's expansive central block, flanked by two wings, consists of two stories; before the entry stand six engaged columns supporting a pediment with the inscription *More Parentum* (In Our Forefathers' Footsteps). A wide stairway guarded by two massive bronze lions leads to the entrance. The west wing, called the "old wing," houses the original residence, while the east wing contains the owner's state apartment and hence is called the "Russian wing." Both wings have low roofs and frontispieces looking onto the courtyard.

Elghammar's most remarkable interior, the Grand Gallery (which probably started out more sparsely and somberly furnished than it is today), is divided into three sections by Ionic columns and embellished with a trompe l'oeil frieze of garlands and lyres, all painted to imitate marble. The room still has much of its original furniture and paintings—for example, the low Swedish tile stoves that

A facade elevation from the original plans for Elghammar from the 1821 work, Fabbriche e disegni di Giacomo Quarenghi. *The actual building deviated somewhat from the original design during construction.*

FACING PAGE *A room as large as the Grand Gallery at Elghammar, situated at the center of the house, is rare in Sweden. The white marbleized walls are articulated by yellow Ionic pilaster-strips and the ceiling is supported by Ionic columns at both ends of the room. In the corners columnar tile stoves serve as plinths for Johan Tobias Sergel's statues. The furniture is a mixture of Gustavian and Empire styles.*

RIGHT *Furnishings from elsewhere in the house were moved to Elghammar's library, seen here, during the late nineteenth century. To the right is a bust from the 1790s of General Curt von Stedingk, who built the palace.*

resemble columns and serve as plinths for Sergel's candelabra statues representing Ceres searching for her daughter Proserpine in the underworld. The beautifully decorated library, with bookshelves framed by white pilasters with richly carved and gilt decoration, suggests Russian influences, thus indicating that Quarenghi was responsible for the room's design.

The international style that Elghammar represents left an impression in the building traditions of the Swedish Empire period. An apt example is Krontorp manor house in the province of Värmland, traditionally attributed to the Danish-Norwegian architect, Hans Ditlef Frants von Linstow, most known for the Royal Palace in Oslo. Like Elghammar, Krontorp also consists of a regal but outsized facade with columns before a low, expansive central block. This kind of architecture was unfamiliar to the people of rural Värmland, and they were therefore not inclined to imitate it.

The front of Krontorp (1825–28), by the Danish-Norwegian architect Hans Ditlef Frants von Linstow, presents a somewhat overbearing portico.

The more common early-nineteenth-century manor house in this region was a two-story structure built of wood and painted a pale color under a slate roof. Size alone differentiated the houses. Occasionally, a simple central marker, such as a pair of columns flanking the entrance and supporting a balcony or a pediment, would be added to achieve a more impressive effect. When Sölje manor house was rebuilt in 1830, the owner used a total of thirty-two columns in the house's two-tiered portico, which probably struck most people as excessive.

CIVIC ARCHITECTURE

In contrast to Copenhagen, Helsinki, and Oslo, where the Napoleonic Wars left a wake of major planning and building needs, Stockholm never experienced such a boom. With the difficult economic situation that followed the most recent war against Russia (1808–9), when Sweden lost Finland—and with it, one-third of her territory and populace—development of the capital came to a standstill. Over the following two decades, only three hundred requests for approval of new construction projects were submitted, with no more than fifteen per year in all of Stockholm. Houses dominated these submissions, but hard times also stimulated demand for utilitarian building such as hospitals, military barracks, and schools. These usually took a severe, toned down form, with unadorned walls and few columns.

The Russian war generated a pressing need for a military hospital. The Garisson Hospital in Stockholm was Sweden's first large-scale hospital and the largest construction project of the first decade of the nineteenth century. Carl Christoffer Gjörwell, Stockholm's city architect who contributed to work at Rosersberg Palace, was responsible for the hospital's final plans. Gjörwell had studied architecture under Louis Jean Desprez and spent time in Rome during the 1790s; at the start of the 1800s, he positioned himself as one of the country's leading residential architects. It is often said that Gjörwell developed the skills he learned from Desprez into a somber, functional classicism. Despite this, he was also open

An exemplary early-nineteenth-century Swedish country manor house—despite the unusually large number of columns at its entrance—is to be found in Sölje manor (ca. 1830).

to new ideas and impressions, and he quickly understood how to translate them into reality. These characteristics, combined with a pragmatic attitude and flexibility, made him popular with patrons.

Constructed between 1816 and 1837, the Garisson Hospital has a traditional classical composition: a long H-shaped building with projecting wings at each end and a frontispiece consisting of six Doric columns. The frontispiece is balanced on the opposite side by a projecting rotunda that houses the stairway. The architect wanted to embellish the front pediment with dentils and a heavily carved relief, but during the construction process, his bold plans were modified and replaced by simple moldings and a clock.

The two main stories have nearly identical floor plans, with eight large examining rooms along a central corridor and in the adjacent wings. From the ground-level vestibule, a magnificent staircase turns with two flights to a semicircular landing, and from there, it continues up another flight to the top floor.

When Gjörwell presented his proposal for the Garisson Hospital, there was already an existing proposal by the Superintendent Carl Fredrik Sundvall, which, had it been realized, would have exceeded the funds allocated to the project. This was not the first time that prosaic reality collided with Sundvall's ambitions. As a Gustavian classicist, Sundvall had more difficulties than Gjörwell in adapting his architecture to the economically troubled times.

When Sundvall was in his sixties, decades after he had designed the Royal Museum for King Gustav III's collection of antiquities (see pages 22–23), the architect was finally given the grand project for which he had always prepared himself: Uppsala University's library. Sundvall's uncle, Carl Fredrik Adelcrantz, had already worked on drawings for a new academic building in Uppsala, though in the end his ideas never came to fruition. The project was given new life in 1811, when the newly appointed university chancellor, Crown Prince Karl Johan, visited Uppsala for the first time. With the precision of the military strategist he in fact was, the prince quickly pointed out the site for the new building:

The Garisson Hospital (designed 1816; completed 1833) by Carl Christoffer Gjörwell today serves as the headquarters of the Stockholm city council.

An 1830 facade elevation of the Garisson Hospital as it was built. Moldings and a clock replaced the rich sculptural relief originally intended for the pediment.

The Uppsala University library designed by Carl Fredrik Sundvall (1819) was completed in 1841 under the direction of Carl Johan Hjelm.

a hilltop at the end of the town's main street. The height provided for effective sighting, but at the same time produced a monumental theatricality better suited to French royalty than to Swedish academia. Invigorated by the prince's enthusiasm, Sundvall presented an ambitious plan that incorporated, in the same building with lecture halls, a grand ballroom for ceremonies and official festivities.

Sundvall worked up a series of different proposals before the final design, greatly simplified from the original plan, was completed in 1819. The new library took the shape of a large rectangle, with three full floors and two recessed mezzanine floors. The upper floor was designated as the university's new ballroom, reached by a spacious staircase in the back of the building between two wings. But this room, with its ceremonious interior, lasted only a few decades before it was rebuilt.

The entrance to the library consists of three arches marked by four columns that support an entablature; to this, a balcony was later added. The similarities between the library's facade and that of the Royal Palace are no coincidence. After all, Tessin's work was held up as an ideal for the architecture of the early nineteenth century and remained a great source of inspiration. Another characteristic clearly drawn from the Baroque was Sundvall's plan for a *säteri* roof instead of the contemporary saddleback roof.

Sundvall's project encountered criticism from various directions, and in 1821 the architect was forced to leave the project. Carl Johan Hjelm, another former pupil of Desprez, who was working as stage-set painter and costume designer at the Royal Theater, completed the library. Hjelm made changes to the interiors and to the building's sublimely simple exterior.

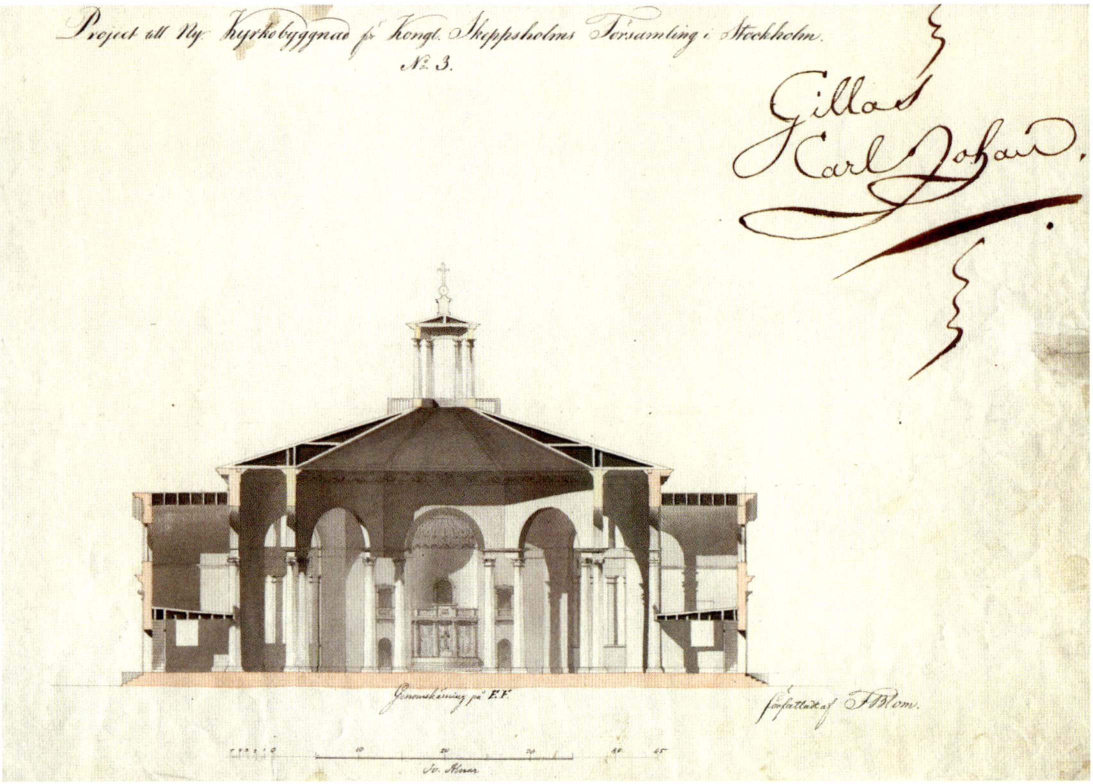

LEFT *This cross-section elevation of the interior of the Skeppsholm church (1823) shows Fredrik Blom's original plan for a central room rimmed by an octagonal arcade. The change in the church's roof (1834) resulted in a round arcade.*

FACING PAGE *The Skeppsholm church has basically been unaltered since its consecration in 1842.*

CHURCH ARCHITECTURE

The somber classicism that characterized Fredrik Blom's architecture won great popularity among private patrons. His repertoire was varied, and his production included military buildings such as his Royal Equestrian Guard in Stockholm; he based some of his architecture for the military on the starkly simple works of the early Italian Renaissance, with their flat facades and scarce details. Thus, while frugality was certainly a consideration, Blom's direct connection to Swedish fortification traditions was at least as influential.

One area especially marked by Blom's architecture is the naval island Skeppsholmen, in Stockholm. Above low barracks towers the Karl Johan Church (now identified instead as *Skeppsholmskyrkan* for its location), which Blom designed in 1823. The Karl Johan Church was designed on a central plan and consists of an octagonal block from which project four cross-arms. Each arm ends in semicircular *thermae* windows and a portico of square pillars. Originally, Blom anticipated a low, tent-like roof, but in 1834, the architect proposed that the church have a dome—a choice the king endorsed.

With this change, the interiors had to change as well. The arcade of paired columns that encircled the central room, reminiscent of the fourth-century mausoleum of Santa Costanza in Rome, became round instead of faceted and was made to carry the classical coffered dome. The final appearance of the church echoes the Holy Trinity Church in Karlskrona, although the Empire architecture of Fredrik Blom has more compact shapes carved out with great precision. The Karl Johan Church was consecrated with great pomp and grandeur in 1842.

Thus, nearly two centuries after the Triumphal Arch composed of perishable materials was erected to honor Queen Christina, the dream of a lasting classical building rooted in antiquity finally became a reality in the capital of Sweden. *Skeppsholmskyrkan* became Stockholm's revered Roman Pantheon.

NOTES

CHAPTER ONE

Historical Overview

10.[*In Swedish history, this epoch is referred to as the Age of Greatness.*] For more on Swedish history during the Age of Greatness, see, for example, *Sweden's Age of Greatness 1632–1718*, ed. Michael Roberts (London: Macmillan, 1973). Also Michael Roberts, *The Swedish Imperial Experience, 1560–1718* (Cambridge, U.K.: Cambridge University Press, 1984); Sven A. Nilsson et al., *The Age of New Sweden* (Stockholm: Livrustkammaren, 1988); and Lars O. Lagerqvist, *A History of Sweden* (Stockholm: The Swedish Institute, 2001).

15. [*Sweden reverted to her humble position as a minor state.*] On Swedish history during the eighteenth century, see, for example, Michael Roberts, *The Age of Liberty: Sweden 1719–72* (Cambridge U.K.: Cambridge University Press, 1986).

15. [*"Here, everyone is behaving like flies . . ."*] From Jörgen Weibull, *Swedish History in Outline* (Stockholm: The Swedish Institute, 1993), p. 58.

20. [*"Venuses and Apollos condemned to lie . . ."*] Quotation from Mary Wollstonecraft's *Letters Written During a Short Residence in Sweden, Norway, and Denmark* (London: 1796, p. 36).

24. [*Despite this, there were a number of substantial advances . . .*] For more on the Karl Johan period, see, for example, Jakob Christensson "Vad stort sker, det sker tyst" in *Signums svenska konsthistoria: Karl Johanstidens konst* (Lund: Signum, 1999).

CHAPTER TWO

The Baroque

28. [*Thus, though the term Baroque serves*] For an overview of the Swedish Baroque, see *Signums svenska konsthistoria: Barockens epok* (Lund: Signum, 1996).

30. [*In 1632, Charles Ogier, a delegate in the French legation*] For more on Charles Ogier, see *Från Sveriges storhetstid. Franske legationssekreteraren Charles Ogiers dagbok under ambassaden i Sverige 1634–1635*, ed. Sigurd Hallberg (Stockholm: P. A. Norstedt & söner, 1914).

30.[*"Not with respect to the quantity or size"*] Quotation from Lorenzo Magalotti, *Sverige under år 1674*, ed. Carl Magnus Stenbock (Stockholm: P. A. Norstedt & söner, 1912, p. 9).

30. [*Sweden's largest building, Skokloster . . .*] For more on Skokloster, see *Skoklosters slott under 350 år*, ed. Carin Bergström (Stockholm: Byggförlaget, 2004).

30. [*The House of Nobility in Sockholm . . .*] For more on the House of Nobility, see *Riddarhuset*, Alf Åberg et al. (Stockholm: Byggförlaget, 1999).

35. [*Jean de la Vallée was well prepared to take over the House of Nobility project.*] For more on Jean de la Vallée, see Claes Ellehag, *Jean de la Vallée: Kunglig arkitekt* (Lund: Signum, 2003).

35. [*A peer and competitor of Jean de la Vallée . . .*] Nicodemus Tessin the Elder and other Swedish architects are treated in Henrik O. Andersson & Fredric Bedoire, *Swedish Architecture: Drawings 1640–1970* (Stockholm: Byggförlaget, 1986).

35. [*Eventually, all of Tessin's time . . .*] An extensive new work about Drottningholm Palace—*Drottningholms slott*, vol. 1, ed. Göran Alm & Rebecka Millhagen (Stockholm: Byggförlaget, 2004)—part of a fifteen-volume project about Sweden's royal palaces, has been published by Byggförlaget in cooperation with the Swedish National Property Board *(Statens fastighetsverk)* and the Royal Court. The author has found especially useful Bedoire's contribution about the palace during the sixteenth and seventeenth centuries.

43. [*Also for the dowager queen, Tessin the Elder designed Strömsholm Palace . . .*] See *Strömsholms slott*, ed. Eva-Lena Karlsson & Rebecka Millhagen (Stockholm: Byggförlaget, 2005). In addition, many residences and other buildings in Sweden are treated in *English in A Guide to Swedish Architecture,* published in 2001 by the Swedish Institute in cooperation with the magazine, *Arkitektur*.

47. [*The most modern country residence of its time . . .*] For more on Sjöö, see Johan Eriksson & Peter Liljenstolpe, *Sjöö slott*. Nicodemus

Tessin d.ä. och Johan Gabriel Stenbock som aktörer vid ett stormaktstida slottsbygge (Uppsala: Uppsala Universitet, 2001).

54. [*In his description of Sweden from his travels in 1674 . . .*] Magalotti, *op.cit.*, p. 101.

58. [*The growth and transformation of Stockholm. . .*] For broader treatment of the Stockholm palaces, see Claes Ellehag, *Palatsen i Stockholm under stormaktstiden* (Lund: Signum, 1998).

63. [*"costly and magnificent, but beautiful and modestly elegant . . ."*] Quotation from Allan Ellenius "Konst och miljö" in *Kultur och samhälle i stormaktstidens Sverige*, ed. Stellan Dahlgren (Stockholm: Wahlström & Widstrand, 1967, p. 80).

63. [*When King Charles II of England first saw Dahlberg's engravings . . .*] King Charles II's statement from Claes Ellehag, *op.cit.*, p. 83.

70. [*The architect of the Kagg mausouleum was Erik Dahlbergh . . .*] On Eric Dahlberg, see *Stormaktstid. Erik Dahlberg och bilden av Sverige* (Lidköping: Stiftelsen Läckö Institutet, 1992), especially Göran Lindahl's article, "Erik Dahlberg och den klassiska arkitekturen," pp. 187–201.

CHAPTER THREE

The Late Baroque

77. [*No architect in Sweden has ever attained the stature of . . .*] The best book about Tessin written in English is *Tessin: Nicodemus Tessin The Younger—Royal Architect and Visionary*, ed. Mårten Snickare (Stockholm: Nationalmuseum, 2002). In this work, some of the leading experts in the field treat the architect and his oeuvre. Many decades later, a standard work in Swedish remains Ragnar Josephson, *Nicodemus Tessin d.y. Tiden – mannen – verket*, vols. 1 and 2 (Stockholm: P. A. Norstedt & söner, 1930–31).

78. [*Tessin the Younger is best known today as the architect of the Royal Palace in Stockholm.*] The most complete work about the Royal Palace is still *Stockholms slotts historia*, vols. 1–3, ed. Martin Olsson (Stockholm: Norstedts, 1940–41).

88. [*"The Stockholm house of my father of blessed memory is by no means . . ."*] Quotation from Birgitta von Haslingen, *Tessinska palatset under 300 år* (Stockholm: Monografier utgivna av Stockholms stad, vol. 143, 2002, p. 170).

91. [*"After much thought on how to decorate it, I decided to paint . . ."*] Quotation from von Haslingen, 2002, p. 120. The author has somewhat adapted the translation of Tessin's description of his plan, which in the original French reads, "Après avoir longtemps balancé de quoi le meubler, je me suis à la fin arresté, de le faire executer en peinture, aussi bien aux plafonds qu'aux murailles, toutes sortes des grotesques . . . Mais pourtant, par tout, entremeslé des figures et petites histories en couleur, comme aussi quelques glaces, et petites bordures de bronze, etc. Dans la Salle, on traitteroit les Beaux Arts, et les Sciences, dans l'Antechambre, le Contentement que l'on tire de la Filosophie. . ."

99. [*Among the properties that the Russians ravaged in the attacks of 1719 was Thureholm . . .*] For more on Thureholm, see Johan Cederlund, *Thureholm under frihetstiden. Återuppbyggnad och nyinredning* (Lund: 1994).

114. [*In 1680, when the city of Karlskrona was established as a royal naval base . . .*] For more on the city planning and architecture of Karlskrona, see *Arkitektur* 1991(3), with articles by Göran Lindahl ("Militärstatens ansikte") and Johan Mårtelius ("Örlogstadens byggnader" and "Idealstaden"), which were referenced by the author.

CHAPTER FOUR

The Rococo

126. [*By the mid-1730s, the French Rococo style had a firm hold in Sweden.*] For an overview of the Swedish Rococo, see *Signums svenska konsthistoria: Frihetstidens konst* (Lund: Signum, 1997). In 1993, the National Museum of Fine Arts in Stockholm (Nationalmuseum) arranged an exhibition on the relations between Sweden and France in the eighteenth century, which was also mounted at the Grand Palais in Paris. The extensive catalogue, *Solen och Nordstjärnan. Frankrike och Sverige på 1700-talet*, appeared in a French translation, *Le Soleil et l'Étoile du Nord: La France et la Suède au XVIIIe siècle* (Paris: Réunion des Musées nationaux, 1994).

128. [*Thus, the leading architectural role went to . . .*] A particularly useful book about Hårleman is *Carl Hårleman: Människan och verket*, ed. Magnus Olausson & Rebecka Millhagen (Stockholm: Byggförlaget, 2002). In this work are contributions by leading authorities, including Bo Vahlne, who writes about Hårleman's interiors for the Royal Palace and Drottningholm Palace. Unfortunately, little about Carl Hårleman has been published in English.

136. [*"Here at my home Drottningholm . . ."*] Quotation from Crown Princess Lovisa Ulrika's letter of May 21, 1748, from *Lovisa Ulrike, die schwedische Schwester Friedrichs des Grossen. Ungedruckte Briefe*, vol. 2, ed. Fritz Arnheim (Gotha: 1910, p. 108).

136. [*Next to the library, in the section that connects . . .*] For more on the Coin Cabinet and its foreign prototypes, see Merit Laine, "En Minerva för vår Nord," *Lovisa Ulrika som samlare, uppdragsgivare och byggherre* (*A Minerva for the North: Queen Lovisa Ulrika, Her Collections and Commissions of Art and Architecture*) (Stockholm: 1998, p. 104). This book is the most extensive work on Lovisa Ulrika as commissioner and collector of art and architecture; it contains a short summary in English.

136. [*One of Adolf Fredrik's and Lovisa Ulrika's primary contributions . . .*] The most useful publication in English about the Chinese Pavilion at Drottningholm is still Åke Setterwall et al., *The Chinese Pavilion at Drottningholm* (Malmö: Allhem, 1974). See also, *Kina slott*, ed. Göran Alm (Stockholm: Byggförlaget, 2002).

139. [*"Everything is distinguished with the magnificence . . ."*] Quotation from Lovisa Ulrika's letter to her mother Sofia Dorothea dated July 27, 1753 from Arnheim, *op.cit.*, vol. 2, p. 329.

141. [*The architect responsible for the new drawings was . . .*] For more on the career of C. F. Adelcrantz, see Stig Fogelmarck, *Carl Fredrik Adelcrantz: ett gustavianskt konstnärsöde* (Stockholm: Natur och kultur, 1995). For texts in English, see *Chambers & Adelcrantz*, ed. Magnus Olausson (Stockholm: Nationalmuseum, 1997).

142. [*"In that taste which we usually call the Chinese . . ."*] Quotation from Nathaniel Wraxall, *Cursory Remarks Made in a Tour Through Some of the Northern Parts of Europe* (London: 1775, p. 121).

149. [*Trained in landscape architecture while in Paris. . .*] Hårleman's landscape architecture is treated in Magnus Olausson, *Den engelska parken under gustaviansk tid*, (Stockholm: 1993), with a summary in English. See also Olausson's article, "National and International Style? From Nicodemus Tessin the Younger to Fredrik Magnus Piper," in *Journal of Garden History*, 1997(4), pp. 267–77.

155. [*"A glorious view facing the fast fairway . . ."*] Quotation from Gösta Selling, *Svenska herrgårdshem under 1700-talet* (Stockholm: Albert Bonniers förlag, 1937, p. 87). Selling's work, considered a classic study of eighteenth-century country palaces and manor houses, was reprinted in facsimile in 1991.

155. [*Sten Åke Nilsson, a leading expert on Swedish eighteenth-century art . . .*] Sten Åke Nilsson, *Det sköna 1700-talet* (Stockholm: Norstedts, 1993, p. 252). Nilsson's book in general has been a valuable source for the author.

159. [*Completed some twenty years after Hårleman's death . . .*] For more about Öved Church, as well as Hårleman's architecture in a modern perspective, see *Carl Hårleman: Människan och verket op. cit.*: John Sjöström, "Hårleman inför eftervärlden," pp. 301–11.

CHAPTER FIVE

Neoclassicism

170. [*In 1753, the French Count of Caylus . . .*] For more on the salon at Åkerö, see Svend Eriksen, "Om salen paa Åkerö og dens kunstner Louis-Joseph Le Lorrain," in *Konsthistorisk Tidskrift*, vol. 32, 1963, pp. 94–120. See also the Eriksen's *Early Neo-classicism in France: The Creation of the Louis XVII Style in Architectural Decoration, Furniture, and Ormolu, Gold and Silver, and Sèvres' Porcelain in the Mid-eighteenth Century* (London: Faber & Faber, 1974).

170. [*In fact, neoclassicism was slow to penetrate Sweden.*] For an overview of Swedish neoclassicism, see Signums *svenska konsthistoria: Den gustavianska konsten* (Lund: Signum, 1998). Texts on the subject available in English include Håkan Groth, *Neoclassicm in the North: Swedish Furniture and Interiors 1770–1850* (London: Thames & Hudson, 1990).

170. [*Creation of the Gustavian style was to a great extent the work of*. . .] For more on J. E. Rehn, see, for example, Anna Greta Wahlberg, *Jean Eric Rehn* (Lund: Signum, 1983).

185. [*Just weeks after his return from abroad* . . .] For more on Olof Tempelman, see Lena Berg Villner, *Tempelman : Arkitekten Olof Tempelman 1745–1816* (Stockholm: Monografier utgivna av Stockholms stad, vol. 127, 1997), which has a summary in English.

190. [*Surprisingly, it was not a trained architect but a military office* . . .] For more on C. A. Ehrensvärd, see Sten Åke Nilsson, *1700-talets ansikte: Carl August Ehrensvärd* (Stockholm: Norstedts, 1996) and the exhibition catalogue, *Carl August Ehrensvärd 1745–1800. Tecknaren och arkitekten* (Stockholm: Nationalmuseum, 1997).

191. [*"Farewell strength and health, reason for beauty and taste* . . ."] Quotation from *Resa till Italien 1780, 1781, 1782* (Stockholm, 1786, p. 26).

201. [*While in Rome, Prince Frederik Adolf came into contact with Louis Masreliez* . . .] For more on the Masreliez brothers' work at Tullgarn, see Göran Alm, *Franskt blev svenskt. Den svenska konstnärs-familjen Masreliez i Sverige under 1700-talet* (Lund: Signum, 1991). In English, see Groth, 1990.

213. [*In 1785, Hall began construction of Gunnebo* . . .] A book about Gunnebo available in English is *Magnus Olausson et al., Gunnebo House and Garden* (Mölndal: Gunnebo slott & trädgårdar, 2001).

217. [*"Carlberg, a man of merit, has transported a beautiful mountain-ous site* . . ."] Sergel's letter is published in Arvid Bæckström, *Gunnebo* (Stockholm: Nordiska museets Handlingar 89, 1977, vol. 1, p. 142). The original letter is preserved at the Royal Academy of Fine Arts, Stockholm.

221. [*These ideals were best realized at af Chapman's Skärva* . . .] For more on Skärva, see Kerstin Barup & Mats Edström, *Skärva: Creating a Place in the Country* (Stockholm: Byggförlaget, 1991); available in both Swedish and English. For further reading about af Chapman, see Daniel G. Harris, *F. H. Chapman. The First Naval Architect and His Work* (London: Conway Maritime, 1989).

224. [*"A Grecian temple on the borders of Lappland."*] Edward Clarke quotation from *Travels in Various Countries of Europe, Asia, and Africa, Part 5* (London: 1819, p. 245).

CHAPTER SIX

The Empire Style

230. [*Rosersberg Palace, on the shores of Lake Mälaren* . . .] For more on Rosersberg Palace, see *Rosersbergs slott*, ed. Ursula Sjöberg (Stockholm: Byggförlaget, 2005).

235. [*With verdant areas, water, and tranquillity* . . .] For more on Rosendal, see *Rosendals slott*, ed. Christian Laine (Stockholm: Byggförlaget, 2003).

241. [*"The roughest of all imaginable beings.* . ."] Quotation from Charles Colville Frankland from *Narrative of a Visit to the Courts of Russia and Sweden, in the Years 1830 and 1831* (London, 1832, vol. I, p. 74).

250. [*When Sölje manor house was rebuilt in 1830, the owner* . . .] About Sölje and other manor houses in the province of Värmland, see Göran Lindahl, "Byggnadskonst i Värmland" in *Ditt Värmland, ed. Anders Hillgren* (Karlstad: Länsstyrelsen, 1988, pp. 132–65).

250. [*Over the following two decades, only three hundred* . . .] For more on the requests for approval of new construction projects, see Göran Alm, "Arkitekturen och inredningskonsten" in *Signums Svenska konsthistoria. Karl Johanstidens konst* (Lund: Signum, 1999, p. 42).

250. [*Carl Christoffer Gjörwell, Stockholm's city architect* . . .] On Gjörwell, see Ursula Sjöberg, *Carl Christoffer Gjörwell 1766–1837* (Stockholm: Stockholmia 1994), which includes a summary in English.

GLOSSARY OF SELECTED TERMS

Note: Some terms given here are French in origin (e.g., chinoiserie, enfilade, trompe l'oeil) but have been absorbed into English and are not treated as foreign words.

aedicule An opening or niche framed by columns or pilasters carrying a pediment or entablature.

antiquity, antique Refers to the cultures of ancient Greece and Rome in pre-Christian, pre-medieval Europe; often used interchangeably with ancient or classical.

appliqué A fixture such as a candleholder attached (i.e., applied) to a wall or a piece of furniture.

apse The semicircular or polygonal termination of a church nave (see basilica) usually housing the high altar.

attic story In a classical building, the story above the main entablature (q.v.).

barrel vault A continuous, concave, semicircular ceiling or vault without ribs.

basilica In ancient Rome, a public hall (later adapted for use as a church), usually rectangular in shape and internally subdivided longitudinally by a central nave flanked by side aisles.

boiserie (French) Wooden paneling richly carved in low relief (q.v.) originating in French interiors of the seventeenth and eighteenth centuries and emulated elsewhere.

broderie (French) In landscape gardening, a method of planting that resembles embroidery in which plantings form images or ornamental forms.

cabinet A small room of private character, sometimes used for a designated purpose in seventeenth- and eighteenth-century architecture; a cabinet of curiosities was a room reserved for the storage and display of precious and/or exotic objects including works of art.

central plan, central-plan church An architectural design based on the Greek cross, which has four arms of equal length; in a central-plan church, the altar stands at the center or crossing of the arms.

chinoiserie A fanciful emulation of Chinese style usually associated with the rococo art and architecture of eighteenth-century Europe.

classicism, classical Refers to the architectural and decorative design conventions and principles of ancient Greece and Rome. As a style classicism was revitalized during the Renaissance and has since found prominence throughout western art and architecture.

coffers Sunken and often graduated multiple concentric squares or hexagons used in fields to ornament a ceiling.

console, console bracket An ornamental bracket, often in a shape of two volutes together forming an S.

cornice The highest part of an entablature in classical architecture, also the projecting moulding running around the topmost portion of an exterior wall.

corps de logis (French) The main building of an estate around which wings and pavilions can be organized.

coulisses (French) The wings at the sides of a stage set.

cove A concave interior molding at the join of a wall and ceiling.

dentils Small, spaced, square projections often found on classical cornices and moldings.

Directoire (French) A transitional style between Louis XVI (1759–99) and Empire in interior decoration.

enfilade The alignment of the doors of connecting rooms in a suite, creating a vista through them.

engaged column Distinct from a pilaster, a column the shaft of which is attached to a wall with half or more of the shaft exposed.

entablature In classical architecture, the superstructure above the abacus (the slab at the top of a column capital) consisting of architrave, frieze, and cornice.

festoon Carved relief ornament made to resemble a suspended garland or wreath of leaves, flowers, or fruit.

fielded panel A framed wall or furniture panel in which the enclosed inner surface is raised.

frieze A running band of decorative relief (q.v.) used on a building's entablature and carrying a symbolic message or historical record.

frontispiece A decorative projecting entrance bay of a building.

greek cross see central plan.

grisaille Painting in gray or grayish monochrome, sometimes enhanced with gold.

grotesque Fanciful ornamentation consisting of animals, foliage, and other fantastic human forms; from the Italian grotto.

hip roof A roof with sloped instead of vertical ends.

loggia A gallery fronted by an open arcade

mansard roof Named for the French architect François Mansart, a roof the lower portion of which is steeply sloped and the top, almost flat.

nave The longest, western portion of a church in the form of the Latin cross, usually consisting of a main central aisle flanked to the north and south by side aisles.

orangery A freestanding or attached south-facing structure that provides an environment suitable for ornamental, often tropical, flora in planters.

order In classical architecture, an assembly of the parts of a column: base, shaft, capital, and entablature; the most common orders are the Doric (without base or capital), the Ionic (usually with a fluted shaft and a capital consisting of two or four scrolls or volutes), and Corinthian (with a fluted shaft and a capital carved to resemble a stylized composition of acanthus leaves).

parterre A level space in a garden arranged with low formal beds of flowers and/or greenery.

piano nobile (Italian) The main floor of a palace or mansion that houses public rooms, usually one floor above ground level.

pilaster An ornamental element in the shape of a vertical section of a column and affixed to a wall.

pilaster-strip A vertical, raised band rectangular in cross-section affixed to a wall and resembling the shaft of a column, without base or capital (also called *lesene*).

plinth The lowest square member of a column or base.

quoin An external angle of a building, often of dressed stone and projecting from a wall.

relief On a vertical surface, carving that is raised from but affixed to its background; low or bas relief is shallow relative to its background; high relief is deeply carved and may be nearly sculpture in the round.

rocaille (French) An elaborate style of rock work, often with marine motifs, applied, for example, in formal gardens and also rendered in wood for furniture; the origin of *rococo*.

rustication Stonework commonly used as exterior trim with roughened surfaces and recessed joints to appear as reinforcement; characteristic of Renaissance buildings and emulations of them.

saddleback roof A normal pitched or peaked roof.

säteri **roof** A characteristically Swedish design consisting of a curving upper section and a lower vertical intermediary often with a row of windows

thermae window A semicircular window subdivided by mullions used in the Roman baths (*thermae*), also called a Diocletian window, referring to the baths of the Roman emperor Diocletian.

transept Reflecting the arms of the Latin cross, the portion of a church that crosses the nave at right angles to it.

trompe l'oeil An illusionary painting or drawing technique that gives the viewer the feeling of looking at actual objects, places, or scenes; from French *tromper l'oeil* (to trick the eye)

trofée **group** From the French for "trophy," an ornamental composition signalling victory and made up of spoils of war such as the helmets, shields, and weapons of the vanquished; often rendered in carved relief.

window reveal The wood or stone interior casing that surrounds a window or door; jamb.

INDEX

Note: Page numbers in *italic* type indicate illustrations.

A

Adam, Robert, 217
Adelcrantz, Carl Fredrik, 148, 157, 167, 181, 185, 251
Adolf Fredrik's Church, Stockholm, 223, *224*, 225
  Chinese Pavilion, Drottningholm, 7, 18, 136, 138–39, *138–43*, 141–42
  Drottningholm theater, 142, *143–47*, 144, 148
  Royal Opera House, Stockholm, 182, 184
  Sturehov manor house, 209, 212–13, *212–15*
Adelcrantz, Göran Josuæ, 142
  Katarina Church, Stockholm, dome, 67
Admiralty Church, Karlskrona (Dahlbergh, attributed to), 114–15, *115*
Adolf Fredrik, King, *16*, 18, *126–27*, 129, 132, 136, 139
Adolf Fredrik's Church, Stockholm (C. F. Adelcrantz), 223, *224*, 225
Age of Enlightenment, 16, 189
Age of Greatness (1611–1718), 10–15
Age of Liberty (1719–1772), 15–18, 76
Ahlfort, Erik, 110
Åkerö manor, Södermanland (Hårleman), 18, 155
  watercolor of interior, *155*
  exterior, *154*
  painted wall decorations (Le Lorrain), *170*
Albertolli, Giacondo, 203
anatomy theater, University of Uppsala (Rudbeck the Elder), *12*, 13
Anckarström, Johan, 23
Andries, Michael, *17*
Androuet du Cerceau, Jacques, 31
Antichità di Ercolano, 203
Arch of Constantine, Rome, Italy, 10, 11, 35
Austria, 10
Avaux, Count d', 78
Aviler, Augustin-Charles d', 96

B

Baltic provinces, 7, 10, 15, 19
Baroque classicism
  architects of, 35
  beginning of, 28, 30–34
  church architecture, 64–73
  city palaces, 58–64
  residential architecture, 43–58
  royal architecture, 35–43
Battle of Lund (1679), 50
Belisarius (Byzantine general), 207
Berain, Jean, the Elder, 86
Bernadotte, Jean Baptiste. *See* Karl XIV Johan, King
Bernini, Gianlorenzo, 78, 79, 87, *91*
Biedermeier style, 228
Bielke, Nils, 50, 52, *54*
Bielke, Thure Gabriel, 100, *103*, 103
Blom, Fredrik, 235, 247
  Borgen pavilion, *234*
  Rosendal Palace, Stockholm, *24*, 25, *226–27*, 228, 235, *236–41*, 237, 239, 241
  Rosersberg Palace, Lake Mälaren, *233*, 235
  Skeppsholm Church, 254, *254–55*
Blondel, Jacques-François, 165, 207
Bolander, Lars, 212, *214*
Bologna, Giovanni da, 155
Bonaparte, Napoleon, 23, 235
Bonde, Gustav, 63–64, 72
Bonde mausoleum, Spånga Church, Stockholm (Tessin the Elder), *72*, 72, 73
Bonde Palace, Stockholm (Tessin the Elder, J. de la Vallée), 62, 63–64
Borgen pavilion (Blom), *234*, 235
Borromini, Francesco, 93
Boucher, François, 141, *142–43*, *155*
Bourguignon, Jean, 131
Boutet de Monvel, Jacques Marie, 181
Bramante, Donato, *91*
Bretano, Giambattista, 121
Briseaux, Charles-Étienne, 165
  Architecture moderne ou l'art de bien bâtir, 148
  L'art de bâtir des maisons de campagne, 152
Bullet, Pierre, 148
Byström, Johan Niclas, 245

C

Caillon, Jean Gaspar, 131
Caps, 15–16
Carlberg, Carl Wilhelm
  Gunnebo mansion, 213, *216*, 217, *218–19*
Carlberg, Johan Eberhard, 166
  colonel's house, 114
Carove, Carlo, 47, *51*, *71*
Cauvet, Gille-Paul, *Recueil d'ornements*, 203
Caylus, Count of, 170
Celsius, Anders, 17
central-plan churches, 64, 67, 68, 69, 115, 117, 223, 254
Chamber, William, *Designs of Chinese Buildings*, *141*, 141
Chapman, Fredrik Henrik af, 191
  Skärva country house, 217, *220–23*, 221, 223

Charles II, King of England, 63
Chauveau, Evrard, 91
Chauveau, René, 86
Chinese Pavilion, Drottningholm (C. F. Adelcrantz), 7, 18, 136, 138–39, 141–42
Blue Salon (Rehn), *142–43*
exterior, *139*
facade drawing, *138*
plan, *138*
Red Salon, *140*
Christina, Queen, 10–11, 13, 31, 35, 54, 76, 223
church architecture
aristocratic contributions to, 15
Baroque classicism, 64–73
central plans, 64, 67, 68, 69, 115, 117, 223, 254
Empire style, 254–55
interior plans, 15
Late Baroque, 114–23
neoclassicism, 223–25
Church of the Holy Trinity, Karlskrona (Tessin the Younger), *116*, 117–18
city palaces, Baroque classicism, 58–64
civic architecture
Empire style, 250–53
neoclassicism, 182–93
postdating Gustav III's Italian journey, 185–93
predating Gustav III's Italian journey, 182–85
Rococo, 165–67
Clarke, Edward, 224
classical, definition of, 7
classicism. *See* Gustavian style; neo-classicism
Consular style, 235
Cotte, Robert de, 131
Council, 14, 15, 58
Coypel, Antoine, *155*
Cronstedt, Carl Johan, 139, 150, 167, 181
Cronstedt, Fredrik, 181–82
Gripsholm Castle, Courtiers' Wing, *178–79*, *182*
Cronström, Daniel, 86, 93
customs house, Stockholm (Palmstedt), *184*, 185

D

Dahlbergh, Erik, 14, 15, 30
Admiralty Church, Karlskrona (attributed), 114–15, *115*
Dahlbergh mausoleum, Turinge Church, Södermanland, 121, *121*
engravings by, *60–61*, *62*, *63*, *69*, *88*
Kagg mausoleum, Floda Church, Södermanland, 70, *70–71*
military quarters, 114
De Geer, Charles, 106, 163
De Geer, Charles, the Younger, 108
De Geer mausoleum, Österlövsta Church, 122, *122*
De la Gardie family mausoleum proposal, Veckholm Church (Tessin the Elder), 70, *72*, 72
De la Gardie, Jacob, 30
De la Gardie, Julius, 99
De la Gardie, Magnus Gabriel, 11, 14, 30, 35, 52, 54, 57–58, 63, 70, 99
de la Vallée, Jean, 12, 44, 58, 78, 96
Bonde Palace, Stockholm, *62*, 63–64
Fullerö manor, Västmanland, *34*, 34–35
House of Nobility, Stockholm, *12*, 31
Karlberg Palace, *56–57*, 57–58
Katarina Church, Stockholm, 64, *64–67*, 67
Oxenstierna Palace, Stockholm, 58, *59*, 64
de la Vallée, Marin, 30
de la Vallée, Simon, 11–12, 35, 44
House of Nobility, Stockholm, 30–31, *31–33*
De Vries, Adriaen, 40, 50
Denmark, 14, 15, 16, 24, 78, 193
Department of Manufacturing, 16
Descartes, René, 223
Désirée (wife of Karl XIV Johan), 24, 235
Desmarées, Georg, *Portrait of Nicodemus Tessin the Younger*, *77*
Desprez, Louis Jean, 199, 225, 232, 250
Déjeuner Salon, Drottningholm theater, *144*
Haga palace proposal, *194–95*, 195
Linneanum, Uppsala University, *188–89*, 189–90
Destain, Joseph Gabriel
Tullgarn Palace, Södermanland, *98*, 99
Directoire style, 232
Doric revival movement, 187
Drottningholm theater (C. F. Adelcrantz), 142, 144, 148
dressing room, *146*
exterior, *144–45*
interior, *146–47*
Drottningholm Palace (Tessin the Elder), 13, 18, 35–36, 38, 40, 78, 132, 134, 136, 172, 174, 177
Blue Cabinet (Hårleman), *135*
Chinese Pavilion (Adelcrantz), *138–43*
exterior from east, *36–37*
exterior from west, *8–9*
grand stairway, *40*
Green Cabinet (Hårleman), *132–33*
Karl XI's gallery, *41*
Lovisa Ulrika's apartment, plan (Hårleman), *131*
Lovisa Ulrika's Coin Cabinet (Hårleman), *137*
Lovisa Ulrika's first study library (Hårleman), *136*
Lovisa Ulrika's new library (Marble Cabinet) (Rehn), *172*, *173*, *174*
Lovisa Ulrika's Natural History Cabinet (Rehn), *174–75*
plan of main floor, *38*
queen Lovisa Ulrika's dressing room (Hårleman), *134*
queen's state bedchamber, *39*
theater (C. F. Adelcrantz), *143–47*
Ducros, Abraham-Louis-Rodolphe, *202*, 203
Dutch classicism, 31, *33*, 34, 44
dynasties, 13

E

Ehrenstrahl, David Klöcker, 39, 76
Ehrensvärd, Carl August, 190–91, 233
drawing, *190*

naval warehouse, Karlskrona, 191, *192–93*
Sergel's sketch of, *191*
Skärva country house, 217, *220–23*, 221, 223
Elghammar manor house, Södermanland (Quarenghi), 245, 247, 249
entrance portico, *246*
exterior, *246–47*
facade elevation, *247*
Grand Gallery, *248*
library, *249*
Elisabeth, Empress of Russia, 18
Empire style, 25, 226–55
church architecture, 254–55
civic architecture, 250–53
residential architecture, 242–50
royal architecture, 228–41
England, 16, 17, 23
English parks
Forsmark, 205, *206*, 207
Haga, *194*, 194
Enlightenment, Age of, 16, 189
Eriksberg, Södermanland, 44, 47
bathing room, *46*
chapel, *47*
exterior, *44–45*
Erstavik manor house (Rehn), 207, 209
Blue Salon, *208*, *209*
exterior, *207*

F

Feretti, Alessandro, 129
Finland, 7, 10, 15, 18, 23, 24, 250
floors, wooden, 150
Fontaine, Pierre-François-Léonard, *Recueil de decorations interieures*, 233, 235, 239
Fontana, Carlo, 78
Forsmark, 205, 207
blacksmiths' residences and church, *205*, 225
English park, *206*
manor house (Rehn), *204*
Fouquet, Bernard, *86*, 86
Fouquet, Jacques, 86, 91
France, 10, 13, 16, 17, 19, 23, 28, 78, 172
Frederick the Great, King of Prussia, 18, 136, 138
Fredrik Adolf, Prince, 199, 201, 203
Fredrik I, King, 15–16, 18, *124–25*, 132, 148
Fredrik's Church, Karlskrona (Tessin the Younger), 118, 121
exterior, *121*
interior, *122*
plan, *120*
French Empire style, 25
French Revolution, 19
Fridsberg, Olof, *155*
Fröman, Georg, 170
Frulli, Gioacchino, 217, *218*
Fullerö manor, Västmanland (J. de la Vallée), *34*

G

Gabriel, Ange-Jacques, 131
gardens
Baroque, 44
formal, simplification of, 149
Garisson Hospital, Stockholm (Gjörwell), 250–51, *252*
Germany, 7, 10, 11, 15, 28
Gimo Manor, Uppland (Rehn), 203, *204*, 205
Gjörwell, Carl Christoffer
Garisson Hospital, Stockholm, 250–51, *252*
Rosersberg Palace, Lake Mälaren, *232*, 233, 235
Göta Canal, 25
Göteborg, 15, 18, 213
government, 14–16, 19, 23
governor's residence, Härnösand (Tempelman), 185, *187*
Great Nordic War (1700–1721), 15, 86
Greek cross plan. *See* central-plan churches
Grill, Claes, *17*, 150, 152
Gripsholm Castle
Courtiers' Wing (F. Cronstedt), *178–79*, 181–82, *182*
theater (Palmstedt), *180–81*, 181
Gunnebo mansion (Carlberg), 20, 213, 217
exterior, *216*
grand salon, *218*, *219*
Gustav I, King, *32–33*
Gustav II Adolf, King, 10, 31, 70, 184
Gustav III, King, 18–20, 23, *126–27*, 159, 167, 170, 177, 179, 181, 182, 184–85, *185*, 187, 189, 191, 193–95, 198–99, 225, 233
Gustav IV Adolf, King, 23, 233
Gustav Adolf's Square, engraving by Martin, *168–69*
Gustavian Age (1772–1809), 18–23
Gustavian mausoleum, Riddarholm Church, Stockholm, 70
Gustavian style. *See also* Late Gustavian style
characteristics of, 19
church architecture, 223–25
Drottningholm Palace, interiors (Rehn), *172–75*
Erstavik manor house (Rehn), 207, *208*
Gripsholm Castle, Courtiers' Wing, *182*
Övedskloster, Skåne (Hårleman), 209, *210–11*
Rehn and, 163, 170, 172, 203
royal architecture, 170–79, 182
Royal Palace, Stockholm, state bedchamber (Rehn), *176–77*
Sturehov manor house (Adelcrantz), 209, 212–13, *212–15*
Gyllenstierna, Christoffer, 44, 94
Gymnasiet, Härnösand (Tempelman), 187, *187*

H

Haga, 19, 194–95, *198–99*
Divan Room, *198*
Grand Salon (L. Masreliez), *199*
King's Pavilion (Tempelman), *196–97*
palace proposal (Desprez), *194–95*
park plan (Piper), *194*
Hall, John, 213
Hammarby (house), *16*
Hapsburgs, 10
Hårleman, Carl, 128, 163, 165, 189, 223
Drottningholm Palace, interiors, *130–37*
influence of, 159, 161, 163, 203

Karolinian mausoleum, Riddarholm Church, Stockholm, 122, *123*
landscape architecture by, 149
Öved Church, Skåne, *158*, 159
Övedskloster, Skåne, *156–57*, 157, 159
provincial governor's residence proposal, *166*
Rococo introduced by, 17, 126
Royal Palace, Stockholm, interiors, *126–30*, 128–29, 131–32
Svartsjö hunting lodge, *124–25*, 148–49, *148–49*
Svindersvik (house), *17*, 20, 150, *150–53*, 152, 155
Thureholm mansion, Södermanland, *74–75*, 99–101, *100–105*, 103–4
Härnösand, 185, 187
Haton, Claude, *80*
Hats, 15–16, 165
Haupt, Georg, 177, *202*
Hedvig Eleonora, Dowager Queen, 13, 35, 38, *39*, *42*, 43, 78, 83
Hedvig Elisabet Charlotta, Princess, *229*, 230
Herculaneum, 19, 170, 193, 203
history, timeline of, *25*
Hjelm, Carl Johan, *253*
Holland, 28
Holstein-Gottorp dynasty, 18, 36, 40
House of Nobility, Stockholm, 30–31, 34, 108
facade, *32–33*
facade drawing, *12*
perspective drawing, *31*
Hultgren, Anders, 203

I

Il Gesù, Rome, Italy (Vignola), *118*
ironworking communities, 106
Italy, 28, 193

J

Le Jardin de Plaisir (Mollet), 44
Jennings, Marshall John, 205
Johan III, King, 35
Joseph II, Holy Roman Emperor, 193

K

Kagg, Lars, 70
Kagg mausoleum, Floda Church, Södermanland (Dahlbergh), 70
exterior, *70*
interior, *71*
Kalmar Cathedral (Tessin the Elder), 47, 68–69
engraving of south facade, *69*
exterior, *68*
plan, *69*
Karl X Gustav, King, 13, 64, 122
Karl XI, King, 14–15, 35, 39, 50, 52, 54, 57, 70, 76, 78–79, 86, 114, 122
Karl XII, King, 15, 78, 84, 86–87, 96, 122
Karl XIII, King, 23–24, 228. *See also* Karl, Prince (brother of King Gustav III)
Karl XIV Johan, King, 24–25, 228, 235, 239, 241, 251
insignia of, *83*
portrait of, *241*
Karl Johan Church. *See* Skeppsholm Church (Blom)
Karl Johan Period (1810–44), 24–25
Karl-Johan style, 25, 228
Karl, Prince (brother of King Gustav III), 23, 230, 232–33. *See also* Karl XIII, King
Karlberg Palace (J. de la Vallée), 57–58
Cabinet of Rarities, *57*
engraving of exterior, *57*
exterior, *56*
Karlsborg fortress, 25
Karlskrona, 15, 18, 67, 114–20
Karolinian manor houses, 108–14, 159
Karolinian mausoleum, Riddarholm Church, Stockholm, 122, *123*
Kartulla Church, Finland, *185*
Katarina Church, Stockholm (J. de la Vallée), 64, 67
dome, *66–67*
facade drawing, *64*
interior, *65*
Katarina Jagellonica, Queen, 35
King's Pavilion, Haga (Tempelman), 195
exterior, *197*
interior, *196*
plan, *196*
Klismos chairs, 198–99, *199*
Konungsund Church (Tempelman), 225
Krafft, Jean Charles, *Plans, coupes et elevations des plus belles maisons*, 235
Krontorp manor house, Värmland (Linstow), 249, *250*
Kungsör, 67
Kvarnholmen, 68

L

Läckö Castle, Västergötland, 54, 57
L'Archevêque, Pierre Hubert, *32–33*, *168–69*, 172, 184
Late Baroque
aristocratic palaces, 88–95
church architecture, 114–23
Leufsta, 106–8
residential architecture, 96–105, 108–14
royal architecture, 78–87
Tessin the Younger, 76–78
Late Gustavian style, 19, 170, 195, *198*. *See also* neoclassicism
Late Karolinian, 76, 96
Le Brun, Charles, 78
Le Vau, Louis, 78
Vaux-le-Vicomte, Maincy, France, 95, *95*
Leclerc, Sébastien, *79*
Ledoux, Claude-Nicolas, 187
Lemke, Johan Philip, 39, *41*
Leufsta, 106, 108
main house, *107*
map, *106*
workers' houses, *108*
Lewenhaupt, Hedda, 242
Liljeholmen manor house, Östergötland, 110, *110–11*
Liljencrantz, Johan, 209, 212–13
Limnell, Emanuel, 239, *240*
Linnaeus, Carl, *16*, 17, 136, 177, 189
Linneanum, Uppsala University (Desprez), *188–89*, 189–90

Linroth, Carl, 161
Linstow, Hans Ditlef Frants von, 249
Krontorp manor house, Värmland, *250*
Ljung, Johan, 177
Ljung, Pehr, 203
Lorrain, Louis-Joseph Le, 170
Louis XIV, King of France, 13, *54*
Louis-Philippe, King of France, *240*
Lovisa Ulrika, Queen, *16*, 18, 132, *135*, 136, 138, 142, 172, 177

M

Magalotti, Lorenzo, 30, 54
manor houses. *See* residential architecture
mansard roof, 149
Mansart, François, Château de Berny, *52*
Marie de Médicis, Dowager Queen, 30
Marmontel, Jean François, 207
Martin, Johan Fredrik, *168–69*
Masonic Order, 232
Masreliez, Adrien, *130*, 131, 144, 174
Masreliez, Jean Baptiste, 184, 198, 212
Royal Palace, Stockholm, *176–77*, 179
tables, Övedskloster, *210*
Tullgarn Palace, grand bedchamber, 201, *201*
Masreliez, Louis, 184, 198, 201
Haga, Grand Salon, 198–99, *199*
Tullgarn Palace, grand bedchamber, *201*
Mauritshuis, The Hague (Post), *33*
mausoleums, 69–73, 121–23
Meaux, Jacques de, 86, 91
Menard, François, 131
military residences, 114
Millich, Nicolaes, 121
Mollet, André, 44
monarchy, 13
monarchy, architecture for. *See* royal architecture
Monnoyer, Antoine-Baptiste, 126, 129
monuments, *6*, *21*

N

Naples, Italy, 19
Napoleon. *See* Bonaparte, Napoleon
Napoleonic Wars, 23–24
National Museum of Fine Arts, Stockholm, 18
naval warehouse, Karlskrona (Ehrensvärd), 191, *192–93*
neoclassicism, 168–225
church architecture, 223–25
civic architecture postdating Gustav III's Italian journey, 185–93
civic architecture predating Gustav III's Italian journey, 182–85
emergence of, 185–93
in Karl Johan period, 25
residential architecture, 203–23
royal architecture postdating Gustav III's Italian journey, 193–203
royal architecture predating Gustav III's Italian journey, 170–82
Netherlands, 11
Neufforge, Jean-François de, *Receuil élémentaire d'architecture*, 172
Nilsson, Sten Åke, 155
Nordic gods, 25
Nordic War. *See* Great Nordic War
Nordin, Lorentz, 174
Norway, 15, 24
Nôtre, André le, 40, 78, 96, 104, 149

O

Ogier, Charles, 30
Oudry, Jean-Baptiste, 134
Öved Church, Skåne (Hårleman), *158*, 159
Övedskloster, Skåne (Hårleman), 157, 159, 209
exterior, *156–57*
gallery (Rehn), *210*
plan, *157*
salon, *211*
Oxenstierna, Axel, 31, 230
Oxenstierna, Gabriel, 230
Oxenstierna Palace, Stockholm (J. de la Vallée), 58, *59*, 64

P

Paestum, 20, 190, 193, 221
painted wall coverings, 104, *104–5*, 163, 163
Palazzo Borghese, Rome, Italy, *58*
Palladio, Andrea, 35, *50*, 217
Teatro olimpico, Vicenza, Italy, 181
Villa "La Rotonda," *117*, 194
Palmstedt, Erik
customs house, Stockholm, *184*, 185
Gripsholm theater, *180–81*, 181
Sophia Albertina's palace, Stockholm, 182, *183*
Stockholm Exchange, *166–67*, 1 67
Pantheon, Rome, Italy, *117*, 225, *245*
Parliament, 14–15, 17–18, 19, 23
Pasch, Johan, 141, *142–43*, 163, *164–65*, 170
Pasch, Lorens, the Younger, *19*
Percier, Charles, *Recueil de decorations interieures*, 233, 235, 239
Peter the Great, Czar of Russia, 15
Petersen, Herman, 207
Pilo, Carl Gustav, 209, *211*
Pineau, Nicolas, 131
Pinnard, Jean, *99*
Piper, Carl, 96
Piper, Fredrik Magnus, 194
Haga, park plan, *194*
Piranesi, Giovanni Battista, 193
Pius VI, Pope, 193
Les plus excellents bastiments de France (Androuet du Cerceau), 31
Poland, 15
Polar Star symbol, 13
Pompeii, 19, 170, 193
porphyry, *226–27*, 241
Post, Pieter
Mauritshuis, The Hague, *33*
Psyche Born Aloft by Cupids (De Vries), 50
public architecture. *See* civic architecture

Q

Quarenghi, Giacomo, 245, 247, 249
  Elghammar manor house, Södermanland, *246–49*

R

Ramel, Hans, 157, 159, *211*
Ramel, Malte, 209
Raphael, 198
Rasonett, Nicolas, *Plans, coupes et elevations des plus belles maisons*, 235
Reduction, 14–15, 72
Rehn, Jean Eric, 141, 157, 203
  Chinese Pavilion, Drottningholm, Blue Salon, *142–43*
  Drottningholm Palace, interiors, 172, *172–75*, 174, 177
  Erstavik manor house, 207, *207–9*, 209
  Forsmark manor house, *204*, 205
  Gimo Manor, Uppland, 203, *204*, 205
  and Gustavian style, 170, 172, 203
  Italian sketch by, *171*
  Leufsta manor house, 106
  Övedskloster, Skåne, gallery, *210*
  Plans et elevations des bâtiments de Suede, 165
  Rosersberg Palace, Lake Mälaren, 228, *228–33*, 230
  Royal Palace, Stockholm, engraving, *14*
  Royal Palace, Stockholm, interiors, *176–77*, 177, 179
  Stora Wäsby manor house (attributed), *162–65*, 163
Reincke, Johan George, Värmlands Säby, Värmland, 159, *160–61*, 161
religion, 15. *See also* church architecture
residential architecture
  Baroque classicism, 43–58
  Empire style, 242–50
  improvements in, 150
  Late Baroque, 88–105, 108–14
  neoclassicism, 203–23
  Rococo, 150–65
  wood painted to mimic brick and stone, 109, 161
Ribbing, Agneta, 70
Richelieu, Cardinal, 10
Riddarholmen, 58, 60–61, *60–61*, 63
Rijf, Jacob, 224–25
Skellefteå Church, *224*
rocailles, 131
Rococo, 124–67
  civic architecture, 165–67
  introduction of, 17, 126
  residential architecture, 150–65
  royal architecture, 128–49
  source of term, 131
Rome, Italy, 13, 19, 170, 172, 193
roofs. *See* mansard roof; *säteri* roof
Rosendal Palace, Stockholm (Blom), 25, 228, 235, 237, 239, 241
  Borgen pavilion, *234*, *235*
  columns, *237*
  dining room, *238–39*
  exterior, *24*
  exterior with vessel, *226–27*
  facade, *236*
  Lantern Room, *240*
  plan, *239*
  Red Salon, *241*
Rosenhane Palace, Riddarholmen (Tessin the Elder), *61*, 61, 63, 64
Rosenhane, Schering, *61*
Rosersberg Palace, Lake Mälaren (Rehn), 228, 230, 232–33, 235
  exterior, *228*
  Hedvig Elisabet Charlotta's dressing room (af Sillén), *232*
  Hogland Hall, *230–31*
  King's bedchamber (Blom), *233*
  overdoors, *229*
  Princess Hedvig Elisabet Charlotta's bedchamber (Gjörwell), *232*
Roslin, Alexander, *135*
Rousseau, Jean-Jacques, 17
Royal Academy of Arts and Letters, 16, 18, 19
Royal Academy of Fine Arts, 16, 19
Royal Academy of Music, 19
Royal Academy of Science, 16
royal architecture
  Baroque classicism, 35–43
  Empire style, 228–41
  Late Baroque, 78–87
  neoclassicism, 170–82, 193–203
  postdating Gustav III's Italian journey, 193–203
  predating Gustav III's Italian journey, 170–82
  Rococo, 128–49
Royal Drawing Academy, 16
Royal Mint, Stockholm (Tempelman), 185, *186*
Royal Museum, Stockholm, 20, *22–23*
Royal Opera House, Stockholm (C. F. Adelcrantz), 182, 184
Royal Palace, Stockholm (Tessin the Younger), 15, 17, 20, 78–79, 83–84, 86–87, 96, 128–29, 131–32, 177, 179, 245
  bedchamber (Hårleman), *130*
  dining room (Hall of Pillars) (Hårleman), *126–27*
  east wing, *83*
  engraving of exterior, *14*
  engraving of north facade, *79*
  exterior, *80–81*
  galleries (for Gustav III's collection of antiquities) (Sundvall), *22–23*
  King Karl XI's gallery, *82*
  lion sculpture and facade, *86*
  Lower Gallery (Hårleman), *129*
  octagonal west cabinet (Hårleman), *128*
  plan, *80*
  plan of surroundings, *87*
  section of portico, *79*
  south archway, *84*
  south wing, *85*
  state bedchamber (Rehn), *176–77*
Rudbeck, Olaf, the Elder
  Anatomy Theater, University of Uppsala, *12*, 13
Russia, 15, 16, 18, 19, 23, 193, 250
Russian War (1788–1790), 19

S

Salsta manor (Spihler, attributed to), 50, 52
  exterior, *52–53*
  interior, *54–55*
  plan, *53*

säteri roof, 34, 43, 57, 95, 96, 100, 106, 109, 114, 253
Scanian War (1675–1679), 14
Sergel, Johan Tobias, 177, 181, 193, 201, 217, 245, 249
altar decoration, Adolf Fredrik's Church, 223, *224*
medallions in Hogland Hall, Rosersberg Palace, *230–31*
sketch of Ehrensvärd, *191*
statues at Elghammar, *248*
Venus aux belles fesses, *126–27*
Serlio, Sebastiano, 235
Sicily, 20, 190
Sillén, Gustav af
Pantheon, gouache drawing, *245*
Rosersberg Palace, Lake Mälaren, 230, 232, *232*, 235
Sperlingsholm manor house, 242, *242–44*, 245
Sjöö, Lake Mälaren (Tessin the Elder), 47, 50
exterior, *48–49*
plan of upper story, *50*
vestibule on upper floor, *51*
Skärva country house (af Chapman and Ehrensvärd), 217, 221, 223
exterior, *220–21*
octagonal salon, *222*
study, *223*
Skellefteå Church (Rijf), *224*, 224–25
Skeppsholm Church (Blom), 254
cross-section elevation, *254*
exterior, *255*
Skokloster castle, 30
exterior, *26–27*
King's Hall, *28–29*
Skottberg House, Karlshamn, *161*, 161, 163
Söderhamn, 67
Södermark, Olof, *241*
Sofia Dorothea of Prussia, 139
Sölje manor house, 250, *251*
Sophia Albertina, Princess, 203
Sophia Albertina's palace, Stockholm (Palmstedt), 182, *183*
Sophia Magdalena, Queen, 179
Soufflots, Germain, 184
Sperlingsholm manor house (af Sillén), 242, 245
entrance portico, *242*
exterior, *242–43*
rotunda, *244*
Spihler, Mathias, 50
Eriksberg, Södermanland (possible attribution), *44–47*
Salsta manor (attributed), 50, 52, *52–55*
Stenbock, Johan Gabriel, 47, 50
Steninge Palace (Tessin the Younger), 94–96
cross-section drawing, *94*
facade drawing, *94*
plan, *95*
Stockholm
city palaces, 58–64
early nineteenth-century, 250
monuments, *21*
Tessin the Younger's plans for, 86–87
Stockholm Exchange (Palmstedt), *166–67*, 167
Stora Wäsby manor house (Rehn, attributed to), 163
exterior, *162*
interior, *164–65*
painted wall coverings, *163*
Storkyrkan, Stockholm, 84, *85*
stoves. *See* tile stoves
Strömsholm Palace, Västmanland (Tessin the Elder), *42*
Sturefors, Östergötland, 96, *97*
Sturehov manor house (Adelcrantz), 209, 212–13
antechamber, *214*
bedchamber, *214*
exterior, *212–13*
garden facade drawing, *212*
octagonal salon, *213*
Sundvall, Carl Fredrik, 251
Royal Palace, Stockholm, galleries, *22–23*
Uppsala University library, 251, 253, *253*
Svartsjö hunting lodge (Hårleman), 148–49
exterior, *124–25*, *148*
garden facade drawing, *148*
plan, *149*
Sveaborg, 16
Svindersvik (house) (Hårleman), 20, 150, 152, 155
antechamber, *152*
distant view, *17*
exterior, *150–51*
vestibule, *153*
Swedenborg, Emanuel, 17
Swedish Academy, 19, 167
Swedish East India Company, 16, 152
Swedish National Bank, Stockholm (Tessin the Elder), *63*, 64
Swedish style, Hårleman and, 17
Sylvius, Johan, 39

T

Taraval, Guillaume, 103
Diana and Endymion, 130
Tavastehus Church, Finland (Desprez), 225
Tempelman, Olof, 194, 199, 225, 230
Church of the Holy Trinity, Karlskrona, dome, 118
Forsmark church, *205*, 205, 225
governor's residence, Härnösand, 185, *187*
Gymnasiet, Härnösand, 187, 187
King's Pavilion, Haga, 195, *196–97*
Linneanum, Uppsala, 189–90
Royal Mint, Stockholm, 185, *186*
Tessin, Carl Gustav, 17, 18, 88, 128, 129, 132, 136, 155, 170
Tessin, Nicodemus, the Elder, 12, 35, 78, 96
Bonde mausoleum, Spånga Church, Stockholm, 72, *72–73*
Bonde Palace, Stockholm, *62*, 63–64
De la Gardie family mausoleum proposal, Veckholm Church, *72*
Drottningholm Palace, *8–9*, 13, 35–36, *37–41*, 38, 40
Eriksberg, Södermanland (possible attribution), *44–47*
Kalmar Cathedral, 47, *68–69*, 68–69
Karolinian mausoleum, Riddarholm Church, Stockholm, 122, *123*
manor house, *43*
Rosenhane Palace, Riddarholmen, 61, *61*, 63, 64
Sjöö, Lake Mälaren, 47, *48–51*, 50
Strömsholm Palace, Västmanland, *42*
Swedish National Bank, Stockholm, *63*, 64

Tessin, Nicodemus, the Younger, 15, 40, 76, 78, 115, 128, 230
Church of the Holy Trinity, Karlskrona, *116*, 117–18
Karolinian mausoleum, Riddarholm Church, Stockholm, 122, *123*
portrait of, *77*
Royal Palace, Stockholm, 14, 78–79, *79–87*, 83–84, 86–87, 96, 245
Steninge Palace, 94–96
Swedish National Bank, Stockholm, 64
Tessin's palace, Stockholm, 88, *88–93*, 91, 93–94
Tessin's palace, Stockholm (Tessin the Younger), 88, 91, 93–94
engraving of facade, *88*
foyer, *88–89*
garden, *92–93*
salon of state apartment, *91*
state apartment, *90*
Tham, Pehr, 217
Thirty Years War (1618–1648), 10
Thoman, Ernst Filip, 203
Three Crowns, Stockholm, *10*, 10, 15, 78, 79
Thureholm mansion, Södermanland (Hårleman), 99–101, 103–4
exterior, *100–101*
facade, *74–75*
kitchen, *103*
plan, *101*
salons, *102*, *104–5*
tile stoves, 150, 213, *215*
timeline of Swedish history, *25*
trofée groups, 131
Tullgarn Palace, Södermanland (Destain), 99, 199, 201, 203
Blue Antechamber (L. and J. B. Masreliez), *202*
exterior, *98*
grand bedchamber (L. and J. B. Masreliez), *201*
Red Antechamber (L. and J. B. Masreliez), *200–201*

U

Ulrika Eleonora, Queen, 15, 18
Uppsala University
anatomy theater (Rudbeck the Elder), *12*, 13
library (Sundvall), 251, 253, *253*
Linneanum (Desprez), *188–89*, 189–90

V

Valsta Manor, Västmanland, 108, *109*
van Honthorst, Gerrit, 50
van Loo, Carle, *135*
Värmlands Säby, Värmland (Reincke), 159, *160–61*, 161
Vasi, Giuseppe, *58*
Vassé, François-Antoine, 131
Verdi, Giuseppe, 182
Vignola, Giacomo Barozzi da, 118
Vingboons, Justus, 31
Vogel, Caspar, *26–27*, 30
Volpato, Giovanni, *202*, 203
Voltaire, 17
von Echstedt manor house, Värmland, 110, 113
painted interior, *110*
privy, *112–13*
von Stedingk, Curt, 245, *249*

W

Wachtmeister, Hans, 117
Wallonia, 106
Westin, Fredrik, *The Day with Apollo Driving his Chariot*, *229*
Wijnblad, Carl, 159, *159*
Wollstonecraft, Mary, 20
Wrangel, Carl Adam, 242
Wrangel, Carl Gustav, *26–27*, 30, 60, 242
Wrangel, Henning, 242
Wraxall, Nathaniel, 142
Wrede, Fabian, 150

CREDITS

Durehed, Lennart 28, 229, 230–231, 232 *both*, 233
École Nationale Supérieure des Beaux-Arts, Paris 99
Glase, Gösta 100–1, 102, 212–13
Håkanson, Philip 182
Hallén, Lars 16, 20–21, 26–27, 28–29, 45, 46, 47, 48–49, 51, 52–53, 54–55, 61, 62 *below*, 70, 71, 72 *right*, 73, 84, 107, 108, 109, 110, 110–111, 112, 113, 121, 123, 127, 128, 152, 153, 156–57, 160, 170, 198, 199, 204 *below*, 205, 206 *both*, 207, 213 *below*, 224 *both*
Hammarskiöld, Hans 32–33, 34
Hofman-Bang, Niels 6, 25
House of Nobility (Riddarhuset), Stockholm 12 *above*, 31 *both* (Hans Hammarskiöld)
Kessler, Herbert L. 1
Korsnäs AB Archives, Gävle 204 *above* (Tommy Westberg)
Lavin Flower, Michael 210, 211, 214, 215, 246–247, 246 *below*, 248, 249
Lindman, Åke E:son 8–9, 22–23, 24, 36–37, 39, 40, 41, 42, 59, 74–75, 81 *below*, 82, 83, 85, 86, 88–89, 90, 91, 92–93, 98, 103, 104–105, 115 (both), 116, 117 *below*, 119, 120, 124–125, 132–133, 134, 135, 137, 139, 140, 142–143, 144–145, 148 *above*, 162, 163, 164–165, 167, 173, 174, 174–175, 178–179, 180, 183, 186, 187 *above*, 192–193, 196 *below*, 197, 200–201, 201, 202, 216, 218, 219, 220–221, 222, 223, 226–227, 236, 237, 128–239, 240, 241, 255
National Archives of Sweden (Riksarkivet), Stockholm 87 (Kurt Eriksson), 138 *both*, 149 (Kurt Eriksson), 166 *above* (Kurt Eriksson), 185, 187 *below* (K Eriksson),
National Museum of Fine Arts (Nationalmuseum), Stockholm 19, 58, 72 *left*, 77, 79 (Hans Thorwid), 95 *below left*, 136, 155, 171, 172, 190, 191, 194–195, 209 (Hans Thorwid)
Nordic Museum (Nordiska museet), Stockholm 17, 212 *below*
Plunger, Max 65, 66–67, 146, 146–147
Royal Academy of Fine Arts (Kungliga akademien för de fria konsterna), Stockholm 181, 194
Royal Archives (Slottsarkivet), Stockholm 148 *below*
Royal Collections (Kungl. Husgerådskammaren), Stockholm 14, 80, 81, 129, 130, 176–177 (Alexis Daflos)
Royal Library, Stockholm 33, 43, 52, 94 *both*, 106, 141
Sandbring. Håkan 158
Segerstedt, Erland 225
Signum Publishing House (Bokförlaget Signum), Lund 56, 57 *below*, 68, 97, 150–151, 154, 161, 208, 234, 242, 242–243, 244, 247 *below*, 252 *above*, 253
Stockholm City Archives (Stockholms stadsarkiv), Stockholm 64, 166 *below*, 184
Swedish Military Archives, Stockholm 114, 252 *below*, 254
Thörnlund, Teddy 188–189
Uppsala University Library 10, 12 *below*, 57 *above*, 60–61, 62 *above*, 63, 69 *both*, 88, 117 *above*, 159, 168–169
Värmlands museum, Karlstad 250, 251
Westberg, Tommy 122